Under The Moon

Under the moon, my baby lives.

Then wide awake with the sun.

He's dead.

Reality leaving me speechless,

Over and over again.

STILL

Making a Whole When Parts Go Missing

Dr. Kimber Del Valle

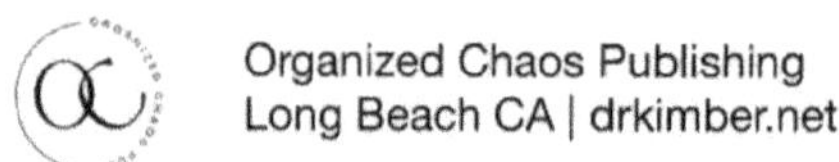
Organized Chaos Publishing
Long Beach CA | drkimber.net

While any stories in the book are true, some names and identifying information may have been changed to protect the privacy of individuals.

Cover design and image compositions: Mali & Friends
Interior Design: Chris Sowers

ISBN 979-8-9870881-0-4 (print)
ISBN 979-8-9870881-1-1 (digital)

Printed in the United States of America

Library of Congress Cataloging in Publication Data
Library of Congress Control Number: 202903857

To Dr. Avedis Panajian

your delight in me was everything,

you created my internal grief container

and when I'm quiet,

I can still hear your laughter clothed in wisdom and brilliance.

In Memory of

Dr. Beth Brokaw

I feel your applause from behind the veil;

I carry you inside of me.

Table of Contents

I've written my story on these pages in hope that it allows you to put words to your experience of loss. What we know about trauma, and pregnancy losses are traumatic, is that in order to heal and transform a loss into something life giving, we have to create a story that makes sense of our experiences. We have to be willing to go into the turmoil. We have to be willing to slow down and stop the impulse to move on by replacing the lost with another child, or worse yet, pretend it never happened.

My hope is that this book, my story, will unearth places in you that need comfort, company, and possibly emotional integration. Much like our bodies need food to be digested to be useful and provide fuel and nutrients, our souls need grief to be processed in order to be metabolized and transformed into something vital. My story will serve you in processing what's disconnected and needs to be part of your bigger story.

Grief, when unprocessed, sticks inside of us like flypaper that never gets replaced. As more and more grief adheres, it takes up all the spare emotional space until eventually it's too much, and we crash under the weight of grief, wondering how we got there and why the pain is so strong.

Our nervous system is akin to that of the mama elephant who returns to the place of her baby's death for decades. Our embodied self doesn't forget. It also doesn't live in linear time so we can be hit with tears of sadness when just moments before, we were enjoying Methow Mud ice cream at Sheri's with the would-have-been-cousins ten years later.

Very few of us ever wanted to be in the grief club, yet here we are. Together, we bumble our way through embodied feelings such as rage, devastation, anxiety, helplessness, and then kicking and screaming, to some sort of acceptance. This is the way through any grief—enduring it together.

It's finding the parts of yourself that were obliterated when you heard the words, "I'm so sorry…" and bringing them out to be seen by the safe people you call community. You may keep finding them years later when you drive by the hospital where he died on your way to get donuts and visit a botanical garden with your living children, now eighteen and thirteen. You may find them when a childhood friend says, "Wow, your kids are far apart in age." These are the times you don't need to keep your feelings to yourself. These are the times when you can call up that friend and say, "I'm missing the face of the one who never entered our family in a physical sense."

If you're reading this book but haven't experienced pregnancy loss, past grief will likely feel invited to reemerge. It's normal for this to happen. But unlike devastating grief that is often unplanned, here I want to invite you to find those people who can hold your grief. This may feel embarrassing if your loss was long ago. After all, we're a science-minded society that often forgets what can't be seen and what can't be proven.

But there are many mysteries out there to be uncovered by the human mind—the weight of grief is one of them. My body carried an unexplainable veil of heaviness after my son's death for six years before one day, while I was dressing, it dawned on me—I felt lighter. Is this interpretation a figment of my imagination? Maybe. But I believe there's a magical essence in every person. The soul finds a way to continue. Our soul finds a way to survive devastation by becoming something we weren't, something we couldn't have been without this brokenness that now won't leave us for the rest of our lives.

I'm grateful to be on this journey with you through my story. Together we can remember we don't need to fear disasters or replace grief with anxiety, something that can happen when it goes unprocessed. By processed, I mean feeling it, sharing it, and creating a story that holds all the parts of our experience. Stories create our reality. Since anxiety can be a compelling storyteller, we have to allow other parts of the story, the less devastating parts, to catch up and calm that which internally feels uncalmable. Processing grief in the form of anxiety allows us to stick our feet into the ocean on a surfboard and anticipate the incoming wave rather than worrying there's a shark nearby.

In trauma, we usually need to go back and rework our memory of what happened. We have to pick up the feelings we disconnected from, displaced, and compartmentalized and rework them into something worth keeping. If it feels right, read this book slowly. Go to the journal prompts in the back and answer them. In trauma, too much happens at once. Allow this time of reflection to no longer traumatize you; instead give words to those things that were unnamable when they happened. What goes underground always resurfaces. Don't be afraid. There's nothing more to lose; you've already survived.

Please remember you're not alone. Let my story hold the hope that what's been broken can be repaired—not into what it was before but into something that you wouldn't have imagined. Into something that has yet to be lived or have form. When it emerges, you'll know. It's waiting to be found. Something that doesn't yet have shape.

As you pick up the pieces, it will find you.

Part One

The Blast

The Day Before

I spend the morning wrestling with myself. Am I being an overanxious mother? Is this an emergency? Should I be concerned? I inspect my stomach in my bedroom mirror—two days away from 34 weeks and ready to get the remaining weeks behind us. Shouldn't I see something? Feel more than I am? Am I feeling movement, or is he only moving when I move?

I start to rub and poke my stomach.

Come on, Baby Long Beach, move.

Kick.

Swim.

Do something.

Come on! It's my wedding anniversary! Nine years.

I watch myself in the mirror, poking, moving the sides of my very obvious stomach protrusion. I shake it while silently pleading, *Show me you're fine!*

He does nothing of the sort. I wait five minutes. Zilch. Nada. Ten minutes and still no movement.

I call the nurse at my OB-GYN's office because I don't feel any kicks and can't tell if the movement I'm feeling is my imagination.

"Are you sure you aren't feeling movements? You know, it doesn't have to be strong kicking movements. They can be light or have a brushing sensation like the baby is swimming. Many women worry about this kind of thing, but it's usually a false alarm."

"I think I feel the baby moving. The baby has never had great kicks. Been more of a swimmer."

"Then why are you worried?"

"Because when I lie down, I can't feel him move."

"How are you counting his movements?"

"I'm counting when I can feel him rub against me from the inside."

"Well, if he's moving then you're fine."

But was he? After all, she's only going off what I'm telling her, and I know I want to believe everything is okay. So I push back, "Today, it feels different."

"Again, if you're feeling movements then everything should be okay, but if you're really concerned, go to the hospital where everything can be checked out and put your mind at ease."

I hate getting help. I hate feeling like an anxious pregnant woman who has gone from noticing some slightly different physical movement to determining a catastrophe has happened in the course of several hours. But with my heart still racing after we've hung up, I realize she's right. I won't be able to put my mind at ease until I hear a heartbeat and have both of us checked out.

~~~

I call a neighbor, whose daughter is Eden's age. She's not available. I try three more neighbors, but no luck.

I decide to bring her. After all, what can be the big deal of bringing your three-year-old daughter to the hospital for monitoring? We're going to be in and out.

On the way to the hospital, I call Dennis.

"Hey, what's up?"

"Hey. This isn't what you'd like to hear on our wedding anniversary, and I don't think there's anything to be concerned about, but I'm on my way to the hospital to have the baby's movements checked."

"Okay."

His tone indicates more words are headed my way. I take a deep breath.

"What's different? Why do you need to go?"
~~~

"I don't really want to get into it if you know what I mean," I say as I glance in the rearview mirror at Eden, who is galloping her stuffed horses through the air. "Listen. I don't think there's anything to worry about. What can be wrong at almost 34 weeks?" We have a share chuckle before I tell him I'll call him later and hang up.

~~~

At three in the afternoon, Eden and I walk through the doors of the hospital and into an empty elevator. I punch the button for the second floor and distract my worry by asking Eden, "How was gymnastics camp today?"

Her hands start our conversation. They wave up and down matching her smile. "It was fun, Mommy. Coach Courtney got to be with me, and we had a bounce house that had a slide." A beep fills the compartment and I ready myself to exit. I nod, rushing my words, "Oh good."

I release the breath I'm unaware I'm holding and mindfully move my tongue from the roof of my mouth. I notice a ball under my ribs I've known for years—anxiety. I still haven't felt the baby move. Tears threaten to flow from my eyes, so I force another exhale.

"Is everything okay, Mommy?" asks Eden's quiet voice.

"I hope so." I say walking while glancing into her big round Hawaiian blue eyes. "We're going to talk to these nurses here and let them help us."

I grip the sign-in pen with a shaky hand. I can't remember my health insurance number, which I've written hundreds of times over the years. I pull the card out of my wallet and write it down. I speak in code to the nurse sitting below the counter window about my situation. "I've been feeling movement all day, but it wasn't until I lay down for a nap that I noticed I wasn't getting any kicks, so I came in."

She nods and says, "Let's get you checked."
~~~

Beside us a door opens, and a nurse with pastel teddy bears on her scrubs greets us with a smile before zeroing in on Eden. "Well, what do you have there?" she points to Eden's books.

"These are books I like to read."

"I love to read, too," the nurse opens a door near the check-in desk as she continues looking at Eden, "Let's get your mommy all hooked up so you can hear your sibling's heartbeat." The three of us walk into a room with beds separated by curtains. I notice I'm not the only one here today; a couple of beds down, I hear heartbeats coming from a monitor.

The nurse continues, "Are you going to have a baby brother or sister?"

"We don't know yet, but I want a baby brother. His name is Baby Long Beach."

She nods. "Wow. That's a special name."

"I named him."

The nurse looks to me. I shrug and mouth, "We're working on a different name."

She nods and smiles back at Eden. Eden rearranges what's she's carrying and pulls out the small, stuffed horses from underneath her books to show the nurse.

"What do you have here?" asks the nurse as she points to the bed to have me lie down and moves to get the straps from the monitor.

"They have babies in their tummies, just like my mommy."

"How cool is that?" the nurse replies.

Eden then lays them on their sides in a row, with their cloth hooves in black, brown, and gray pointed toward me on the monitoring bed.

"Look, Mommy, they're lying down, just like you."

The nurse rolls the ultrasound machine over to the table and smears cool gel on my belly. She moves the instrument around my midsection, trying different angles.

"Hmm," she says, "I can't hear anything. Now when did you last feel movement?" I repeat the coded information I gave the check-in nurse. "Okay. Let me get the doctor."

My heart takes off like I've been spooked. It doesn't take medical knowledge to understand that this isn't a good sign.

~~~

The doctor greets me with a friendly tone--maybe a bit too friendly, as I can see the anxiety on her face as she takes the ultrasound wand. "So what do we have here?" she smiles—nervously?—as she squirts more gel on my belly and picks up the heartbeat monitor. She asks me the same questions the nurse did.

"How far along are you?" *Thirty-three weeks and four days.*

"When was your last appointment with your OB-GYN?" *Two weeks ago.*

"When's the last time you felt movement?" *I thought this morning but now I wonder if I was imagining it. For sure I felt a few kicks and flutters last night at dinner.*

After each of my answers, the doctor nods, keeping her eyes on the monitor screen. Then, glancing briefly at the nurse, she asks, "Do you have someone who can pick up your daughter? It would be best if it wasn't your husband so he can be here with you."

"So does this mean you can't find a heartbeat?" I whisper, so Eden can't hear. The doctor nods before whispering back, "So you're going to need to stay here. I'll explain more once you get admitted." Both of us have tears though none fall.

All I can think to say is, "Could you tell me the sex of my baby? We don't know."

She swallows. "It's a boy," she whispers.

I answer with a nod and don't allow my imagination to go much further as I'm aware of Eden sitting beside me.
~~~

I have a son.

He doesn't have a heartbeat.

As I inhale, I look at Eden and slide her next to me, put her hip to hip, my arms surrounding her. I glance up and nod as the doctor and nurse leave the room, grateful for the privacy. She's taking me in, waiting for me to speak, "Eden. I'm going to have either Mandy or Alicia come get you because it looks like I need to stay here for a little while."

She nods but her usual curiosity has grown silent. I pass her the butterfly book we've brought along with another picture book.

I call Dennis but he does not answer, so I call a few neighbors, friends, and my two employers as if ordering a pizza: I need a sitter, undergraduate substitute professor, and the counseling center secretary to cancel my psychotherapy appointments. I make the calls using code language.

"I'm at the hospital. The worst possible scenario you can imagine has happened."

In fifteen minutes, I've settled all urgent matters. Our friend Mandy is on her way; she isn't teaching at the community college today so she's dropped everything to drive the hour to the hospital to pick Eden up until Sharon, Dennis's mom, can fly in to help. Dennis's brother Ryan has offered to pick Sharon up at the airport for us. He's an hour and a half away, but he's leaving work now to be at the airport when Sharon arrives. The university has found a substitute for my statistics class, or they will. My counseling center director, where I'm finishing my post-doctoral clinical psychology hours, tells me not to worry about my clients; they will reach out to them and provide another therapist if they need an immediate appointment.

I think but don't ask, "Do you want back the onesie and gift card you just gave me?"

After taking care of these immediate needs, I watch Eden, who slides off the bed to play with her stuffed animals. I see her turn her horses one by one onto their other sides. Glancing up, she tells me her horses and their babies are sick and their mommies are sad.

I whisper, "Oh I'm so sorry." I pat the bed beside me, "Do you want to come back up here, and I can read you your books?" I try to focus on the words on the page, forcing my mind away from "*Your son has died*." Eventually, there are no words left. We sit staring at the horses, hoping someone comes along soon to make them feel better.

~~~

Mandy comes for Eden. I feel outside of my body interacting with her. We speak few words, and all are cryptic. No tears fall though our eyes are full. "Oh, Kimber," she whispers.

I nod. I'm afraid to open my mouth for fear I'll fall into Mandy's arms and weep. For Eden's sake, I don't.

Mandy matches my lead perfectly and reads my unspoken message, "We can't talk about this now. Eden can't know, yet." It isn't that Eden can't handle my tears and my sadness; I believe she could—but she'd want an explanation. I don't want to give her one without her dad being here. I also don't want her to wait for Dennis, be told her brother died, and then have to leave with Mandy, processing her brother's death without us.

When Eden and I say good-bye, I tell her the simplest facts about what's going to happen—she's going to play at Mandy's house for a little while, and I need to stay in the hospital and be with the doctors. I tell her that Grammy will come to our house, I will be home very soon, and she can always call Daddy or me if she wants to talk to us. I don't tell her everything is okay or will be okay. False assurances are usually for the good of the giver, not the receiver.

I phone Dennis again. No answer.

I start watching the clock, regretful I didn't bring a book and feeling as if I'm once again that 6-year-old girl who lay by the dryer
~~~

waiting for her favorite shirt to be ready. With each passing minute, my irritation grows, along with my determination not to fall apart by myself. I try not to feel the sorrow that keeps showing up in the tears falling out of the corners of my eyes onto the stark white sheets.

~~~

Nearly an hour passes before I hear his voice. He'd turned off his cell phone. Listening to him explain why he hasn't been available, it dawns on me that he too thought nothing would be wrong.

I tell him our son has died.

His words pour out without pause, "What? How could this happen? You said it wasn't a big deal you were going to the hospital. How could this be? Oh my goodness. We are having a son? I was going to be a dad to a son. Oh this is awful." I feel his tears through the phone and start crying with him.

"It is awful. It is absolutely awful."

We hang up, leaving him to cancel the rest of his clients and finish up a few things at work. Still annoyed but also relieved he's on his way, I call my former therapist, hoping he'll have time to talk.

"Can you have Dr. P call me?" I ask his receptionist. "My baby died."

There is an awkward silence, followed by, "I'm so sorry. I will let him know. I'm sure he'll call you right away."

~~~

"Hello. This is Kimber." My voice sounds as if I ran to the phone.

"Kimber," his Armenian accent feels like home. I take deep gulps of air as if coming up from underwater.

My eyes fill with tears and make their way down my cheeks as I speak. "Hi, Dr. P. Dennis and I have been expecting our second child, but he d…" I try again. "My baby died, Dr. P. They don't know what happened. He just didn't have a heartbeat."

"Oh, I'm so sorry. This is terrible, absolutely terrible." His empathy wraps itself like a blanket around my heart. "When are you coming to see me?"

When am I coming to see him? Could I? Would I? Four years out from my last session, that option hadn't even crossed my mind.

"I don't know," I tell him. "I hadn't considered it." I pause for a few seconds. "When works for you?"

I hear what sounds like papers being shuffled in the background. "Let's see. July 11. I have 1 pm."

"Yes. Yes, I think that would work," I answer. "Thank you. I look forward to seeing you."

"Okay," he answers in a manner that tells me, "This is good." "See you Thursday."

His words linger in my ear. "When will you come to see me?" His invitation unleashes longings, and I realize I wanted desperately to ask but did not even imagine asking, "Will you come to the memorial service?"

<div align="center">~~~</div>

I've put off the call to my parents for last to give them more time before their world, like mine, gets shattered. I know they'll be busy working at the golf course, surrounded by loud familiar voices, most of whom I've known my entire life. I worked at the clubhouse from high school until I moved away at twenty-three. If it's a typical day today, Dad will be out on the golf course changing sprinklers, and Mom will be at the cash register or cooking while she acts as a greeter to both members and visitors.

I take a deep breath, heart pounding as I dial the number I memorized at six years old. 5-0-9. I drop the phone, feeling like I'm going to have a panic attack. Once I'm breathing normally, I start again. 5-0-9-9-9-6-2-8-4-7. It rings. I force another deep breath, but it doesn't loosen the tightness in my chest. We haven't talked much in the last few months. and our last visit was Christmas.

"Golf course," my mom says.

"Hi, Mom. I…" My voice wavers. I try again. "I'm not sure how to say this, but our baby has died." The end of my sentence is pressured, like I'm trying not to cry because I'm trying not to cry.

"Oh, no." A long pause but I can hear her sniffling. "Where are you?"

Oh good, facts. I can stick with facts and not fall apart. "I'm at the hospital. They couldn't find a heartbeat."

We're synced—facts. "What happened?"

"We don't know. Neither does the doctor. There isn't a cord wrapped around or anything. I haven't cramped. I haven't bled."

"I'm so sorry. So you'll have to give birth?"

"Yes. They're going to induce me."

"Oh, Kimber, I'm so sorry that you have to go through this."

I hear her words but don't want them to crack me open, so I respond with reassurances. "Thanks. Sharon is flying in as we speak, and she's going to be with Eden. We'll be okay."

"I wish I could be there." I hear sadness in her voice. "I'm hugging you from afar. Have Sharon give you a real hug from me."

I picture her sitting at the desk I know well, voices in the background carry through the phone line, and I know our conversation needs to end. "I will. Thanks, Mom. Can you please tell Dad and call my brothers? I just can't talk to everyone right now."

"Yes. I know they'll want to know. I love you, Kimber. I'll be praying for you. Please let me know if I can do anything. I'm going to call my prayer warriors and put them to work for you."

I close my eyes and feel the pounding of my head as I say, "Thanks, Mom. I love you, too. I appreciate the prayers."

It's interesting to me that in this moment I've never felt so relieved in having people to ask for help. Today I'm not alone. I picture Ryan driving to get Sharon at the airport. Mandy driving Eden to her house. I rehearse the condolences from work and offers of help. I won't go through this alone; I'm not going through this alone.

The Story of Us – Part I

I met Dennis in Greek Literature class fifteen years ago. He introduced himself one day as I was walking into the library. He grabbed my arm with a light squeeze and said with a smile that reached from ear to ear, "Hey, we're in Greek Literature together. You're Kimber, right?"

"I am." I felt impatient, not wanting to be interrupted as I attempted to get my schoolwork done before basketball practice.

"I'm Dennis. I'm friends with a few people who you play basketball with, Greg and Tim."

"Oh my goodness, yes! I think you are who they keep saying I need to meet. In fact, Angie and Heather keep saying I should meet you, too."

"Oh my gosh! You know them too? That's so funny. We have so many common friends. I didn't even know."

"Well, it's nice to meet you. I've gotta get in and get studying before practice."

"Oh right. Would you like to have lunch in the café sometime?"

"That sounds fun. Let me see when might work for me," I leaned over and used the gray metal book drop for a table as I pulled out two day planners from my backpack.

"Look at you. A bit organized, aren't you?"

I joined his laughter. "Hey, what can you say, I'm a bit of a perfectionist and well, you know – gotta stay on top of practice and class."

"Just a bit of a perfectionist, huh?"

"Now, now. We just met. Don't ruin it," I chuckled so he knew I could take some ribbing without getting defensive. "How about next Tuesday at 12?"

He looked skyward exaggerating a thinking expression. "Next Tuesday. Let's see," he paused, "Yup, that should work." He looked around and grabbed a napkin off a small table nearby. Then he waited beside me while I penned it in both day calendars before asking, "Can I borrow that?" pointing to the pen.

"Yup," I laughed as I watched him write the day and time on his napkin. "Well that's a great system. Make sure you don't wash it because I don't do redos."

He looked me straight in the eye, "Believe me, I won't forget."

Hour Four

The room closes in on me as I can't stop listening to the chorus of baby monitors all around me. I try to stop the mantra of "*my baby died*" from consuming every part of me.

I wiggle my toes. Wiggle my fingers. I rock my head back and forth, but I don't want to seem like I'm having a mental breakdown should the nurse open my privacy curtain. In my profession, having my mental shit together is advertising.

What I want to do, but don't do, is rub my belly. I want to rub my son back to life. I want to wake up this body of mine that shows no sign of heading into labor.

Traitor.

I practice yoga three days a week.

How pathetic.

I want to pound my belly. Make it wake up. Make it magically turn into something useful, for now it's an embarrassment. So I curl up tighter on my bed. Tuck my arms so I can hold the side of my face in my palms. I focus my attention on my ice-cold hands touching my warm face. I try to spread the warmth. I fail.

~~~

When Dennis shows up, by the redness of his eyes, I can tell he's been crying.

"Hey there," he says, as he sits down on the bed and gives me a long hug. I can't make any words come out of my mouth. What's there to say? He speaks, "I never thought something like this could be wrong. I never imagined our baby dead. How does this happen?" I hear the agony in his voice but feel my own numbness.
~~~

I squeeze his hand, pulling back from our embrace, and nod. I hold his hand and gently rock back and forth until words form a sentence. I whisper, "We have a son. Can you believe it?"

His head bows and tears drip onto the mattress as he shakes his head, "How did he die? Do they know? Can they find out?" He looks up at me as if I can answer his questions, but I can't.

"They don't know anything. Only that he may have died before to-day. But they don't know what could've happened, and they really don't think we'll find out. The doctor said it happens more than we might think." I keep nodding and rocking with our hands still held.

"How long will we have to stay here?"

"I don't know. They haven't told me much. I wanted to wait until you were here."

Our silence is eventually interrupted by a nurse "Dr. Del Valle, we're ready to get you into your room now." *Dr.* Del Valle. If only my doctorate weren't so meaningless right now, my mind unrecognizable. She reaches to shake Dennis's hand. "I'm so sorry for your loss." Dennis shakes her hand while wiping his face with his other hand.

As Dennis and I follow her hand in hand, we pass families, women with bellies taut and full. Not even in my own room and already I want to trade places so that my baby is living and theirs has died.

When we get to my room, a nurse with short brown hair greets us with the presence of someone who knows what she's doing. "I'm so sorry. We're going to get you through this."

I nod.

"Something we don't like to talk about is that this happens more often than we think. Here, have a seat and lie down while I ask you some questions." She peels back the sheets and tucks me in like she'd done it millions of times before. She grabs my rolling bed tray and sidles up next to me, leaving room for Dennis to sit at the end of the bed. If I were asked, at a future date, "When did you feel safe?" this would be the moment.

"Your doctor will be in after I get you fully admitted. I apologize; I know you answered most of these questions before, but I'll also need to hear your story, so we get it right in this chart and you won't have to keep sharing it over and over again."

We converse back and forth, the two of us, like we're having a friendly tennis volley.

When did you feel the last movements? *Yesterday but now I'm not sure.*

When was your last prenatal appointment? *Last week.*

Anything unusual? *Yes, I didn't gain weight or gain inches though both were still in the normal range, and heartbeat was normal and strong.*

Was your 20-week ultrasound normal? *Yes. Everything looked good.*

I pause to find the words and swallow the lump in my throat. "He was shy or uncooperative and didn't show us he was a he, so we just found out today we were having a son."

She reaches over and squeezes my hand. "I'm sorry this is how you found out."

She turns to Dennis, drawing him into our dialogue. "Do you have a good community of friends and family to support you?"

Dennis nods, wiping his eyes. "Yes. We have amazing friends and family. Our church is great, too."

"That's going to be important. You don't need to grieve alone." He nods as he keeps wiping.

"Do you want to hold your baby?"

"We can hold the baby? Why…" I'm interrupted before I can finish, *would we want to? What's the point?*

"It's a way to say good-bye."

As I hear her words, I realize how frozen I am. I would have never thought to ask to hold the baby even though the thought of never holding him seems devastating to me. I look at Dennis, trying to read his thoughts. He nods up and down at me before saying, "I want to hold the baby."

"Great, I'll make a note in your chart. We'll make sure this happens."

Then as if we've been talking about the weather she says, "I imagine you haven't eaten."

On cue, my stomach growls. "Not for hours."

"Well, let's get you something to eat, if it's okay with your doctor. I'll be back later to check on you before I end my shift. And I'll be keeping you in my prayers when I go home. I'll check back in with you tomorrow to make sure you're doing okay even though I'm off."

Tears run down my cheeks. "Thank you. I think I'll need all the checking in on I can get." She reaches forward and gives my hand another squeeze. "You're going to get through this." I want to believe her, but my anxiety is on high alert. This part of me has my attention, *"So many things can go wrong. You've got to be prepared."* I don't find words, so I nod slightly as my eyes fill again with tears.

As the door clicks closed behind her, Dennis turns to me, hand on my shin. "I'm thinking of going home and grabbing some toiletries and my pillow, doing some things while we wait. Would you be okay with that? Would you like anything? Your pillow? Books? What can I get for you?"

"Sure. I'll be fine," I respond automatically because that's what I do, say I'm fine even if I'm not so I don't inconvenience anyone. "I'd like my pillow, my Bible, *The Other Side of Silence*, and *Blink*. And my journal."

"Okay. I'll be back. I was also thinking of grabbing some dinner with a couple of friends, so I might be a while. Will that be okay?"

"Sure." Before he reaches the door, I add, "Have a few drinks for me, but not beer because you know—I don't like it. A margarita with salt sounds good. Maybe a peach flavor."

He chuckles on the way out, "Peach, huh. I'll see what I can do."

"Be safe," I respond as the door closes. The walls are blank with nothing to entertain my eyes. So I start naming the wall color as if in a contest, *Winter White Out. Snow Bunny. Milk.* I've exhausted my imagination and close my eyes, letting my mind wander to the beauty and excitement of my childhood home, where I played in a barn and had horses. *In my imagination, I became that little girl again. She didn't have this pain making it hard to breathe.*

I'm too numb to call anyone. So I wait. For directions. For a clue. For something to hold onto about what comes next on this awful path I find myself on.

I attempt to practice mindful eating and taste every bite, which for some reason releases a new flood of tears. I know I should be tasting gravy and roast beef but only salt in the gravy gets past my numbness. Usually my head would be spinning with ideas to make this unexpected trip to the hospital a great story-telling experience, a great blog post. Today it's beyond my powers. There is very little I would like to remember about today. There will be no color commentary.

Words Never to be Spoken

At least.
God has a plan.
What happened?
I understand how you feel.
It happened to me. You'll get through it, too.
You'll see your baby again.

Doctors and Birth Day

Two men enter my room, and by their dress and stethoscopes hanging from their necks, I know they're doctors. "Hi, Kimber," says the taller of the men. "I'm Dr. Green and this is Dr. Sylvan. First of all, I'm so very sorry for your loss." Their postures and glances say it's true. I don't sense they feel like they've drawn the short straw; instead, I get the feeling they are really here for me. "We are going to take care of you with the absolute least amount of burden we can give you. Since your body isn't giving us signs of having started the birth process, we're going to give you induction medicine. We'll start with a small amount and then see what your body does. If it jumpstarts the process, we won't do any more, but it wouldn't be uncommon to need another dose tomorrow morning. We'll just need to wait and see. Do you have any questions?"

I nod. "How long does it usually take before..." How do I put this? Expelling? Giving birth? Delivering?

He saves me from finishing my sentence, "It's hard to say. Everybody is different. But this medicine works like a train. It starts off slow, but once your body is engaged in the birthing process, everything will go fast, so we want to make sure you have the pain medication you need in order to be as comfortable as possible. We'll order an epidural as well as oral analgesics. Please let your nurses know if you need anything. For now, can we get you any medication to help you get more comfortable?"

"Yes, please, I'd like a side of a hallucinogens, maybe a benzo, and an anesthetic that would knock me out until this whole thing is over."

They join me in my fantasy escape with a slight chuckle, "That would be nice. We're going to take care of you. Please let us know if you need anything."

A baby. I'd like a baby, please.

~~~

It's 5:21 a.m. The lump in my throat, the numbness surrounding me suggests reality didn't get rewritten during my dreams. I'm still here, clothed in a light blue hospital gown, sleeping on sheets stiffer than my own.

Still, I wait for him to kick me at any moment. I want to remember everything about him, yet already my memory fails me. *Did he snuggle more into my right pelvis or the left? What did it feel like when he swam and moved?*

My hands avoid my belly, creating an unaccustomed awkwardness. Dennis is sleeping in a chair, behind me, not close to my bed. I know all I need to do is ask Dennis and he'll come to my bed to hold me, but I have no experience asking for connection when I feel so vulnerable. So I keep my wishes to myself. I notice numbness inside me, and though I know sadness is there, I can't reach it. So I lie here, pretending I don't hear Dennis's rhythmic breathing. Pretending I can get through this by myself.

~~~

The rattle of the door handle doesn't startle me. I wish it had. It would mean I'm not wide awake, desperate to escape into sleep, as Dennis has.

An unfamiliar woman in steel-blue nurse attire wastes no time with introductions as she comes toward my bed. "Your nurse is busy, so I'm doing her rounds," she says, like a diner waitress tired of reciting the morning special.

I open my mouth to greet her, but she cuts me off. "Why isn't your baby on the monitor?" she asks. My heart takes off as if someone had dropped a plate. Without waiting for a response, she grabs the baby blue elastic monitor band and begins to hug my belly as if putting on a belt. "You didn't feel like it?" she snaps. "It's important that we follow your baby's heartbeat, so we know it's okay."

"My baby is dead," I whisper, though if I wasn't so exhausted I may have screamed it.

She stops wrestling with the monitor band and backs away, speaking like she's catching her breath. "They... they didn't tell me. I'm so sorry."

I watch the nurse as she retreats toward the door. I say nothing more though I would love to remind her it's her responsibility to check my chart but what would that really gain me? Definitely not my son. She states her condolences again and flicks off the lights as she leaves.

A sound escapes my mouth. I don't recognize the groan as my own. Tears run down my cheeks as I torture myself in my fantasy of a different, live birth. I imagine talking to him quietly, sweetly, as I hold him against my belly, his skin like fine powder. I imagine putting his tiny mouth to my breast and gazing into his periwinkle eyes. I imagine hearing the squeal of delight from his sister as she opens the door and sees him for the first time.

But all I hear now is another family on the other side of my room's adjoining bathroom. I recognize that they're speaking Spanish but identify only a few words. *Bebe, bueno, MaMa.* I hear the thump-patter of a baby monitor and the mother's protests as her labor pains intensify. What will my labor be like? How will I sound? I would give anything to trade places, to have that pain, that suffering accompanied by the heartbeat thrums from the monitor.

Silence screams at me as I long to hear something, anything, from my baby's monitor. Instead, like nails on a chalkboard, I hear my husband snoring.

<p style="text-align: center">~~~</p>

It's 7:35 a.m. I should be stuck in a sea of cars on the 405 North commute from Long Beach to West LA. I'd probably be passing LAX by now. I should be feeling him swim and kick. I should be pushing his head away from my pelvis toward the center, so I don't have to pee. I should be thinking about the good-byes to my therapy clients, my supervisors, and the staff because it's my last day of work at the counseling center.

Instead, there's no swimming, no kicking, and no bladder jive. There will, however, be a good-bye.

~~~

It's 8:10. Nothing in my body feels different, occasionally I think I feel some mild cramping. Since last evening, we've had to decide his name, declare a funeral parlor, fly in a grandma, and realize that there will be no milestones met.

Dennis has left to find breakfast in the cafeteria while a new-to-me nurse pushes my IV stand as we move toward another unit where I'll be showering. She's arranged everything, including a toothbrush. Walking the corridor, I focus all my attention on her turquoise garb so I can pretend I don't see the other women—the ones walking with their hands under their ballooned bellies or those in wheelchairs with their hands resting on top of their bump while nurses push them down the hall.

I'm tempted to rub my belly so no one knows the hell I'm going through. I just want to get to the other unit, the one with the shower. The one where no mothers are walking around, taunting me with what I don't have.

We make it to the shower, only one of us wondering if I can focus long enough before losing my shit in the form of whatever socially inappropriate messiness would leak out of my reserve. I have yet to
~~~

lose control of my grief bubbling inside me. The hot water massages my skin, caresses my belly as I cannot do for myself. Or him. I've stopped touching him, inside my belly. It's too much. Too connected to his death, his dying. It's as if it's barren already, disconnected from me, like my body stops at my ribs and reconnects at my pelvis. I watch my skin turn pink then red before turning the temperature down to comfortable. I turn my body so the water pounds my back. I gently touch my belly with my lemon scented shower gel. I think of *his* first bath and burst like a raincloud, shoulders shaking, but no thundered sobs emerge, only guttural clicks from the back of my throat. I deflate onto the shower floor, my legs no longer holding me. My head leans against the tiled wall, wishing it were warm and had arms. I finger the tile, tracing the grout around the squares. My hand makes its way to my belly and caresses. It's the beginning of our good-bye. Still, I stay on the tile floor until the storm passes and I feel cold air in my bones.

<center>~~~</center>

It's 10 am. Dennis has gone home to shower. Mandy is back, sneaking in cookie dough and some nuts. "Oh my goodness. You're my savior. Would you stand by the door in case a nurse tries to come in? I want to hide this."

"How's this?" She places her right foot on the door as if doing a calf stretch. I give her a thumbs up while I chew. "Or this?" she asks as she stretches her entire body out as if trying to cover the whole door. I laugh. "Or this," she asks as she does a combination swan dive and airplane yoga pose, balancing on one leg and then the other. Our banter lasts for several minutes as I try to both savor my treats and avoid getting caught eating them.

After our shenanigans, she settles by the bed. No questions asked. No expectations of me, only words of comfort. "I don't know what to say or do to make you feel better. I don't think there is anything." I nod in agreement looking into her eyes.

I share the awful experience about the nurse who scolded me for not having my baby monitor on. Her face shifts to read anger. "Come on! You can't be serious! How hard can it be, put up a damn sign!" She pauses, taking a breath before sadness enters her voice. I feel like getting some paper and writing, "Family grieving. Use care."

I nod, allowing her protest to validate the unnecessary pain I was put through this morning, "Even a simple, 'Baby died' would work."

"We could even use medical language, 'Baby expired.'

I push down the lump in my throat. Find my voice, "Read the fucking chart before interacting."

We linger side by side before walking the corridors. "You would tell me if my underwear was showing, right?"

She looks behind me. "Absolutely. You're good."

"Are you sure? I feel like it's showing."

She looks again. "Nope. All covered."

"It doesn't feel like it."

"Let's have you twirl. Good. How 'bout making a circle with that IV pole?"

I begin a version of pole dancing while she views me from behind, chuckling. In this moment I'm struck with an unfamiliar mix of feelings—joy to be with this friend who lightens my anxiety that my underwear is showing, alongside a deep, deep sorrow that's still looking for words. "I think you're good," she declares as she moves to my side at the same time Dr. Greene walks through the double doors.

"Oh good. You're up walking around," he says, moving toward me.

"I am. This is my friend Mandy. She's helping me escape."

As they exchange words, I feel their concern and care for me all the way down into my toes covered in hospital socks. I try to keep that feeling inside of me as we continue walking the halls. I meet the gaze and respond to the "hello" of every friendly staff member but purposefully ignore everyone else, especially the pregnant women. I notice the weight I've had on my chest since yesterday afternoon is lighter out here where I am not stuck in a windowless room waiting for the inevitable. As we pass the Family Waiting Room with its storks, balloons, and "Congratulations!" gift bags, Mandy puts her hand on my arm to let me know it sucks to be walking by here. I ignore my longing to put my head on her upper arm while we walk because it feels as exposing as showing my underwear.

I take a deep breath—one I hadn't realized was stuck inside of me. As we look out the window to the courtyard below, commenting on the birds of paradise blooming there, I tilt my head sideways in her direction, knowing in this moment what safe feels like.

The Story of Us – Part II

"I brought you some ice cream."

"What?" I say into my dorm room phone. Before he could answer I rush in, "Are you serious?"

Dennis laughs. "I am. Ben and Jerry's—your favorite Chocolate Chip Cookie Dough.

I laugh. "I can't believe you're here. Where are you?"

"Downstairs."

"Downstairs, downstairs?"

He laughs. "Where else would I be?"

"I can't believe you brought me my favorite ice cream during finals. You being a working person with a job. Impressive."

"I can't have my favorite senior starving."

"I feel so understood."

"Well, are you going to come down? It's melting."

"Yes!" I pause unable to stop myself as my excitement is replaced by anxiety, "You aren't expecting me to eat it with you, are you?"

He laughs. "Of course not. I know you too well. I'm sure you have every minute of your studying planned out until your graduation party where I'll see you."

I laugh. "You do know me."

He laughs. Letting it linger over the phone before saying, "I do. Now come down."

"Coming."

Sharks On Land and In Disguise

I hear Eden's excited voice outside our door, "In here? In here?" I sit up in bed. I take in our caramel-haired, ocean-blue-eyed beauty, alert to her every movement and breathe easier when her eyes find mine and she exclaims, "Mama!"

I match her tone. "Eden!" She's all here in her plastic heeled Snow White princess shoes, navy blue leggings, and a lime green t-shirt with an embroidered butterfly. We smile at each other, and she moves toward my bed after hugging Dennis. I want to bury my head in her hair and feel her in my arms. She's full of life.

"Do you want to sit up here?" I ask patting the bed beside me.

"Yes, Mommy!" she says. I put both hands out to help her up, but she pulls back and puts her index fingers in her mouth.

"What's that?" she asks pointing to my hand.

I had forgotten that I was hooked up to a bag hanging over my bed. "This is called an IV. It's giving me important vitamins and water. It's kinda like food so I actually don't have to eat. It looks super weird, but it doesn't hurt me."

She stares at my hands unconvinced of my reassurance. I pat the bed, "Come up here and snuggle with me. It doesn't hurt me." She needs no more encouragement. We sit hip to hip. Snuggling. Squeezing each other as if to confirm we're really together. We snuggle even more as her bottom rocks back and forth until she's satisfied with our closeness. Then she starts in about her day: who's marrying who in her stuffed animal families of Shark, Siamese kitty, and Snip, a stuffed cat. She folds her hands together and looks directly at me. "Mom, let's play fish and shark. You be the fish. I be the shark."

I respond to her as I've done hundreds of times, my right hand stretching into a breaststroke while I sing off key because I can't do otherwise, "Swimming, swimming, swimming in the water, I hope I don't see a shark, shark, shark." Eden growls, softly at first and then louder. She bares her teeth, scrunching her face. Her hands become the jaws. She chomps my arm. She eats me. I scream.

She rocks with laughter, "Let's do it again!" She can play shark for hours. I'm usually used up after ten minutes, but today I, too, would do it for hours if it meant avoiding this conversation.

Eden eats me several more times before Dennis sits down beside us and says to Eden, "We need to talk to you about Baby Long Beach." My eyes fill with tears. I pray silently, "Lord, help me tell her the truth in a way that won't overwhelm her."

She moves her body slightly away from mine, her face no longer playful. I take a turn. "We have some very sad news. Baby Long Beach didn't grow all the things he needed in order to breathe and live here with us, so he's gone up to heaven to be with Jesus."

She looks away to Grammy, who is crying at the foot of the bed, and then down at the tiled floor. "I don't want him to be there. Why can't Jesus fix him and send him back?"

"That's just not the way it works, Sweetheart. On earth, you get only one chance to grow, but with Jesus, Baby Long Beach will be able to live until we can see him one day."

Eden's eyes become shiny as she moves away from me toward Grammy, who is watching her intently. I bite my lip to stop the quiver. I don't want her to move away, but I give her the freedom to choose. My eyes sting. My chest feels tight and it's difficult to breathe. I search her face looking for a sign she's going to be okay. I want to whisper, "I'm so sorry I'm shattering your innocence" but my lips don't move.

I glance at Dennis, but he's turned partially away. His upper body shakes and his hands covering his eyes can't contain the stream of tears flowing down his cheeks.

"Is he going to ride home in my car seat?" she asks begging me to say, "yes," with her eyes.

"No," I pause catching my breath, "He isn't coming home with us at all. He didn't grow like he needed to. He's in heaven now." She's just out of reach. I can't hug her. I hope my eyes say what my mouth doesn't dare, "I'm so sorry. I can't bring him back. I can't take away this hurt."

Eden only nods before she moves farther away from me, toward Grammy. Eden puts her arms out to her, and I catch her small voice saying, "I want to go home."

"Please don't push me away," I whisper, hoping the words won't carry.

I speak again this time to be heard, "Eden, I see you're sad. Can I comfort you?"

Without looking at me she slowly inches her bottom back toward me and places her head on my lap. I rub her forehead, brushing her hair away from her face. She stares at the blank, white wall, not speaking about the hurt I see in her eyes. I reassure her of my health and that I will be coming home soon.

I don't contain my tears, but Eden has none. We all lose our words until Eden finds hers again. "I want to go home, now." She sits up and moves away. "Grammy, let's go home," she says with certainty.

I get a hug from only one of them, the one without the princess shoes. Dennis walks them downstairs. I grab a box of tissues. Self-doubt sets in over her reaction. Did I do something wrong? Could I have said it differently, so she wanted my comfort? Other questions join the mental circus: Could I have prevented her brother's death? Why didn't God stop it? Is her soul destroyed?

I lean back. Push my call button.

"Can I help you?" a nurse asks through the static.

"I need some pain medicine, please."

<div align="center">~~~</div>

Someone is nudging my shoulder, moving me. I try to wake up, but I'm stuck in my dream. It's a familiar place from long ago. The sounds here remind me of scissors cutting paper, but it's the tall bromegrass against my pony's legs. I'm riding bareback, jeans against horsehair. Ladybug is heading home.

She's gone this way a hundred times, maybe even several hundred. But suddenly she turns sharply. *What is she doing?* My legs grip her back as she takes off toward the trees. Terrified, I see the tree branch coming. My heart pounds to the rhythm of her hooves. The stiff grass rattles as she runs. *How will I fit below the branch?* The tree is coming too fast. *Duck! Duck! Duck!* I scream silently to myself.

My body jerks but I'm still falling. Someone is touching my arm. I hear my name. "Kimber." I never make it to the ground as I come back into the room in blackness. Someone is tapping my shoulders, and I try to speak but nothing is coming out. It's a female voice and it's persistent, and I can't ignore it though I want to. I lift my eyebrows up, then down hoping for enough force to open my eyes, but blackness remains. I try again—up, then down. Same result. Finally, through my brain fog, my eyelids flutter, and I see blue. A nurse.

"What?" I whisper with the politeness of a roused adolescent.

"Your friend is here. She brought her baby with her," she pauses as if to let these words settle in before asking, "Do you want me to let her see you?"

"Yes," I reply, thinking nothing about the content of her words, only to appease with hope she'll let me go back to sleep.

She repeats herself slowly, as if talking to a child. "She has her baby. Do you really want her to come in?"

The word baby catches me this time, startling me awake to mull over the situation as much as my narcotic haze will allow. How difficult would it be really—to see a baby?

When I don't answer, she repeats again as if I'm an even younger child, "She has her baby."

"It must be Robin," I hear Dennis say from behind me, his voice groggy. He moves closer, "She left a voicemail an hour ago. Are you up for seeing her? I can tell her you're sleeping."

We now see each other eye to eye. It hits me that I'm the one in charge and these are my guards, looking out for my needs. I'm aware that what I really want to do is enjoy the rest of my narcotic escape, but I feel guilty to say so since I know Robin has driven an hour. So I say, "It's okay. She drove all the way. But tell her—I'm drugged."

Almost immediately, I hear a rattle and can see her moving toward my bed. She's just a bit out of focus, like I'm looking through dirty glass at a blonde headed figure wearing jeans and white top with a smallish lump being carried on her hip whose blonde hair lets me know it's her son.

She greets Dennis and me with warmth and concern, but she's a bit breathless, like someone late for an appointment. "I just had to come see you and find out what happened. But I need to feed Daniel first." She looks around noticing what I can only imagine are the sheets on the bed-chair that is also in the down position and nowhere else to sit. "Do they have a lounge somewhere?" she says, not quite looking us in the eye.

I have no access to the "sometimes overly helpful" part of me as I respond, "I don't know. I don't really know what's on the unit."

She doesn't press and walks towards the door. "I'm going to go check. I'll be back."

I nod, close my eyes, and lie back down, happy to get some more rest. As I drift into deeper sleep, I hear Robin returning to say she's found nothing.

Dennis says, "I can leave the room, so you can feed him."

"I'm so sorry for the inconvenience. I wanted to get here as soon as I could, but he's hungry."

As I hear her moving around, setting the chair up, I reconsider my invitation to let her come in. I feel a bit like I'm on a diet and she's come to eat chocolate cake in front of me—nursing her living, breathing baby in a space I can hear his slurps and burps. I don't have it in me to hold a grudge or feel angry. I know this is a person who loves me. I love her. I'm willing to give her grace, realizing she's in shock along with me—unable to process the death of my child who she, too, was looking forward to meeting.

While she's feeding Daniel, I try unsuccessfully to stay awake. I hear voices and background noises but nothing's computing as words. I'm teetering on the edge between wakefulness and slumber.

Just as I have the sense of being in a hypnotic state, I feel words coming to me that suggest I need to wake up, get back into the room when every part of me wanted to escape, stay in my mental state far, far away from here. I know the voice—Robin's. I hear my name over and over until I'm able to open my heavy eyelids. "Kimber, I'm so sorry. How are you feeling? What are you on?" I notice she's sitting on the bed now, next to my legs.

"Narcotics. Where's Daniel?"

"Dennis took him out of the room so we could talk. They let you take narcotics?"

I answer bluntly, "It won't hurt the baby. He's dead." Her grimace suggests I'm not playing nice.

I forget momentarily that we're having a conversation until I hear my name again.

"Kimber?"

I open my eyes, feeling as if my lids weigh a pound each, and mutter, "So sorry. It's the drugs."

Through somewhat blurred vision, I see Robin as she leans in and asks me, "What happened? How did you know something was wrong? Do they know how he died? Are you going to find out? How are they going to know? What symptoms did you have?"

I feel the questions like shots from a firing squad, one right after another.

Words to be Spoken

I just want to be here with you.
Please forgive me if this is poor timing…
I want to help but I don't know what my role is.
I'm available. Let me know how I can help.
I am not tired of hearing about your grief.
It makes sense you have nothing to say.
Let me sit here and hold your hand.
No words are needed now.
Let's sit together and let that be enough.
I don't know what you're feeling, so I'm not sure if this
will bring you comfort.

Mixed Company

"**O**h good. You're awake."

"Hi, Ann," I say, remembering the nurse's name from this morning. I look for her cart with her blood vials but see she's come with only a shopping bag. As she approaches my bed, I can see her eyes have tears in them.

"I feel so helpless. I didn't know what else to do so I went to the Christian bookstore during my lunch hour and found this book. I don't know if it's any good…" She looks at me as she hands me the book.

My eyes fill with tears as I take it. "How sweet. Thank you." I open it up, noticing its journal style before reaching out and touching her arm. "Really. This is so considerate of you. I feel blessed in this moment."

She looks at me again before looking away. "I didn't know what else to do."

"Thank you. I feel cared for. I will remember your kindness every time I see it."

~~~

"We're going to give you another suppository boost to keep this labor progressing since your body hasn't shown any signs of labor."

"Sounds good," I reply, trusting Dr. Greene because he's been very specific about what he's doing, what he will do, and when he's going to check on me, which he has.

"Any guess as to when this delivery will happen?" Dennis asks as he leaves his bed chair behind me and comes around to the side of my bed.
~~~

"It's really hard to say. I think before tomorrow, but sometimes the body doesn't cooperate. As I've mentioned before, we expect it to go quickly once her body starts labor."

I nod my head. "Dr. Greene, you mentioned yesterday about us having an autopsy. I wanted to clarify a few things."

He gives me a nod as Dennis sits on the side of my bed. "It likely won't reveal anything. Is that right?"

"That's right. Most of the time, nothing is found, but they do look for infections and the health of the umbilical cord, placenta, the baby's organs to get any clues around what may have happened."

"Why doesn't everyone do it?"

"Some don't need answers. People don't likely find things out, and that can feel disheartening all over again. If you're having a service and showing your baby, it could impact how the baby looks."

Dennis looks at me before saying, "I think we should. Why not?" he pauses and takes a deep breath as his tears fill his eyes and he looks at me. "What do you think?"

I squeeze his hand before looking at the doctor. "We'll do it."

Dr. Greene nods with understanding on his face. "You have my card, right?"

"I do."

"I can go over the results. Answer any questions you may have about future pregnancies."

"Thank you. I'd like that."

After he's gone, we keep the question to ourselves, "Will we be trying to have another baby?"

<div align="center">~~~</div>

Open! Open! She's touching my arm. "Kimber," she says softly.

I know her; I know that voice, it's my regular OB-GYN, but I can't wake up. She keeps saying my name, but I can't do more than flutter my eyes. I want to wake up. I want to tell her, "See something was wrong. I told you that last week."

I can do nothing but stare as my lids finally pry open. I nod as she gives me her condolences and I believe her. She looks sad. My words finally come, but only the polite type. I thank her for coming. Thank her for her words. I eventually work up the courage to say something about our last appointment, but I can't even understand what my mouth is saying so I hardly expect her to understand. *Damn narcotics.*

However, as I watch her leave, I realize the situation is unresolved. I remember our last visit when I did directly communicate my fears. My mind takes me right back there as if it's happening now.

"I feel like something isn't right with this baby. I'm worried," I tell her from my exam table after noticing I didn't gain any weight and I'm not measuring in my belly on the high average range like usual.

She raises her eyebrow at me, "He's making his ten movements every two hours, right?"

"Yes, but it's taking the full two hours."

Her eyebrows return to the up position, "Is this different than before?

"No. He's always taken around two hours."

"Then you have nothing to worry about. But just to be sure, let's listen to the heartbeat again." We listen together. It's strong, clearly beating. "That sounds strong. Nothing obvious here."

"I didn't gain any weight and I haven't changed my eating habits. That worries me."

"Sometimes this happens even this late in pregnancy. Your stomach measurements are still within the normal range," she says as she re-measures my front bulge. "He has a good strong heartbeat. Your last ultrasound didn't have anything suspicious in it."

She might as well have said, "You're being ridiculous. You have no reason to worry. Stop being irrational and just enjoy the baby's health.

"But he's so different from Eden, who kicked and moved all the time."

"You have to remember that every baby is different. This baby isn't as active as your last but he's still hitting his growth markers. He's doing fine."

Hindsight is 20/20. He wasn't "doing" fine. He isn't fine. I want to blame her. But my self-awareness nudges me to spend energy elsewhere. I know I feel like the victim who needs to find someone to blame. But logically, how can I? His vitals were never outside the normal limits. I just wish I would've marched myself down to labor and delivery for monitoring. Before. When his heartbeat was still there.

I start an internal mantra, "It's not my fault. It's not my fault. It's not my fault." I say it as the nurse comes in to give me another hit. Slowly thoughts blend with one another, and thinking doesn't matter. I'm at the gates of the place where babies don't die.

<div align="center">~~~</div>

"We want you to have your epidural before your pain levels get too high. Let's keep you comfortable." Drs. Greene and Sylvan are once again at the foot of my bed discussing my delivery, which they anticipate would be sometime tonight or early morning. "Let's get your nurse in here so we can get that ordered now for when you need it since the computer system is down."

I nod. "We just want you to be comfortable," says Dr. Greene as Dr. Sylvan turns to greet the nurse who just came through the door.

"Hi, Marissa. We'd like to make sure that Kimber gets on that epidural rotation. It looks like she's progressing well, and we anticipate within the next few hours she'll be delivering." Marissa nods. Dr.

Sylvan looks at me, but continues talking to Marissa, "We just want to make sure she's comfortable so make sure she's given what she needs to manage her pain."

"It shouldn't be any problem. We have plenty of time to put in the orders."

The Story of Us – Part III

"So you're not going to tell me where we're going?" I ask as I climb into Dennis's 4Runner.

"Nope. It's a surprise."

"This isn't going to make it weird in our friendship, is it?"

"What do you mean?"

I look out the window as we get ready to enter the freeway. I know if I look at him I might chicken out, and I've been a ball of anxiety ever since he asked me out two nights ago. "Going on a date," I pause, glance over at his face that remains blank, and continue after looking back out the window, "I'm finding myself. I have no interest in dating, and I want to make sure we're on the same page."

He chuckles, leans over, and pats my knee. "I'm making you nervous. Trust me. This won't be awkward."

He always could read between the lines. "Listen. I'm not going to relax unless you tell me. I hate surprises. You should know that by now."

"Oh. I do know. I just don't care." He laughs seemingly to himself. "I'm taking you to a seminar at the psych hospital I work at."

"You're finally having me admitted?" I hope the sarcasm is dripping in my tone.

"It's on perfectionism."

"Perfectionism?"

"Uh-huh," he glances over at me. I can see the twinkle in his eye. "You're perfect for this, and you know it, Miss "win awards and never feel like you've done enough."

I laugh and notice the tension releasing out of my body. "Maybe." I look out the window again, not wanting to show my excitement and express too much. I need to keep my emotional cards close—otherwise, it will in fact get awkward.

We're off the freeway. Waiting to turn right on Bristol. "First! We're going to dinner. My treat. Nothing fancy. I don't want you getting any ideas." We look in each other's eyes and laugh.

I take another deep breath and turn my body toward him. It's all going to be just fine. "So tell me about your job…"

Go Time

Someone's kicking me! Someone's kicking me! *"Wake up! Wake up!" I'm screaming from the inside out as if an anesthetic has left me awake but unable to move.*

I scream but don't make a sound until roused out of my narcotic sleep. *What the?* A pain shoots through me like I've been kicked in the crotch by a steel-toed boot. My pulse races. *What's going on?*

The room is dark except for a slit of light coming from under the bathroom door, illuminating the black hands of the clock high on the wall. 10:17. It must be evening.

My breath stops as another pain rips through my gut. Oh my goodness! Oh my goodness! Breathe! Just Breathe!

I recall the doctor's words from yesterday, "This induction gel starts like a train. It's slow in the beginning, but once it starts moving, it works fast."

My train's leaving the station. I'm going to meet my son. He won't come home with us. He won't meet his sister. There will be no balloons, no congratulatory signs. I will hold him one time. I won't watch him grow up. I'm leaving him here.

The next abdominal strike reminds me I'm aboard a high-speed monorail. Frantically, I stretch my right arm, trying three times before successfully pushing the square orange button for the nurse's station.

Static buzzes in before a voice answers, "Can I help you?" She sounds like she's in a tunnel.

I work to keep the panic out of my voice so I can speak full sentences. "I need my nurse. I need my epidural."

More static. "I'll let her know."

While waiting for the nurse, my contractions, which feel like the hand of God squeezing my belly, hit every few minutes. I breathe loudly, making a guttural sound, hoping to make enough noise to disturb Dennis from his slumber. But I don't ask for what I need, a birthing partner.

When Marissa arrives, she hardly waits until she's in the room to inquire, "What can I get for you?" I can tell she's in a hurry to go somewhere by the quickness of her pace and glances to the door.

"I need my epidural. I'm in a lot of pain."

Her eyes widen and her eyebrows arch as she says, "You want your epidural *now*?" She moves toward the bag of fluid that drips into my vein, checking the machine it's hanging from. "You have to finish your IV treatment first."

The IV bag is two-thirds full; it has taken two whole hours for it to deplete by a third. *Holy shit, this is not happening to me.*

The nurse avoids making eye contact. I know she doesn't think I'll get the epidural in time. *Does she remember I'm being induced? Does she remember my labor won't be a normal progression?* My heart feels like it's being swallowed by my stomach. My face is tingling. My breath comes faster, shallower. My crisis mode self wakes up, and she's pissed off. This chaos wasn't supposed to happen to me. I asked for the epidural hours ago—I asked her.

Another wave of pain jolts me into a seated position. "Oh my goodness, oh my goodness," I yell, making her hear my pain. I say it over and over, hoping the lack of cursing is saying something to her: This is your fault. I want to slice this twenty-something nurse a little. Make her suffer. Is this happening because she forgot about me? Did she set the drip rate on my IV wrong? Why can't I get it now?

I shake off the knife imagery and slice her with sharp words. "The doctor promised me I could have an epidural. You need to make that happen. How long is this bag going to take? A half hour? 45 minutes? You can't leave me like this! This is your fault."

She continues to avoid looking at me and moves to the end of my bed. "I need to go out to deliver a baby, so another nurse will be covering for me."

"*What?* When will she be in here?" I stare at her, daring her to acknowledge me with her eyes, but she doesn't. I know I'm on my own.

She interrupts the scene, "I'm sorry. I have to go. I'm sure someone will be here shortly."

She's leaving me, the bitch! I feel panic rising like high tide along with anger and determination. I make noise with each contraction.

My midsection feels run over again and again. I groan. I pant. I breathe, exhaling loudly. Dennis finally stirs, gets up and goes into the bathroom. I moan louder as the pain hits, so I know he hears me. The bathroom door opens. He moves past my bed back to his. I ask nothing of him.

I rock back and forth, grabbing the side rails. Contractions come every few minutes. I breathe through them trying to focus on anything but the pain. This induction drug is like a steroid version of the Pitocin I'd had when Eden was induced. That labor, in hindsight, has become the warm-up. Then, I'd envisioned the 9/11 firemen team from New York completing the Eco-Challenge a week after the event officially ended. They had to carry one of their members for days—their pain helped me get through the pain of that labor. Now, I'm unprepared. I have no inspiration besides what's inside of me. I'm having only thirty-second breaks between contractions now.

I internally coach myself. *You only need to last through each second.*

(It's coming too fast! I can't! I can't!)

Focus.

You can do it.

(No! No! I need relief! I need help!)

Tears flow down my cheeks as groan after groan escapes my mouth. I scan the barely lit room for something to ease my fear. I find my answer on the wall. The clock, though barely visible in the dim room, ticks off the seconds with its smallest hand. I count with the hand, riding through each second. "One, two, three, four, five…," I whisper through gritted teeth.

God, I need you. Have mercy on me. Don't hide your presence. I start reciting my favorite psalm…"Though my enemies attack me I will not fear…"

My body shifts from helpless to alert, from panic to determination as I stare at the second hand. I refuse to cave to terror. I block everything out but counting seconds. I rock myself back and forth using the metal railings on my bed, repeating out loud like a mantra, "Give me strength. He never leaves me nor forsakes me."

While the train continues its trip the pain intensifies, if that's even possible. I can't count anymore. What can I do?

"Dennis?" I say in a tone known to get his attention.

"Ya," I hear through his groggy voice.

"Go find a nurse. I need a nurse." I pant my words, adrenaline coursing through my entire body.

"Okay," he says, seemingly relieved to have something to do.

I watch him out of the corner of my eye. Slipping on his shoes and feeling around for his glasses on the floor, he looks like he doesn't quite know where he is. However, once he's collected himself, he moves quickly out the door.

Five eternal minutes pass before Dennis reenters the room, alone. "The hallways are empty, and no one is at the nurses' station."

What the hell! She lied to me. I knew she was passing me off and not following through.

"Keep looking! You need to find someone!" He stares at me blankly, so I raise my voice even more. "I'm supposed to have an epidural! Find someone, anyone! Go in rooms if you have to!"

"I'll try."

"You got this, Kimber," I say to an empty room. The clock and I wait. Flashes of my life intrude—a broken toothpick stuck in my foot for three hours, my knee split open by a broken off fence post, an Achilles heel injury, playing a basketball game with a broken wrist, running the 800 meters—every single time wondering why, a broken sesamoid bone, an induced pregnancy without pain medication—each scene I see I've made it. I rock and rock, holding onto the safety bars on my bed. I count with the second hand--"29, 30, 31." I want all other thoughts gone—"43, 44, 45."

Several times around the clock and still alone, warm water gushes from between my legs as the train runs over me again and again.

I scream.

I find anger to cope.

I scream loud enough to be heard by every nurse on the unit.

I want them to know

I. Am. Here.

I want drugs.

I want attention.

I want them to squirm—as if hearing someone being burned to death.

"Help me! Somebody help me. Help me. Please help me!!"

Dennis rushes back in, now by my side. I grab for his hand and squeeze one of his with both of mine. Eye to eye, he reassures me, "I found someone. She's coming. She said she'd be right here."

I nod and whisper, "It hurts so much! It hurts too much!" I groan again trying to equal the level of pain inside of me. As it reaches my ears, I want to look around to see who's being tortured. It strikes me seconds later—I am.

When the contraction breaks, he shifts me to his other hand and flexes the one I let go of. "Oh good, it's not broken." He half laughs. I half smile, feeling like we've taken a time out. All too soon the pain is back. The past fades away. I have a teammate. I can see in his eyes that he hates I'm in pain. Part of me wants to whimper as tears run down my checks. My shoulders shake as I sob.

He coaches me, "Kimber, you can do this. Breathe. You can do this. One pain at a time."

I nod and rock—knowing the truth that one felt pain means one less in the future.

We enter a dance.

Rock, yell, breathe, and squeeze.

"You can do this, Kimber."

Rock, yell, breathe, and squeeze.

Eight minutes later—a lifetime—a nurse and anesthesiologist barge in. The anesthesiologist, a man, drags some kind of machine next to him as he announces he's here to give me an epidural.

"I feel like pushing," I gasp to this nurse I've never seen before.

She moves to the foot of my bed quickly, but her voice is calm as if we have all day. "Let me check you. You have to lie down all the way." She might as well have asked me to tie my shoes. Impossible.

"I can't lie down. It hurts. It hurts. I can't." She looks at me with her eyebrows up. I get the message—if she doesn't check me, I can't push. I let go of Dennis's hand, placing my own on the steel side rails positioned with my knees bent, legs spread. I rock my upper body back and forth.

"In between contractions, I'll check you." She stays at the foot of my bed. Dennis, at my side, shakes out his hands, probably recovering from my grip.

"But they aren't stopping. I can't do this. I need drugs. Give me my epidural!"

Her mouth tightens before she says in a forceful tone, "You need to be checked, and you have to be still to get an epidural, too. Lie back or I'll have to hold you down." She reaches to lift my gown.

I grab Dennis's forearm with both hands and lower myself back, in agony. I squeeze his arm as if I'm about to fall off the bed. He winces but lets me hold on. The nurse checks me. We go into battle.

"I need to push!" I tell her with greater certainty.

"You can't push. You aren't dilated."

"But my body feels like pushing."

She stares me down. "You can't push. You're only at six."

Now the anesthesiologist steps up to the bed and begins asking questions. He seems to ask the same questions repeatedly, using slightly different words. "What medications are you allergic to? Are you allergic to any medications? Have you had any allergic reactions to medications before? Have you ever been allergic to medicines?"

I answer each question mechanically. "Codeine. Penicillin. Codeine. Penicillin. Codeine. Penicillin."

The anesthesiologist asks Dennis to leave the room. He protests, "Why? I shouldn't have to go. This doesn't make any sense." He steps closer to me, away from the doctor.

"Protocol," he replies, unmoved. We consult with our eyes, and I nod my approval for him to go, hoping I'm minutes away from numbness.

Now I hold onto the nurse's arm while she one-handedly moves my legs to the edge of the bed, then tugs the rest of me into a seated position.

Pain shoots up my center. "Oh, that hurts! Please, please let me lie back down."

She grips my forearm harder, but I feel her calmness and know she's helping me. "No. This will only be for a minute, then you won't feel anything. You need to stay still. He's going to put a needle in you."

Another pain shoots up my core. I try to pull away. "I can't. It hurts too bad. I need to lean back."

She grips my arms steady. "Listen, you asked for the epidural. You need to stay still until he gets the needle in."

I acquiesce and clench my teeth, grip her arms. Grip to grip we are locked in a rescue posture. I can feel cold liquid being applied to my mid-back with something soft, like a cotton ball.

Then, without warning, I'm overcome by an urge to push that can't be put off. As I push, I can feel his body moving down my birth canal and then stopping. He feels like a heavy sandbag, plugging my vaginal opening. Then I feel another push coming and my body moves without permission, informing me that my son is ready to be birthed. I feel his head crown, as I move my head to the foot of the bed and tip like a felled tree until my shoulder meets the mattress to make room for his body exiting mine. My lower half twists, with my knees sticking up in the air—in a love making position. A warm liquid oozes down my back and makes me aware of having a bowel movement, but self-consciousness is a luxury I can't afford. The baby's shoulders slip through next. The labor pain suddenly stops. I do not feel one ounce of pain. It's as if I have a huge tampon down there, not a baby. Tears roll down my cheeks. I think I've made it.

My eyes travel to my son's shoulders at my vaginal opening. My baby, my son, partially birthed, still needs to be expelled.

I hear the anesthesiologist say softly to the nurse, "Looks like I'm done here."

Dennis flies into the room as the anesthesiologist leaves, his voice frantic. "What the...? What's going on? Did you have the baby? I'm so sorry, Kimber, this isn't the way it's supposed to be. This isn't the way they said it would be. They promised you'd have drugs."

Suddenly I'm the coach as I look at him. "We can talk later about what went wrong."

I hear a familiar male voice. "What the hell?" he says. It's Dr. Greene, my attending physician. He's here. Someone called him. Thank God. He's been so kind to me since I was admitted. I think to myself, "The madness will stop. I'm saved."

He looks serious but his facial features are soft as he says, "I need you to push when I tell you to, Kimber. Are you ready?"

"Yes."

I barely tense my muscles before my son slides out. There are no smiles, no shouts of joy, no words of welcome. No admiring glances or whispers of, "Just look at him." The nurse wraps him in a white blanket with cartoon bunnies—pink, baby blue, yellow, and spring green. I watch her as if she's stolen my greatest treasure. She walks to the corner of the room and places his partially bundled body in a stainless-steel bowl before leaving him there, with his feet hanging out.

While mortuary-toned conversations carry on around me, my eyes never leave his feet. My heart bolts as if a gun went off when I hear the doctor say to the nurse, "Dead at twenty-three thirty-six hours." It's official. Our son is dead.

Not Another Day

A funeral motorcade passed me while I ran

Pain of an internal force caught my breath.

Tears mixed with sweat.

A living soul is no more.

Gone.

I find no peace in the idea of a future reuniting.

I long only for the now.

For what I don't have.

Helpless, At Least That's My Belief

I watch him, lying there all alone. I'm helpless to move, but I want to hold him. Before I can ask, the doctor informs me that he needs to reach up into my uterus to retrieve my placenta because it hasn't birthed. It's been ten minutes and he can't wait any longer.

My body tenses as I take in the sympathy in his face. I know this can't be good. As his arm enters my uterus, a tortured wail travels from my vagina up into my throat and emerges full volume out my mouth. I convulse forward. His arm feels as rough and as wrong as a baseball bat, even more so as he clears my uterus by blindly battering it before pulling out the placenta. He turns to the nurse and says, "Placenta delivered at twenty-three forty-seven."

He looks at me apologetically and says, "I need to go in again to check for any remaining tissue." With tears in my eyes I request, "Please take some fat cells while you're in there." He gives me a semi-smile and a nod while he goes in. I squeeze my eyes shut, waiting for my brain to signal the assault. I scream again, not recognizing it as mine but knowing it because of the burning sensation at the back of my throat. Pain rams me over and over again as I feel his hand sweep my insides. I whimper once he's out, wanting to curl up into a ball but remain straight. I tune him and the nurse out as they converse with one another. Tears slide one after another across the bridge of my nose. I say nothing.

Now there are two nurses in my room. The smell of ammonia fills the room. My eyes never leave my son's feet in the corner. I imagine he's cold. Lonely. But his tiny heart isn't beating. He doesn't feel any of these things.

<p style="text-align:center">~~~</p>

As I climb into bed now in a clean light blue hospital gown, I ask for pain medication for my afterbirth discomfort. Tylenol arrives in a miniature white paper cup. It's par for the course here; this night shift is tight with the drugs.

After my nurse leaves, we're alone with baby Long Beach, who's still in the corner. I ask Dennis as if he's psychic, "When are they going to come and clean him up?" "Why are they taking so long?" "Do we need to ask them to clean him so we can hold him?" Ten minutes pass, and then Dennis asks me similar questions. We have no answers and are too frozen to go pick him up. I'm also too frozen to say what I really need to say to him, "Please hold me because I'm devastated."

As I lay in bed, my belly aches as though the doctor's hand is still in my uterus and is now squeezing all my organs. In my pain, I wonder why God allowed this. That's the question isn't it, when we, as God's children, suffer what would've been so easily taken away by Him. I wonder how Mary's mind must have questioned God being with her as she gave birth in a stable. I imagine her questioning whether she'd imagined the whole thing—the angel appearing, her impregnation by the divine, finding no room at the inn. Maybe it's God's faithfulness to Mary as it's unfolded in history or maybe it's God's faithfulness in my life up until this point, that I trust in my frozen state, in Dennis' frozen state that He's present. I imagine him weeping with us, seated at the right side of God, groaning on our behalf to take away this cup. I grab a strand of life inside of me and reach out for connection to Dennis, "I'm cramping a lot. I don't remember this much pain after giving birth to Eden."

"Ask them for some drugs," he responds. "Before the doctor left, he said you can have anything you need now."

"I did. She gave me Tylenol."

"Tylenol? Shit. Where was I when this happened, talking to the doctor in the hall?" He begins pacing next to the bed. "What you need is Vicodin. Where's your doctor?"

My young nurse reenters my room. Dennis stops pacing and says, "My wife needs some stronger drugs. What can you get her?" *Whoa. Something comes alive inside of me, now we're talking. Thank you, Dennis.*

She answers me, not Dennis. "I gave you two Tylenol. I don't think I can give you anything else, but I'll ask." I nod over and over again, preparing like a wind-up toy to spring forward at the appropriate time.

Before the second hand has gone around twice, she returns with a middle-aged garbed woman whose badge reads, "Charge Nurse."

"Can I help you?" she asks with what seems like barely contained irritation.

I try to keep the anger out of my voice but hear it as I speak. "I want some stronger pain medication."

"I can give you some prescription strength Motrin, but that's it without an order."

I feel my forehead scrunching together and I lean forward speaking slowly as if to do otherwise might unleash all the anger and pain inside of me. I keep my eyes focused on hers.

"Am I missing something? My baby is dead. I can't do him any harm. My doctor told me I can have any pain medication I want, and you're telling me I can only have Motrin."

Her lips pucker as if tasting a lemon. "I'll need to ask your doctor. He's delivering a baby."

Oh no, you don't! "What you need to do is check my chart. In my chart you will find he has ordered a whole host of pain medication. It's probably right next to the epidural order I should have received at 10 before I delivered my baby."

She backs away from the bed with an expression I can't read. "I'll see what I can do."

I sigh, lie back, and close my eyes, allowing the tears to come. Who knew things could go so wrong? In a redo world, we could've had a friend here to advocate for us. It feels like we're in quicksand, the weight of our situation making it hard to breathe. I keep thinking something is going to relieve the pressure, but then the next thing happens, and I feel stuck.

My child is still in the corner. He hasn't been touched. They cleaned my blood clot from the floor sooner than they cleaned my son. I take a deep breath and practice my meditation. Breathing in God's words, "I love you." Breathing out my response to Him, "I love you."

I'm lost to the time but eventually the door opens, and the charge nurse returns with a pill and water. "Here's some Vicodin. It was ordered in your chart." I take the pill without a smirk because a victory about drugs is trifle compared to the battle I've lost: my son's ability to live.

Another nurse comes in and clears my son away with no words or explanation. Fear kicks in, "Will she remember to bring him back? Where is she taking him? How long will he be gone?" Another part of my mind chimes in, "Just breathe, Kimber. You're okay. It's okay. They won't forget."

Dennis and I wait together, yet apart, anticipating our first, and last, meeting with our child. Neither of us says a word, and left to myself, my dread takes over. Over and over, I remind myself to take my tongue off the roof of my mouth. Over and over I remind myself, "This is it—have no regrets. Be present. Be here. Be right here." I feel the cramping subside, grateful to have that distraction removed. So, we wait for ten minutes, then twenty. According to the school styled clock, it's past midnight, yet I'm as alert as if the sun is high in the sky.

I'm in anticipation mode, *"What if my heart doesn't feel love?"*
What if I'm repulsed by how he looks?
What if they have to tear him from my arms, prying finger by finger?
What if my next drug is Haldol, an antipsychotic?"
Dread is winning. I feel it in my tightening chest, my clenched jaw. Part of me is yelling to get up, leave, and never see him. I could ignore the fact that I've given birth to a dead baby and start over, get pregnant again—my mind is capable of that much denial.

But his feet pop into my mind. Sticking out of the tin pan. The size of miniature chocolate bars. I want to hold him. I do. I want to put my cheek on his and whisper "I love you." I want to tell him everything I'm going to miss—not mothering him. I want to unfreeze the emotional numbness that has invaded my body since they told me he died. Now, more than anything, I want to be with him and be able to cry.

The Story of Us – Part IV

"We're kissing."

"We are," I say feeling a flush of warmth covering my face. We continue looking into each other's eyes. The ocean breeze coming up the cliff moves pieces of my bangs to block my view. My fingers push the hairs back behind my ear. "It's all my fault."

He laughs. It's the laugh I love that reaches his eyes, and I feel like I'm the most important person in the world. "Oh, I see. It's your fault that you stole my job when I went to Europe with Steve and Ken two years ago, so I picked up shifts on the other psych unit, and we commuted together."

"Yes. That was your turn to say you only wanted to be friends."

"Right so you began playing your vocabulary tapes on our drive, claiming you needed to for your GREs."

"I did."

He leans in. His lips soft on my lips before leaning back so our faces were a few inches apart. "You did." He pauses before adding, "The timing seems suspect."

"Maybe," I move the hair out of my eyes again looking out at the ocean before returning to his gaze. "Still. I asked you to my Rosemead dance last month so I'm back to it being my fault that you're here kissing me." He raises his eyebrows. I continue, "You had a year and never made a move."

"Maybe," he leans in stopping right before our lips touch, then whispers, "That doesn't mean I wasn't plotting."

We lose our words, finding other ways to communicate in this new layer of our friendship.

Holding, For A Lifetime

Baby Long Beach enters the room in the arms of my nurse. She carries him with care, as if he's alive. I'm grateful. He has another bunny blanket, though a different color—light green. As she lays him in my arms, I notice the splotches of blood on his blanket.

"You can press your call light when you want me to come and take him." She acknowledges his place in my world as she tells me, "He's 2 lbs. 8 oz. and 15 inches tall." She doesn't linger.

For several minutes, I hold him as one might hold a bomb. Stiff. Afraid. Unsure.

I try a silent mantra hoping to relax, "He's your son. He's your son. He's your son."

I feel his skin, caress his hands and eventually, snuggle toward him. His head is perfect, not the a-bit-misshapen-because-I-went-through-the-birth-canal shaped head. Its size reminds me of a small ostrich egg I'd once held at the county fair. I cradle him in the crook of my right arm and bring him close to my face. I sniff. He's a bit antiseptic. I'm too scared to deeply inhale.

What if infant death smell is disgusting? I don't want to feel disgusted.

He's so still. His chest doesn't rise and fall. He never moves or opens his eyes.

I get braver and breathe deeply.

What does death smell like? Some type of cleaner. I forgive myself for not having Dennis go and pick him up from the bowl. We're getting him second hand. But now isn't the time for regret; now is the time to love.

I study him like a masterpiece painting I never want to forget. He has white baby goo all over his body and face, normal for preemies.

His coloring isn't pink like mine, but it isn't blue like I expected. His veins seem close to the surface, and his wrinkled skin seems olive toned but I'm not certain. I caress his skin, soft, but not baby soft. It's more weathered, like something having incubated in liquid. Looking at him, he's peaceful as if he could just be asleep.

He's a miniature version of his dad. His ears, the size of quarters, are angled away from his head. His lips are oval, thick, and plum-colored, with a flat upper lip. From head to toe, the resemblance is present in his broad forehead and wide, flat feet. I run my finger along his faintly colored eyebrows, perfectly shaped over his eye. His face has one characteristic of mine, a bunny hill ski jump nose. His sister has one, too.

My hand dwarfs his doll-size hands, which are almost all fingers. Long and narrow, they would've been perfect for catching passes, playing the piano, or opening jars. I trace the lines on his perfect palms. *No fortune to be read.* Teardrops fall from my eyes as I move my caress to his feet. My thumb is as big as his entire foot, the smallest toe the size of the cotton of a Q-tip. His second toe is longer than his big toe. This is characteristic of a great athletic jumper, according to my dad. My tears cover his feet as I grieve all the things I will miss because his feet won't grow: first steps, first run, jumps, bear crawls, walking to kindergarten, walking for high school and college graduation, walking down the aisle.

His body is light as a doll yet feels as heavy as a boulder. "Would you like to hold him?" I ask Dennis, who's been watching us from his bed. He nods as he scoops him up gently. I shut my eyes and hear Dennis sobbing.

I really want to check out, but my mental coach takes over. *I know you're exhausted and want to escape; put those feelings aside.*

What's the point? He's dead.

Be here. Be in this room. Memorize him.

Impossible. His image is slipping away, and it's only been two minutes.

You've got to hang in there.

Why?

You can do this.

But why do I need to?

Because he matters. Because he's real. Because he's a part of you. Because if you hadn't seen him, you wouldn't know that his feet are the size of miniature chocolate bars.

Trying to stay present, I feel the bed beneath my body rub the sheets between my fingers as my breathing deepens, I open my eyes and watch Dennis walk around the room, soaking his son with tears. Love washes over me, surprised it's not anger that he hasn't been more present, as I take in Dennis' tears, sharing his devastation with his son. I catch bits of it, "never going" "throw" "wanted to be your dad."

Sometime later, I hold him again, speaking to him without moving my lips, caressing his tiny feet.

Hi, Long Beach. I'm your mom. I miss you already, not having you in my womb. I miss chiding you to move around more because I need to get those ten kicks. I miss feeling you swim. I really wanted to get to know you. I wanted to see the color of your eyes and hear the sound of your voice. I wanted to see those feet grow into a man walking in our door with your own son in your arms. Are you in heaven? Your great grandmas and grandpas will take such good care of you. They loved your mommy and daddy. They're probably loving you right now.

Tears blur his features as I waver on what to do next. How do I push the call light? How do I let him leave knowing he'll be in an urn the next time I hold him?

Dennis sits next to me and my mountain of tissue, I lean on his shoulder before deciding I don't want to push any button. "Can you hold him?" I say.

"Yes. I'll take him." I close my eyes and put my pillow over my head, hoping to stop the anguish. I know Dennis has taken him away when I hear the faint click of the door as it opens and closes. A pain, sharp and insistent, rams my heart. My chest feels like it's caved in, making it hard to breathe.

Dennis returns alone, and we both lay in the dark in our respective beds. Quiet. Like a tomb.

A Voice In Need

I'm sitting here with nothing to give.
A shell of a human full of grief rather than fulfilled desires.
Can you sit with me, my friend?
Can you sit with me and not try to move me out of my despair?
Can you trust that I, in time, will move myself – but only with your company.

Only with your patient, enduring company.
I need grace.
I have none.
I think I killed him.
Surely, I did something wrong.
Surely it has to be so, so I don't have to sit in the uncertain promise of "This may happen again."

Can you free me from my bondage without uttering a word? Without trying to fix me? Without telling me it's been too long to stay in this pit of grief while those women I was pregnant with have babies in their arms. While I know they are up late at night feeding baby mouths while I'm up late feeding only my own.

Can you be with me?
While I only have need.

The Day After

In my dreams, I float on my back in the ocean. Sea salt stings my eyes and parches my mouth. I can't see the shoreline, only endless waves. I question how much longer I can float and swim. Breathing becomes difficult, and my muscles feel exhausted. I fight to keep my head above water until I can resist no more. Water fills my lungs and I start to sink. Then an impulse to live springs up in me, so I fight once more.

Then, I'm sitting up in my bed, gasping. As my surroundings sink in, I notice I'm cold and wet from my sweat. A click at the door reminds me I'm not at home. My nurse tells me she's having trouble finding a bed. We let the unsaid remain between us, "You can't go to the postpartum ward."

The clock tells me it's 2:35 am. I've barely slept since *his* birthday. I try not to think about my pillow-top bed with its light down comforter and 1,000-thread-count sheets that Dennis is sleeping in right now. I'd sent him home since I knew he wouldn't have a bed next to mine.

As I wait, now in some recovery ward, for him to come back, I take the opportunity to get reacquainted with my body. I caress my arms with my fingers. *I wish I had scented lotion and a masseuse right now.* I move to my breasts, smashing them to my chest to see what they know about giving birth. A nurse told me they'd never get the message the baby died, I'd have to deliver that myself, which I'm unsure about. My hands move to my stomach. It reminds me of dough, especially the donut dough I'd kneaded when I was a kid. Kneading it now, I want to punch it. Blame it. See if it will rise again.

I drift off until 6:00. I refuse to call anyone, even Mandy, who I know is an early riser. I tell myself it's because it's so early. But I know the truth. It's because I don't want to feel. I don't want to sit in my need for others. I'm used to being the helper. My neighbor behind the curtain separating our beds makes this hard to do as her phone starts ringing with well-wishers. My eavesdropping informs me that her daughters, her granddaughters, her son, her neighbors, and what I surmise are her church people, are the ones blowing up her phone.

During a rare break in her conversations, she asks me behind her curtain with a friendly, curious tone, "I'm recovering from hip surgery. Why are you here?"

What will it be like to speak the truth aloud? Do I really want to share? "I gave birth…I gave birth to my son who died."

I hear her take a quick breath. "I'm so sorry," she says.

"They didn't let me recover in the postpartum ward so I'm up here."

"One of my grandbabies died. It's a hard time. You sound young. How old are you?"

"36."

"Give it some time. You'll have another one." I appreciate the sympathy I hear in her voice, but it doesn't help to know I may have another one. I know she wants to be positive for me, but a new pregnancy still isn't *him.* Besides, how does she know my next baby won't die in my womb? I get it—this need to see the hope, the bigger picture. Hell, if I thought it would work, I'd surround myself with it. However, 48 hours into this, encouraging words don't even take a small piece of my sadness away.

In fact, encouragement makes me feel like there's something wrong with me, like I should be looking on the bright side. Yet, I know there's no remedy, no way out of this sadness. There's no cure for a broken heart grieving someone who's never coming back. How many well-intentioned platitudes will I receive as I tell my story? Still, like her phone line, I realize after speaking with her, I'd love to be surrounded by words of comfort and support. I know I have family, friends, and a whole church congregation who'd take my call at any hour. Part of me wants someone to talk to right now, someone I can vent to, or cry with, or just sit in silence with. Yet, I don't pick up the phone. It's complicated inside of me to need. I'm usually the one being needed. Instead, I just stare at the ceiling tiles before remembering Dennis brought my Bible. I pick it up and wonder where to begin.

Lamentations seems like a natural choice. But after skimming a few verses, I realize its David's emotional honesty, not Jeremiah's exhortations, that I long to hear. I find what I'm looking for in Psalm 139.

> *Where can I go from your Spirit? Where can I flee from your presence? If I go up to the heavens, you are there; if I make my bed in the depths, you are there; if I rise on the wings of the dawn, if I settle on the far side of the sea, even there your hand will guide me, your right hand will hold me fast. If I say, Surely the darkness will hide me and the light become night around me, even the darkness will not be dark to you; the night will shine like the day, for darkness is as light to you.*

<div align="center">~~~</div>

Grief surges up from the well of my soul and spills down my cheeks. I lie on my side and curl my legs to my chest as if in the womb. I pray, "Why, God, did you let this happen? Why didn't you prevent it? At the very least, why couldn't you have given me a few hours with him? Why haven't you shown favor to me? To us? I've been faithful to you. Why don't you work on a system of rewards? Dammit! Why don't you protect your children?

Yet, I know he protects with a different lens—death isn't death to him. Suffering isn't the same to this God of the universe.

Longing for comfort, I pull out my journal and write a psalm of my own, something I've been doing since high school when my Mom gave me a psalm she'd written. I've been inspired ever since.

Praise be to the Father who created me in my mother's womb.
Praise be to the Father who created my son in my womb.
The whole universe belongs to you, Lord.
You know it all.
You reign over all.
You, Lord, are gracious and righteous, full of compassion.
Be compassionate to us now.
Give us healing.
Give us your love.
In sickness, in health, in joy and in pain, You reign.
Forever and ever.
Amen.

~~~

Dennis should be up by now. I reach above my head and grab a dingy cream-colored oblong receiver that delivers a loud, low dial tone, replaced with electronic beeps as I punch in our home number. No answer. *Oh good, he must be on his way.*

No answer on his cell, either. Instantly, I imagine him upside down in his car on his way home earlier this morning, dead from a collision with a drunk driver. I change the channel and picture him picking up Starbucks coffee, his sleep-deprivation drug, and then driving here.

I force myself to count the 12 by 24 ceiling rectangular tiles five times before I pick up the phone again to call Dennis. 8:30. I dial again and again with a growing sense of urgency, as if I'm stuck in a car slowly sinking in a river. As each ring goes to voicemail, my urgency transforms into rage. I want to break the receiver over the phone's cradle. Instead, I set it down loud enough to make a clanging sound. I close my eyes and wait.

My quiet mind fills with thoughts reinforcing my adrenaline rush, only they have death on their mind, not anger. Eden would be to school by now.
~~~

An image of an ambulance taking her and Sharon off to the hospital, a car having run a red light.

I shake my head only to see Eden running down the sidewalk in our neighborhood and being run over while a car was pulling out its driver rushing to work.

I put my hand over my ears, as if that will help my racing heart. *You're going to have a panic attack. Stop!* I curl my body and see the dad who has a restraining order showing up at Eden's school with a gun. That image is quickly replaced by the one of Dennis upside down in his car somewhere.

I focus on my breath using words, "I'm safe" on the in breath. "Everyone's safe" on the out breath. Over and over, I repeat these words until my heart rate and breathing returns to normal.

My limbs become heavy and my breathing deeper. I'm vaguely aware I'm dreaming as I float down a river into the ocean on nothing more than a giant leaf. I notice two boys on the shore, fair skinned with blonde hair, about three or four years old, not far from me. They are laughing as they splash each other with their feet. One notices something in the water and points. The other's gaze, along with mine, follows. What are they looking at? I can't see anything. But soon my answer comes as they pull small fish from the water. Blue, yellow, orange, and red, the little creatures flop and flip in their fingers. Their laughter is musical, and I can't help but smile as they hop up and down with the fish before opening their hands to set them free.

"Are you feeling okay?" a female voice pulls me out of the sea and into my white starched sheets. Who's talking to me? It feels like minutes before I can open my eyes. "Are you doing okay? Do you need anything?" I see my nurse's face floating above me.

"Yes," I say, still groggy. I keep to myself, "What I need you can't possibly provide." I look at the clock again. 9:13. No Dennis.

My eyelids close again and I try to recreate the boys' laughter from my dream. Is he visiting me in my dreams already?

~~~

When I woke at 6:13 this morning, I asked for more pads. Three hours later the squish between my legs lets me know it's time to try another approach.

My stomach has a feeling like a hard pit. I hate asking for things. I have this awful feeling inside that actually feels sorry for the person I'm burdening with my needs.

I waddle to the counter in the center of the room, keeping my legs close together. "Hello," I say to the only nurse at the nurse's station trying not to cringe on his behalf. "I'm sorry to inconvenience you but I need a replacement pad."

"We don't have anything like that up here."

"I wasn't given anything when I transferred up to this floor."

"Okay. I'll see what I can do but I'm not sure how long it will be."

I squeeze my lips together as the pit in my stomach grows. I force myself to take a deep breath. *Don't go off. Don't go off.* I bite my lip, take a deep breath, and look around the room before returning his gaze.

"It's like this. I just gave birth to a dead baby. I'm supposed to be in the postpartum ward but for obvious reasons I'm here. Earlier they hadn't transferred any of my drug orders so that gal, pointing to the black-haired nurse coming towards us, found my orders so I could have my thyroid medication. Now you're telling me they didn't give you the right supplies."

"I'm so sorry. I will try to help you as soon as I can."

"I appreciate it. I asked three hours ago and I'm not sure what happened. I really need a new one if you catch my drift."

"I'm really sorry I don't have one to hand you. I do have an adult diaper if you'd like it."

"I might as well, given what I think is going to happen."
~~~

Where's your bed?"

"Second one over there," Pointing behind me.

"Okay. I'm going to take care of that right away. Again, I'm sorry for your loss."

"Appreciate it."

I head to the bathroom, before returning to my bed.

I close the door and head towards the toilet. Plunk. *Shit.*

I look down at my feet. A piece of blood and tissue falls; it's the size of a golf ball.

"No better time than the present to ask for my needs," I mumble to myself as I make my way back to the nurses' station. "Uh, there's a clean-up issue in that bathroom," I say pointing to the one on the left, "Dropped something the size a golf ball. So sorry."

I feel proud I didn't add, "It could've been avoided had I had a new pad."

<div style="text-align:center">~~~</div>

"Here's your prescriptions to get filled at the pharmacy. You can take one pill every eight hours as long as you need them for pain management."

This charge nurse has come up from the labor and delivery unit. I know this because she said as much when she introduced herself. "Is there someone to take you home?"

"Not yet. I don't know where my husband is."

She looks as if she doesn't know how to respond. "Well, we can't release you until someone is here."

"I'm sure he'll be here soon. He likely just needed to get some breakfast."

"Okay. Let me tell you the orders and when he gets here you can go."

I nod as she starts giving me my discharge orders. She moves her finger to the next number, number two. I look ahead—there are six numbers here. Six. I keep nodding as if I'm understanding what she's saying. As if I could remember more than a sentence right now. As if I could comprehend anything other than my baby is dead.

"Now." She looks at me as if I really need to get this one, so I stop nodding. I try to concentrate so that I can take a piece of something in. "Your body will produce milk…" I start nodding. Hoping against all hope that it's written on that yellow piece of paper because I only hear sounds. Words aren't computing.

The weight has returned, and I feel like I'm sinking back into quicksand without anyone to pull me out.

The Story of Us – Part V

We move apart after our hug. Tears in our eyes and we're standing on the cliffs, this time a few miles north and two years from our first kiss in Laguna Beach. "I know you know what I'm going to ask you." I nod. "But first, I want to do something for you."

He takes my hand, taking me along a cement path leading down the hill as if we're heading down to the beach. We pass his dad holding a camera, who I didn't know was in town, but I now know he flew in for our engagement day.

Dennis leads me to a blanket with a small stool alongside a pitcher of water and bowl. He pours the water into the bowl as he motions for me to sit on the stool. He looks at me as he takes each of my feet and puts them in the water, "Just as Christ did this for his disciples at the Last Supper, I want to do this for you. I want you to know that I will always do my best to serve you." I look at him with tears in my eyes as I nod, wiping them before they go down my cheeks.

"Thank you," I whisper. A short time later, I say "yes."

Faking It Until Your Mood Changes

The clock now reads 10:40. I could go home. But I'd need to take a cab. Dennis is AWOL. So far, I've controlled my impulse to throw the phone when I hear his voicemail greeting, "Hi, you've reached the cell phone of Dennis Del Valle," blah blah blah, "leave a message." I stop counting after forty. What's almost worse than not being able to reach him is that he hasn't thought to call me, to let me know where he is. I curb my impulse to shout expletives. I want to scream, pound my fist into my pillow. Call him names. I don't know what to do. I can't call friends because then everyone would know my husband is being a complete moron. To send him home for a few hours of sleep seemed kind. He's exploited my goodness.

The curtains at the foot of my bed move. A familiar voice, high-pitched and warm says, "Hello-o." I mouth "Hi" to greet Sharon, Dennis's mom, but no sound comes out.

She looks at the chair next to me. Empty. "Where's Dennis?"

Blood rushes to my face, heating it like an oven. I clench my fists. Hard. I take a deep breath before answering as unemotionally as possible, "Good question."

I look at Sharon's long, straight black hair that brushes her shoulders before falling down her back, almost to her waist. How do I tell a mother her son is an asshole who's completely disappeared and forgotten me?

I figure the facts will do the telling so I continue, "I've been calling him every fifteen minutes for the past several hours and he isn't answering. I have no idea where he is or what he's doing."

"I should have swung by the house first after dropping Eden off at preschool."

She shouldn't have to. But my lips don't move until I find a safer topic, "How's Eden?"

"Eden's doing okay. She's quiet, not telling me stories like she usually does. I can tell she's disappointed her baby brother won't be coming home." She pauses before adding, "She's been drawing pictures of her family and baby Long Beach is always in them."

My throat gets that narrow straw sensation again. I know my voice will crack so I just nod my head.

"When she went to school, her teachers came to her immediately. They gave her a hug. Told her they loved her. And were there for her. She looked a bit uncomfortable, but I think it calmed her. I even heard her tell one of her friends, 'My baby brother went up to heaven to be with Jesus and then went off to fairyland.'"

I lose more words. A long silence passes before I ask, "How did she sleep?"

"We watched *The Little Mermaid.* Then Eden and her stuffies had a tea party with her princess books. She tossed and turned before finally falling asleep. She left me a sliver of the king-size bed. With a chuckle she adds, "I felt like I was sleeping on a diving board all night. I was so afraid I was going to fall off the edge. Or roll over on her."

I smile at the image. "That's my girl—a snuggling bed stealer."

"When can you leave?"

"The nurse said I can go home anytime. I just need to tell them I'm ready."

Sharon takes out a brush and asks, "May I?" I nod as I slide into a sitting position so she can reach my hair. She continues, "There's something I would like to do, with your permission. I've called a woman in San Diego who does bronze imprints. It's the same company that did Eden's bronzed hands and feet. I thought it would be good to have this kind of memento to remember Baby Long Beach by. How do you feel about that?"

"That sounds good, but how will we make it work?" *My baby's in the morgue.*

"I'm going to call her back in about twenty minutes to find out when she could be here. I wanted your approval before I finalized it."

"I'll call Cheryl, the social worker, and ask about logistics. She left me her card."

After our calls, we settle in together as Sharon moves to massage my feet while I relax, close my eyes, and attempt to clear my mind.

I allow tears to fall through closed eyes while she continues to rub my feet. I ask my mind to stop replaying scenes that provoke my anger. I just want a break.

I want to enjoy this foot rub.

The strawberry smell from her lotion.

The care of Sharon who flew out here immediately to be with us.

The care of our friends who have called, offered help, and organized a food chain.

<p style="text-align:center">~~~</p>

It's arranged. I'll see him again. We'll take his imprints. A hand. A foot. My mind goes to work preparing me for the worst with mental questions, "Will he smell rotten? What color will his skin be? Bloody? Blue? Or will he look the same as he did last night?"

It's noon. Sharon has gone out to buy us fast food while we wait for Tessa, the woman who bronzes imprints, to drive the hour and a half to the hospital. Dennis hasn't checked in or answered my calls. Where is he, having breakfast with his friends? The pull to call again is too strong to ignore.

I hear the ringing for what feels like the hundredth time. Bull's eye. Dennis's sleepy voice answers.

"Hello?"

My heart races, jaw clenched. I rapid-fire questions at him. "Where have you been? I've been calling you for hours. Why aren't you here? You were supposed to go home, sleep for a few hours, shower, and come back! Why haven't you answered your phone? I could've hemorrhaged, died, and you'd be the last to know!"

"What do you mean? You told me to come home and sleep, so I did." *Not for nine hours!*

"I can't believe you didn't even keep a phone beside you in case I needed something. Which I did!"

"What did you need?"

"To know where you are. To let you know I can go home," I say, getting louder and louder with each sentence.

"I'm sorry. I'm exhausted. I didn't hear either phone. Have you been alone?"

What has that got to do with anything? I answer in a growl, "Now I am. Your mom was here, but she's out getting us some food."

"Well. That's good."

My hand hurts from squeezing the phone, but I can't loosen my grip. "What do you mean, 'That's good?'" I'm practically yelling into the phone. "What's the relevance of whether or not your mom is here? *You're* not here."

"Why do you need me there? I hear you're angry at me, but it's not like you're all by yourself."

"So I can be justifiably angry with you if your mom wasn't here, but since she was, I'm not supposed to be angry? Is that what you're saying?"

I can hear him let out a long breath. I imagine him running his fingers through his brown curly hair. "No. Listen. I'm just saying it seems like a win-win because I got to sleep, and you got to have company." *You're missing the point.*

Adrenaline courses through my veins so I remain quiet, knowing nothing but future regret will emerge.

"Do you want me to come now?"

I sigh and take a deep breath. "No. It's a little too late for that."

After a pause, I add in a quieter tone, "I'm expecting to go home soon. Why don't you go pick up Eden from school at 1:00? She'll be glad to see you."

"Okay. Are you sure? I know my mom wouldn't mind picking her up. Then I could come and be with you."

I give him my standard bullshit line, "I'm fine." But after a deep breath, I say something genuine. "Give Eden a hug for me. Tell her I'll be coming home soon."

"Okay. I'm sorry you're angry with me." His voice is softer, no longer defensive.

"Bye," I reply. A stranger would have gotten more warmth.

I put the phone down with more force than a gentle placement, then replay the conversation in my mind, my anger building once again. He didn't even really apologize. Expressing regret because I'm upset isn't an apology. I hate it when I feel like a victim, but for now I don't care. For what feels like the umpteenth time today, I sob into my pillow.

I force myself to move on from our conversation. I'm going to see Baby Long Beach one last time. I long to touch his feet. His hands. His fingers. His lips. His nose. His eyebrows. The pile of rumpled tissue continues to mount on my bed.

~~~

Tessa goes right to work, pulling clay out of her cooler. I stand beside her holding Baby Long Beach's arm and leg while she carefully imprints each finger and toe into the clay. Five minutes later, I hold him to my chest. He's a bundle of blankets with a body wrapped in them. I hold him out now in front of me so I can see him. Sharon stands near me, tears running down her cheeks.
~~~

I can't get over how much he looks like Dennis: the flat forehead and strong jaw lines, the square face, the flat, wide feet, his ears, his thick lips. I caress his hands, his face, and unwrap a foot before stroking it one last time. I tuck his foot back into the blanket and talk to him in my mind as I swaddle him. *Good-bye, son. I love you.*

I set him back down on the narrow table in his bundle of blankets, noticing the lack of anxiety about whether he'll fall off. Sharon picks him up and says her good-bye. It strikes me then I wonder if any of our friends would have wanted to hold him. I never thought to ask.

~~~

Sharon and I ride the elevator in silence. At the curb, I sit down on a bench while she gets the car. The birds chirp. People smile as they walk into the building. What fresh hell is waiting for them? Two weeks ago I was at a routine check-up at the office building next door, listening to my son's heartbeat. Two days ago, I entered this hospital thinking I was going to get reassurance my baby was okay, just acting sleepy.

Now, I'm leaving without my baby and I'm unsure how Dennis and I are going to make it back together. What will be left after our shock fades, and we're left with this huge chasm of disconnection between us?
~~~

For Kimber

He lives,
in the gorgeous memory
of floating the eternal sea
of your womb,
the sweet pulse of heart
and amniotic
bathing him
in a world of blanketed
wonder;
oh, how he loved
being inside
this place you created-
this temple of
sacred community
carved out
of soul and sabbath;
a waiting room
of love and maternal
commitment
before entering
the holy of Holies.

with tears and all of my love, dear friend,
Gina Mammano Vander Kam

Precious LB Del Valle

In the blink of an eye, life as we know and understand it is gone.

Life as Jesus knows it is eternal, never gone.

LB, we didn't have the pleasure of meeting you this side of heaven,

But you've made an impression on our hearts.

You were a small warrior with a short mission before you were called back

home.

Heavenly angels rejoiced in your homecoming.

Grandmas, Grandpas, uncles, aunts, and cousins were there to greet you.

Our earthly minds will never fully understand God's ways,

We will never know why your life was so short and we didn't get to spend

time with you here,

But we know you have carved out a place in our hearts that will last until we

meet you on the other side of heaven.

God is with you.

All our love, Mimi and Grandpa Court

Part Two

Confetti

The Place Where Babies Don't Die...Yet? Forever?

Sitting in the car with Sharon, I realize my prayers for the Iraqi women losing their sons and husbands in the war we started have been full of ignorance. I was ignorant of the actual devastation of losing a son, ignorant of legacy endings, ignorant of the overwhelming collapse and shock that grief leaves. We travel past familiar landmarks: a discount fabric store, a Shell station, the boys' Catholic high school, then the girls' school, Papa John's Pizza, the liquor store, and Allen's Tire Company where the marquee says, "Sorry. Yesterday was the deadline for complaints." I want to smile, but I can't gather the strength.

I'm realizing very few things seem the same to me. My body doesn't feel like mine. The round bulge above my waistband sags, rather than sticks out tautly above my black cotton pants. I feel nervous, fidgety, which is unusual for me.

I turn on the radio. Out of the speakers comes the American Rejects. "Move along, move along, like I know you do. Even when your hope is gone, just to make it through, move along." A pep talk and we're not even two miles into the drive.

I push the off button. Silence, except for the tires spinning on the road. The voices in my head are loud. You're the American reject, losing your baby. You could've done something to save him. Your body is incompetent. It couldn't nurture and develop your own child. Hell, it couldn't even deliver the placenta. Surely when you pull up in your driveway some neighbor is going to ask, "Do they know what went wrong? Do they think it was something you did?"

Soon I see the Liquidamber in my front yard, glowing with tiny spring leaves. Its greenness feels too bright—too much living color. I feel like stripping the leaves and shortening this year's lifecycle like my son's life has been shortened. I glance away, taking a moment. My neighbor's dead grass across the street seems easier on my eyes.

I lose sight of the grass as we pull into my driveway. The internal judge shows up, noticing the gray stucco on my house looks dirty. Balloons and signs are absent, of course.

I realize a number of things didn't come home from the hospital. My pregnancy glow—gone. The to-do list for setting up the baby's room—removed from my purse and in the garbage. Bookmarked web pages for car seats—deleted by Dennis at my request. The next entry in my pregnancy journal—absent and now complete.

I take only a few steps from the car when I hear a sound I'd know anywhere—SMACK! The screen door.

"Mommy! Mommy!" It feels like a week since I've seen her. Eden's short pig tails fly back, carried by the wind of her momentum. She's sporting a light pink shirt with a green butterfly embroidered on the front and a pink flowered fabric skort.

"Hi, Sweetie!" I reply as I step out of the car and walk towards her, searching her eyes for signs of grief but finding nothing unusual behind her long brown lashes.

She hands me a piece of paper. "Look, Mommy, I drew you a picture of our family."

There are four stick figures: two big, one medium, and one small.

"See, Mommy. Here is you and Daddy and me and Baby Long Beach. We're all holding hands and we're together."

My eyes fill with tears, longing for this scene to be true. Unsure of how to navigate this new territory of loss, I hold back some of my sadness but bend down to meet her eye level. "It's such a nice picture. I wish we were all together." She looks at me with her big blue eyes, as if I can pull Baby Long Beach out of a hat.

I pull her in with a one-handed hug while I hold her important picture with the other. "I've missed you so much." We walk together hand in hand before I sit down on the front porch rocker and awkwardly pull her onto my lap. My still swollen gut makes it impossible to cuddle her close, but I pull her shoulders near enough for her hair to tickle my chin. "I'm so lucky to have you as my daughter, Eden," I whisper.

I see movement out of the corner of my eyes and see Dennis as he comes through the screen door. "You're home. Can I get you anything?" His somber tone lets me know we're on the same page.

"I'd love some water, thanks."

I head to the living room with Eden. We settle in together on the worn brown leather couch. Eden snuggles next to me, adjusting her position like a cat in a box. I realize everything's the same, except it isn't. The entertainment center and bookshelves are still full of books. None are relevant; we don't have one that tells you what to do when your baby dies.

"Mommy, I want Baby Long Beach to be with our family. I want him here with us."

"I wish he was with us, too."

"Why won't he come home?"

"He didn't grow the way he needed to, so he went up to heaven."

"I want to go up to heaven. I want to play with him."

"He would've loved playing with you. You would've made a great big sister."

"I want him here." She pauses before asking, "Why didn't he grow right?"

"The doctors don't know. Sometimes babies just don't grow the way they're supposed to when they live in their mommy's tummy."

I watch her eyes get big as she asks, "Are you gonna die because Long Beach was in your tummy?"

Her words sting and my eyes fill. "No, Sweetie. Mommy is healthy." *Why worry her with the reality that I don't know when I'll die?*

She squeezes my arm with her tiny hands. "I don't want you to die, Mommy."

"I want us to be together forever, too."

She changes the conversation channel and tells me stories about her and her "boyfriend" Alex at school.

"I want to marry him like you and Daddy."

"You really like Alex, don't you?"

"Yup, and I'm going to marry him!" she says with a certainty of one whose mind has no other possibilities.

In my stomach, cramping is taking over. My uterus muscles feel like they're the width of a dishrag being stretched over a trampoline. Pretty soon I won't be able to talk without pain in my voice. I don't want Eden to see me in pain, especially after our conversation about dying.

"Eden, Mommy is going to lie down." Her lips tighten, but I don't pause. "I'm not sick or going to die but my body needs to rest and heal after growing baby Long Beach. Daddy and Grammy are here with you."

She looks down and vice-grips my arm. "I don't want you to go. I want to rest with you."

"I know you do, Sweetie. I want to be with you, too, after I rest." I mouth to Dennis, who's sitting at the dining room table watching us, "I need your help."

He comes over to the couch, puts his hand on her shoulder. "Eden, Mommy needs to lie down now. Let's go outside and see what Grammy's doing."

"No! I don't want to leave Mommy," she protests, squeezing me tighter.

I lift my arm and peel her body from my midsection. I give her shoulders a loving squeeze with both hands as I move away and say, "I'll be out in a little while."

She scrunches up her face and flares her nose. "NO! I don't want you to!" She stretches across my lap and grips my arm again.

"I'd rather play with you. But I need to rest. You can make a choice: come sleep with me or you can play outside with Daddy and Grammy."

"I don't want to rest."

"Okay. You start playing and I'll be there as soon as I can."

I feel her fingers unclenching. Dennis picks her up and carries her outside, until she can't see me anymore.

Once in my bedroom, I take my pain medication, strip down to my underwear for comfort, and slide between the sheets. I strain to hear outside. No screaming. I imagine her climbing our tree as she does every day. My eyelids get heavy. I smile in my mind when I hear Eden squeal with delight. "Mia!" She's found her neighborhood friend.

My room is suffocating from the heat. It sticks in the rafters, refusing to cool even at night. The bear is back on my chest and my breathing feels forced. However, I know that soon Vicodin will take me to that place where babies don't die. They play in the ocean and catch fish.

Darkness

Though darkness surrounds me, you are there.
I don't care.
I want to sit and mope.
Can't you go away?
Can't you allow me to be in peace?
I don't want to face my brokenness.
I only want to sulk in the wrong that has been done to me.
Don't bother meeting me in the darkness, you aren't welcome.
Do I have to reject you?
That type of darkness is scary – it's cold.
The type of cold that hurts as it unthaws.
At least here, in my complaints against you, I feel the safety to
pout.
So Leave me be.
Wallowing.
Moaning.

But don't go too far.
I need you to hear my complaints.
Until I'm sick of saying them.
Until I'm ready to pick up the pieces to find a whole

With your help.

Sitting in the Ashes with Warm Brownies

Periodically, Eden walks through my field of vision with her arms over her head making an 'o.' I recall her ballet teacher calling it high fifth. Her brown curls once again in pigtails, she wears her layered pink dress with dainty ruffles and red flowers. She's performing her ballet routine from last week's recital. I watch her through the slit in my bedroom door, but she's aware only of the two on the couch, Dennis and Sharon.

I've just woken up from another Vicodin escape.

"Aunt Lisa!" I hear Eden yell as I sit up just in time to see her soar across the room with eagle arms before collapsing around Dennis' sister's legs.

"Hi, Eden. I've missed you so much." I watch her pick Eden up for a chest-to-chest embrace.

"Where's Austin and Natalie?" Eden asked while jumping up and down.

Before Lisa can answer, another voice cuts in, "Hey, where's my hug?" Rachael, Dennis's sister-in-law enters the house behind Lisa.

"Aunt Rachael!" Eden squeals again as Rachael grabs her from Lisa and gives her a wrap-around hug.

I wonder how my son would've greeted his Grammy and Aunties.

Still sitting up, I whisper to my long-haired Sylvester look-alike cat, Oedipus, "Time for me to get myself out of bed." Oedipus opens one eye before closing it again and returning to purring.

Before standing, I do an internal body check to make sure all parts are working—wiggling toes, circling my ankles, flexing my fingers before jiggling my legs. With all parts alert, I stand. No Vicodin foggy hangover seems present.

I close the door just enough that the slit disappears, but it doesn't click shut as I step to my closet. I hear Dennis and his mom exchanging greetings with the newcomers before Rachael asks to be shown something in the kitchen.

"Aunt Lisa, do you want to see my new stuffies in my room? Some of my stuffies have been sick, but a new bear has joined them, so they are feeling better now."

"I'd love to see your room." Their voices become more muffled. "Watcha got?"

I hear Eden saying each animal's name, "Here's Chip, Snip, Big Bunny, Siamese Kitty, and Raven. Here's my baby. Her name is Cor'la." She pauses. "Aunt Lisa, my baby brother went up to be with Jesus," she says matter-of-factly.

I take a step back and sit on the bed. I wasn't expecting this conversation so soon. I lean towards the door, careful not to make a sound so I can hear what she's saying, "When Jesus saw him, he gave him a big hug and then took him to fairyland."

"Wow. Fairyland? Who's in Fairyland?"

"That's where all the fairies play. They eat their lunch together and color."

"Is Jesus there, too?"

"No. Jesus just took him to fairyland and went back to heaven."

"Was he lonely without Jesus?"

"Oh, no. He had all the fairies to play with."

From my bed, I study myself in the mirrored closet doors: swollen belly, red streaks around my nose from blowing it, bloodshot eyes, pale skin, and a blonde ponytail. I pull out my black cotton pants along with a maternity-shaped raspberry, ruffled sleeveless shirt, hoping it will give my face some color. In the other room, I hear Eden tell Lisa, "Come on. Let's go outside to see blackberries!"

I lean over and give a body length pet to the cat, before whispering, "Okay, Oedipus. It's time I made my appearance. Wish me well."

A brief, 30-degree head lift acknowledges my words and the purring resumes.

I walk into the living room before heading to the kitchen. "Hi, Rach. Thanks for coming."

She emerges through the kitchen doorway with puffy, water-filled eyes. Her long ash blonde hair swings across her shoulders as she moves to greet me. She stops an arm's length away before saying. "I'm so sorry. I just had to come and see you."

"It's good to see you."

"I feel helpless. I know there's nothing I can do, but I had to do something. So, here I am, with Lisa." At the same height, five feet four inches, we're eye-to-eye. "Lisa and I brought you Ghirardelli Triple Chocolate brownie mix—your favorite. We wanted to make them here since you like them hot and gooey."

"That's so thoughtful. I feel so known."

Her arms enfold me like a ribbon on a package before squeezing me. I take a deep breath, feeling her arms securely around me and smell her light woodsy perfume.

The screen door shuts, and I hear behind me, "Hey, there."

I turn around to see an older and darker hair version of Eden. "Hey, Lisa. Good to see you."

She pulls my body close to hers, my head to her shoulders.

As we part, we both wipe our face and eyes with our hands. "I wanted to be here in case you needed anything."

"Please just sit down and relax. I know we didn't call to warn you. Just make yourself comfortable on the couch," Racheal says from the kitchen doorway.

With a sheepish half-smile, Lisa adds, "Where's your vegetable oil and measuring cups?"

I come into the kitchen and grab one from the cupboard above the stove and the other from the drawer. As I hand them to her, she half-grins and chuckles, "Now you can sit down."

I smile as I make my way to the couch.

"How are you?" Dennis asks as he returns inside from sitting on the porch. He walks over, sits down next to me.

"Invaded." I answer.

"By my family?"

"No. My mind."

He nods with empathy in his eyes.

"Every other thought in my head shoots me with 'My baby is dead.' I can't get away from it."

He rubs his eyes. Wipes his nose with the back of his hand. "I know. I never knew him. I just can't get over that."

After a few moments, Dennis asks, "Do you want a foot massage?"

"I'd love one. Thanks." He moves down to the other end of the couch and lifts my feet. I lie back against the arm rest and close my eyes. The smell of brownies enters my nose, Dennis's fingers gently relieve pressure in my high arch, and Eden's sing-song voice floats into the house through the screen door, "These blackberries aren't ripe, Grammy. They need be very dark. These too light."

Rachael's voice brings a different sort of enjoyment, "Brownies are ready."

Outside, I hear Eden say, "Grammy, brownies are ready. Come on! Come on!"

"Mommy!" Eden runs over to me as the screen door slams. "Mommy, we get brownies! We get brownies!" She jumps up and down, holding her elbows by her side and flapping her arms as if trying to fly.

"You're so excited. Aren't we lucky that Aunt Rachael and Aunt Lisa made us brownies?"

"I'm so excited. Come on, Mommy. Come up to the table." She reaches out and grabs my hand, pulling me toward our solid oak dining room table.

"I think Baby Long Beach would've loved brownies. I want him to be here!"

"I wish he was here, too. And if he was anything like you, he'd love brownies."

Her scowling eyebrows return to their normal position. She grabs her brownie and takes a bite. She looks across the table to her dad. "Daddy, I'm gonna savor this. Are you?" *Our family eating habit that we'll never share with Long Beach.*

He nods, wipes his eyes with his index finger and thumb, and responds in a quiet tone, "Yes, Eden. I'm going to savor this."

~~~

Rachael is quiet as are Dennis and I as we sit at the dining room table. Lisa and Grammy have taken Eden to the neighborhood park.

Dennis finds his voice. "I'm so angry. I feel robbed. This is completely fucked up." Rachael and I nod. "I've been doing all this work in therapy. Preparing to be a father to a son and now," he pauses blowing his nose. "I'm not going to be."

Rachael allows the words to linger. "Do you think God will give you another chance?"

"I don't care about that. I can't even think about it."

"That makes sense."

"It's not happening now and that makes me angry."

"Does it feel like God took him away?"

"Yes. He could have stopped this."

She turns to me. "How about you, Kimber? How are you processing God?"

"I'm sad. I'm trusting for his loving kindness to show up. Like you driving the two hours to be here with us."

"What does that do? Me showing up?"

"It means I'm not alone."
~~~

She nods.

"It means that Eden gets to make brownies with her aunties."

She nods again, with tears in her eyes this time. "I want to share a song with you. I don't know if you'll feel comfort, but it says a lot. Can I read it to you?"

"Sure. I'd love to hear it."

"It's called *Held* by Natalie Grant."

It's unfair.
When the sacred is torn from your life and you survive.
This is what it means to be held.

"I don't know if that will bring healing or not."

I open my eyes, having listened to the song with them closed. "Thank you."

"You're welcome."

She leans over and gets something from her bag on the ground. "I also brought you some beer for your sorrows, and now we're going to feed you." She gets up, squeezes our shoulders as she passes us on her way into the kitchen.

I want to say to her, "Thank you for taking care of us." But I will not disturb her.

I want to say, "Does God really answer prayers?" But it seems like the moment has passed for questions like that.

A Brief History of My Relationship with God

Singing hymns and standing in the pew at Winthrop Method-
ist Church,
I believed in God as a five-year-old can.
In seventh grade I charted horoscopes to get His attention.
It didn't work. A dark spirit came.
My mother exorcised it when I went to college
and my brother took my room.

At school, I thought a Bible study might work,
but ended my basketball career
with an injury. We'd had a shot at Nationals.
I tried again with intensity and an open heart,
learned about the martyrs,
crucifixion and the hairs on my head.

Frozen

My teeth ache from the icy cold, but my body is warm under the winter sun. According to the clock-like thermometer posted on the hillside, it was 25 degrees Fahrenheit when I left several hours ago. As I come around the corner, I catch a glimpse of red on the stack of snow dropped from the roof. I ski closer. I notice it's Eden in red pajamas and what I believe are black snow boots on her feet. I do a full arm wave so she can see me. She waves back.

I hear the slide before I catch a glimpse of chimney high snow sliding into another chunk near the bottom. It's a foot thick. My brain registers it's going to fall on her before my mouth can respond.

"Eden!" I scream. The snow covers her. I'm breathless but find a way to yell, "Help! Help!"

I take off in a sprint with arms pumping at shoulder height, trying to drive my body forward. I'm 300 meters away on my cross-country skis, usually an easy sprint but after a 20-mile trip to the lake and back, I'm hitting a wall. My quads feel like jello and my hamstrings tighten.

Where's Dennis? Where's somebody? Who's watching her?

I yell again but only a whisper comes as I can't catch my breath long enough to project it out. I watch the front door area like a hawk, hoping for movement. Hoping to catch red. Hoping she doesn't suffocate.

She's going to die. I'm not going to get to her in time. My calf muscles spasm and I collapse, jolting myself forward. The nightmare ends as my mind transitions from dream to reality. I try to grab for my foot but miss it, swallowing a moan, maybe even a scream. My calf is in a full-blown cramp that feels like the muscle are being wrung dry like a wet cloth.

Shit! Shit! Shit! Get it! Get those toes!

Pain shoots up through my body, as I struggle again to maneuver around my large midsection. I want to writhe in pain but focus on my toes, knowing they are the ticket to relief. After several attempts, I finally angle myself so I can reach my foot, easing the pain.

My breathing and racing heart eventually slow down. I shiver despite the heat in the room. I focus on the finches singing outside. Sweat slides down my spine. I flop back onto my pillow.

Really, God? A cramp? You couldn't even give me a break regarding cramps? My body feels like it's a war zone. Fire nipples from no baby to feed, tortured muscles, drooping core.

~~~

The clock reads 1:03. I pull on my black cotton maternity pants and a coral t-shirt. Dennis's snores meet me as I open the bedroom door. His size 12 feet, bare, give away his location on the couch.

I look for Eden. With three and a half years of practice, I turn the knob like a master intruder, my eyes look at her bed, anticipating seeing her there.

My heart takes off and my stomach drops as I register her bed is empty.

She's been stolen!

My eyes dart around the room looking for clues. My legs move before I consciously register she's on the ground. In a pile. Stiff. Like she has a metal rod in her spine. Next to Raven, her stuffed golden retriever.

I rush towards her, "Eden? Eden, honey. What's wrong?"

I kneel, rub my hand up and down her arm before spooning her, careful to avoid lying on my pain-filled, milk-filled breasts.

She's shaking and stiff.
~~~

What the? I've seen this sort of stiffness on the adolescent unit in the psych ward when I worked there.

A 10-year-old girl with catatonic schizophrenia comes to mind. "Eden, honey. I'm here with you."

She says nothing but I know she hears me because she responds by clinging tighter to her stuffed Golden retriever, Raven, who's almost as big as she is.

"Hey there, sweetie. I'd like to help. You're safe. I'm here." I stroke her hair, the side of her face until I feel her take a deep breath and her body relaxes.

I watch the huge tear drops fall down her cheeks before disappearing beyond her cute ski jump nose.

What happened? Why isn't she in her bed? "Eden, what's wrong?"

This time she answers.

"I'm scared. I called out but no one came."

"I'm so sorry, Eden. I didn't hear you. Why didn't you come and get me?"

"Da-daddy said not to bother you. He said you needed your rest."

"Oh, honey. You can always get me. I never need rest more than I need to be your Mommy."

She snuggles closer to me, but still faces Raven. "But why don't you get to take care of Baby Long Beach?"

Tears fill my eyes and my breath catches.

"Baby Long Beach didn't develop correctly. He didn't have the things he needed to live on Earth, so he went to be with Jesus."

"Why doesn't Jesus fix him and send him back?"

"That's not the way God made us. We don't get to come back."

"But I want him," she says, "I want Jesus to fix him." She flips around and hugs my arm.

"Me too, Eden. I feel very, very sad that he's not with us. But Eden," I move closer, nose to nose, "I will always, always be his Mommy, and he will always, always be part of this family. Just like I will always be your Mommy. Forever."

Her eyes widened like saucers before saying, "Will he get birthday cakes?"

"Sure. We can make them to remember he's always in our family."

Eden snuggles into my shoulder, saying nothing. I rest my chin on her head, feeling her heartbeat, and noticing her breath. After thinking about the stiffness I saw earlier in her, I ask, "Eden, why didn't you go get Daddy when you were sad?"

"He's too scary," she says as she lifts her head to look into my eyes.

"What do you mean?"

"When he sleeps, he's loud."

"That's just snoring. You know he wouldn't hurt you." I stick her curls behind her ears.

She shakes her head with wide eyes again, "No, Mommy. He's loud."

"He would've stopped being loud after you woke him."

She avoids my eyes and snuggles back into my shoulder, "No. He's scary."

"Let's go take a nap in my bed."

As we enter my bedroom, my heart slams into my chest as I see the golden-brown bottle of Vicodin.

Was I so out of it, I couldn't hear her?

I pause over the kitchen garbage before dropping the Vicodin in. Those pills have been the only support I could count on for my rock-hard breasts. I leave them in the trash, a vision of Eden's stiff body front of mind.

Back in bed, I pull Eden's body close to mine, until she wraps my arm under hers and pulls tight. Our rhythms blend—first her breath, then mine. Over and over, we leap-frog, until hers fall behind.

~~~
~~~

At one time I wore dull. I wore it with a smile. I wore it with awards and success. I wore dull until people believed it was joy. Only I knew it wasn't. Even now I remember the wind and the cold ten years ago. I remember the bridge where I'd stood and watched the water pass, 100 feet below. I remember wondering whether I'd join the rush like a leaf before feeling nothing.

It took two years in twice-a-week therapy sessions with Dr. P to feel real, not dull or numb, after I walked away from that bridge. Suicide hasn't been a consideration for years. It isn't one now. But I have no idea the way forward. I can't wait to talk to him this week. He'll give it to me straight—tell me if Eden is emotionally ruined.

The Story of Us – Part VI

"Dennis and I fight a lot; do you think I should be worried?" I'm lying on the couch in Dr. P's office wondering if I should break off our engagement.

"What do you make of it?" he asks after a long pause.

"I think we're both stressed. He's finishing his master's, and my third year of graduate school is kicking my butt. Also, I have to decide if I should take a year off because I'm not sure if I really want to be a psychologist."

"I think you're working out some of your childhood dynamics with him."

"What do you mean?"

"Well. You seem to mistake conflict with intimacy."

I laugh before I protest, "Hey!"

He laughs. "You know it's true. You're not easy to get along with."

"Wow."

He pauses, letting his observations fill the room. "I like Dennis. He's a good guy. He's interested in growing. That says something."

"But what if we're wrong? What if we really don't get along and I'm destined to a conflictual marriage?"

The question lingers while the ticking of the clock fills the space. "Do you want to give him up?"

Tears fill my eyes. "He's my best friend. I tell him everything. He's the one I want to call whenever something good," I swallow, "Or bad happens."

"You're scared."

I nod though I know he can't see me. Eventually I find my voice and say, "I am."

"Am I, what do you say, chopped liver? You aren't alone to figure this out. I'm here." I keep nodding, letting the words settle inside. "Okay."

The word sits in the air. I turn to my right side and push myself up, looking into his eyes before I grab my purse. "I'll see you Thursday."

As I go down the elevator alone, I find the question I don't want to ask myself, "What if I can't say good-bye to Dennis, even though I should?

I'm Breathing, It's a Start

In the light of the waxing crescent moon, I retrieve the bottle I'd thrown away earlier. I take the little white pill. I return to bed in the same manner I used to catch wild barn cats in my youth—tip toes and very slow movement. I lift the covers at the same speed, wondering if my arm muscles will tire. I slide next to Eden, scooting her body over toward the middle, hoping she doesn't wake up. Hoping dreams will stop my nipples from feeling like a cigarette meeting a lighter.

~~~

A door handle rattles, startling me awake. I didn't realize I'd been sleeping. Eden bolts out of her room and stops by my bedroom. "Eden. I'm in here on the couch."

In front of me, she begins twirling back and forth in her favorite princess pajamas, an empire-waist dress with the face of a red-headed princess on top. She smiles, stops and grabs the sides of her dress as if preparing to take a bow but stops short of doing so before saying in her matter-of-fact tone, "Mommy, you missed the dinner fairies."

"Who are the dinner fairies?"

"They're taking care of us. They leave food on the front porch at dinner. Last night they left chocolate chip cookies."

"Chocolate chip cookies? Did you leave any for me?"

She nods her head several times. "Daddy made me save some."

She tips her head over to the right and looks at the wood floor before looking at me from the corner of her eyes. "Can I have yours?"
~~~

"Maybe," She climbs up and snuggles into my ribs, her head on my shoulder.

She looks me in the eyes, "I really want one, Mom. It's my favorite."

"I see."

"Mommy, are you sad?"

"Yes, Sweetie. I'm sad about baby Long Beach."

"Me, too. It's not fair I don't get to play with him."

I brush her caramel-colored bangs out of her eyes with my fingers. "I wish you could play with him, too." She snuggles her head deeper into my side and puts her arms around my center.

"Do you have a baby in there?" she asks, looking at my stomach.

"No. This is what my body looks like when a baby has been in it."

She squishes her face. "It didn't look like that after you had me."

"Yes, it did. You don't remember because you were a baby."

Her forehead wrinkles together in the middle, "I remember things when I was a baby. I don't think it looked like that."

"What do you think it looked like?"

"It looked normal."

Thirty minutes later, alone in bed, I'm still thinking about normalcy as I take one of those little white pills and wait for it to relax my body. The scene had all the components of normalcy: Eden and Dennis at Grammy's hotel eating waffles, me resting in bed after delivery. But the silence, the no sucking sounds, the no gurgles, the no tiny smacking sounds next to me, makes this scene anything but normal.

As I drift off to sleep, I remind myself, *I'm alive. I'm breathing. Normal is out there.*

~~~

I haven't been able to write. No words. My grief tornado has been on a rampage since my son died, destroying sentences and thoughts,
~~~

while uprooting any sense of wholeness inside of me. Yet, I sit with my journal on my lap waiting for them to come. My pen sits poised above the white paper in the proper writing triangle of middle finger, index and thumb of my right hand.

"Dinner, Kimber," Dennis says.

I startle, finally making contact on the page in the form of a random line. "Coming," I say.

At the table, I point at the creamy yellow cube in the middle of the table, closer to Dennis than me.

"Butter?" he asks.

"Yes, butter," I say, "Butter, that's it," I remind myself without moving my lips, without sound. "Thank you." I remember that phrase easily. No rehearsal necessary.

I'm weighed down with absence. I have no room to worry when the forgetting will stop. The absence of his swimming body along my pelvic bone replaced by flesh hanging-over-the-beltline. Flesh. I finger it now. Pinch it a little. Send a shot of pain to my brain. That I recognize. Maybe it's fat. Or organs plus skin. What is it exactly that hangs once the baby is gone?

I look at Dennis with the feeling I have something to say. But the words have gotten lost.

I forget what it's like to want to be understood. I forget what it's like to be anything other than a mother who has an empty car seat.

~~~

I'd love to numb myself with my prescription drugs, French fries, chocolate chip cookie dough, and ice cream while staring at sentimental television shows where the plots stay the same, one happy ending after another.

Instead, I push the answering machine button so I can find connection through the words of comfort from others. My brother
~~~

Brian's voice plays first. "Please let us help you. We're here anytime, anyplace. Just let us know and we'll drop everything."

My mom's voice: "I wish I was there to give you a big hug."

Bruce, my graduate school advisor: "I just got the news. We're grieving with you."

Another friend's: "We're brokenhearted with you. Please let us know if you need anything."

And another: "Words seem so empty, but they're all I have right now so I wanted to call to let you know I'm thinking of you."

And another: "Call me if you're up for company."

Fresh tears fall on my lap. I need others and here they are, reaching out to me through my answering machine. There are no questions in this space—no questions asking for me to tell them what happened. No one asking me to string together thoughts I can't grab through the fog that's taken over.

~~~

I'm stuck in a loop. Eden and I draw pictures and play stuffies. I stack used tissues one after the other as Eden draws and explains her pictures, "This is Baby Long Beach and here we are with him." "Look! I'm with him—floating with Jesus and the angels! You can't come. Only I can!" "Look here's Baby Long Beach and Jesus. He's sad. Jesus is there to comfort him, but he wants me to be there." And then there are others—less hopeful, where babies suddenly die, and mommies become sad.

~~~

I dream I'm drifting in the ocean on my back, pummeled by the waves. I know I'm dreaming, but I can't wake up. I'm searching for what I can't find. *Him.* There are no boys playing by the shore today. No boys for me to pretend are him.

In my semi-conscious state, I'm aware that in this dream my drifting has turned ominous. My raft has flipped and I am clinging to the rowlock. My breasts throb and my chest sinks like it has an anchor attached to it, dragging me down into the ocean. I'm going under and can't breathe.

"Aah!" I throw my body forward, sitting up. It's dark, and I can't get enough air. Hand to chest, I press with firmness until my gasping stops. I keep it there long after I've returned back to my pillow, staring at the ceiling. Sweat collecting on the mattress until hours later, sleep returns.

~~~

"Mommy!" I jolt up, before I turn toward the middle of my bed, remembering Eden is next to me as she has been since two days ago when I found her on the floor with Raven.

The clock next to my bed reads 3:14 a.m.

Eden shifts and squeezes my arm. I'm unsure if she's awake or asleep.

"I'm here. You're safe," I whisper.

I tuck Eden into my side. She's my unwanted heat warmer in a room that doesn't cool down without a cold night, which we haven't had in a couple of weeks.

While my heart pounds, I remember before. Before her brother died, we'd been on the steady path toward individuation, sleeping in her own bed, feeling comfortable with her school, having playdates. Now she's regressed. We've regressed. Leaving her with someone who might accidentally let something happen to her, specifically death, I find myself unable to do it. I want her with me or Dennis at
~~~

all times. I can't even entertain the offers of going to friends' houses who have a pool. What if she drowns? I couldn't bear it.

I know sleep won't come easily. So I pray, sharing my heart with God:

How can you do this to her, Lord? She was innocent. Now she thinks you've stolen her brother. Will her heart become hard, like the Israelites being delivered from slavery in Egypt? Don't let Eden be driven from you. Don't let more harm come to her. To us. Tell me you will never do so! You say in your Word, "Blessed is he who has regard for the weak; the Lord delivers him in times of trouble." I have regard for the weak. I've spent thousands of hours volunteering with people on Skid Row, homeless pregnant women, inner city kids. And yet, God, you have not delivered me, or my family.

<p style="text-align:center">~~~</p>

It's 8:00 am. Time to get ready for church. But I won't be going today. Part of me wishes I could do it. There are caring, sensitive people in the congregation, lots of them, as proven by the endless stream of cards, emails, phone calls, flowers, meals, and playdate invitations that come every day. I knew we were part of this community, but I guess I didn't *really* know until now.

I reach for the latest stack of cards we've received.

"We prayed very specifically for you tonight, knowing that only our Father can comfort you completely."

"We grieved for you when we heard the news."

"We can't imagine what this experience has been like, but we have held you three in our thoughts and prayers every day."

From the 2-year-olds Sunday school teacher, "I'm so sad I won't get to hold his hand in class two years from now."

What I don't want to hear, but would likely hear at church by well-meaning people, are phrases like "Time will heal" or "You'll have another one" or "God's in control." I also don't want to be told that my son is with Jesus unless it's by people who are shorter than my waist. In fact, what I long for most, is people who can just say *I'm sorry* and trust the Holy Spirit to remind me of God's presence.

It's too soon to go. Too soon to fall apart at every sympathetic nod, word, or expression. Too soon to answer questions that could trigger traumatic flashbacks. Too soon to walk by the church nursery, the nursing room, and the pregnant bellies. Instead, today I'm doing church in my bed with the blackout shades drawn.

Anger

It's difficult to justify being angry at the One who with but a breath created me.
Who gave me his son, willingly.
Yet, in my brokenness, I feel angry.
Why didn't I have a healthy son?
So many others do.
Why not me?
For how long must I suffer?
I feel a fool to be angry.
Who am I in light of You?
Maker of heaven and earth
Eternal God
Omnipotent God
Yet, my wee small, whiny voice explodes,
"I made a connection. You took him away. I can't make another. I don't want to tell Eden her baby brother can't come down from heaven to play or sleep in her bedroom. I detest that her 3-year-old innocence was robbed June 29th. She is no longer a stranger to death. No, she knows it intimately now. And you could have stopped it. Why didn't you?"
In my pain, I want to punish You.
Retreat. Believe less.
Yet, I'd be the fool – punishing me.
I love You because I was first loved by You.
I serve You – a God who chose to lose his son so that I may live.
Sacrificed.
For me.
His blood shed for me.
His body broken for me.
Angry?

Only in my pathetic, self-centered brokenness – which is real.
My pain is real. The perseverance is real.
Yet, I am not alone.
I haven't been abandoned.
I have been given eternal life.
I will meet my son one day because of Your plan, Your will,
Your kingdom
You live in me.
You hear my anger and don't respond likewise.
Your love pours over me even when I am angry.
Take my entitlement from me.
Transform my anger to humility.
Who am I?
I am the daughter of the eternal and one True King.
Who loves me and deserves my recognition.

When Homes Shift

I wake to silence. A visual feast greets me in the dining room: assortments of tiger lilies, Gerber daises, carnations, sunflowers, and roses.

I eat alone, unsure of where Dennis, Eden, and Sharon have gone.

~~~

George Sander's Funeral Home - Dignity Memorial, says the big black sign.

As Dennis and I pull up to the mortuary, I can't help but think, *what's dignified about being dead?*

Having never been to a funeral home, I expect the whole building to be black and shaped like a box. Instead, it's peach colored with a Spanish brick roof, trimmed with thick white molding. Like a house, with people inside who celebrate birthdays.

On the left of the circular driveway, two white statues gaze at each other between four white Romanesque pillars. With the attractive landscaping, white benches, and raised brick patio it looks like a European garden. I can see it now, "Have a picnic while we embalm your loved one. Better yet, convert your loved one into a statue."

I'd take a statue. I imagine caressing my son as a statue marble figurine, outlining his face with my fingers, massaging each toe, pretending there wasn't a good-bye.

Dennis and I walk hand-in-hand through an open doorway. Orlando, the funeral director, opens a three-ring binder. My heart drops into my stomach. Here we go, the custom packages for the dead.
~~~

Before he has a chance to speak, I say, "We don't need any services except cremation. We're burying him next month in Washington State, and we're holding a service at our local church."

"Have you thought about family plots in this area?" he replies.

This time Dennis replies, "We don't need anything else right now. We aren't in a place to discuss anything except my son."

"I understand that. Let me show you briefly what we have so I don't leave anything out."

I hear his voice, but nothing registers as words, only sounds. I watch Dennis as he listens to Orlando. He's leaning forward, nodding his head.

He's got this.

I sit back in my chair, trying to ignore the pain throughout my body as it regroups from giving birth. I look around at candlestick lamps and glossy cherry wood. It reminds me of hotel furniture.

The sound of confusion in Dennis's voice pulls me back into the conversation. "What kind of container will we need?"

"Something that will seal," Orlando replies.

"Can you be more specific? We've never done anything like this before." After a pause he adds, "We've never buried anyone."

I'm reminded of an urn-like vase I'd purchased from one of my favorite potters in Washington, the Almquists. "Would an urn about this size work?" I ask Orlando, holding my hands about a foot apart around the invisible container.

"Does it close?"

"Not now, but I could try a wine cork. The lip is about that wide."

"As long as the opening isn't too big, I think we can find something here."

I hold my hands up to show the size again. "So a container like this is big enough?"

"Oh yes. There aren't a lot of ashes."

My eyes burn and I look down at the table. I nod my head and whisper, "Of course."

I withhold spewing my anger directed at no one but the situation I find myself in. "So are his ashes about the same as a medium-size dog? A large dog? A cat? Do you cremate animals here or is that done at the vet?" I have the information I need; my son will fit easily.

Their voices fade away again until I hear Orlando say, "We'll need payment for the cremation today. Then, if you can bring me your urn, you'll be able to pick it up next week."

On autopilot, I bend down and pick up my purse to get the check-book and my calendar. While Dennis writes the check, I pen in "Bring urn to George Sander's Funeral Home" on my calendar. Like it's an ordinary appointment.

We walk out as we came, hand in hand. I hear Dennis take a deep, gulping breath as we settle into the car. He looks at me with an anguished expression. "That was the hardest thing I've ever had to do."

I notice the absence of feelings of any kind as I slightly nod my head before turning my head to stare out the window at the statues frozen in place. I have a casket-sized weight on my chest.

~~~

I wait, pen poised over my spiral notebook. Sharon has suggested having the memorial service in a couple of days since family has driven out here to be with us. I try to express what my son's life meant to me.

On the page I write, "I wanted to be his mom."

I wait, hoping for the next thought. Tired. I put down the pen. Language floating somewhere inside but there's no eighth word. No start of another sentence. No thought of how I feel. How I'm moving forward. What he's left.

There will be no memorial service in two days.
~~~

I'll let Dennis say the words.

I twist the bottle cap and grab my white pill.

Ahhh. At last.

A place where no words are needed. Only pillows and bed sheets.

The Story of Us – Part VII

"You look beautiful," Dennis says as he enters the church bridal room.

I look at him and grin. "Thank you. You look great in your tux." He leans down to kiss me. I turn my head. "You can only kiss my check for the next two hours. You'll ruin my make-up."

He laughs. "Okay. But there will be lots of kissing afterwards."

"Promises, promises," I say as we stand nose to nose. "I love you."

"I love you, too."

Later, I'm caught off guard, as he grabs me under the knees and carries me down the aisle in my wedding dress. We said, "I do."

As he sets me down, he whispers, "You're mine."

"I am." I pause, looking into his eyes, filling up with the love I see there. I know we'll be joined by our friends and families in moments. I lean forward, "And you're mine."

Before I know it, we're standing next to each other holding cake. "You're gonna get it," I say over the hoots of our friends.

"Get her, Dennis!" I throw my head back in laughter as I shake my head.

"Don't you dare."

In neck-break speed, I feel my head snapping back as he smears cake on half my face. Anger surges up through my middle and comes out through my arms and hands as I return the favor.

Later on, when we meet again for our first dance, after I've been in the bathroom with several friends picking the cake out of my hair and dabbing it off my face, so we don't ruin what's left of my make-up. "Kimber, how you respond is up to you right now. What do you want to remember about your wedding?"

I snap, "Certainly not that I got cake smeared on me."

"Listen. I'm sorry. I got carried away. I thought you were going to smear it all over me."

"You're not wearing make-up."

"I'm sorry. And I don't want you to be mad at me because I want to enjoy what's left of the reception."

"So do I."

"So do you forgive me?" We move together—front to front, the only ones on the dance floor.

"I'd like to not need to forgive you," I say talking over his shoulder not looking at him. I take a deep breath. "I forgive you."

"Thanks," he says. "I forgive you too for smearing the cake all over my face."

I roll my eyes. "You 100% deserved that." He chuckles. We kiss. Glasses are being tapped with silverware. If the walls could breathe, they do it then.

Buried

I tap my fingers lightly over the computer keys in hopes that the clicking of nails on plastic will spark some coherence. How does one announce that her child's life was over before he took a breath?

"We regret to inform you…" Strike. *Too formal.*

"With devastation, we…" Strike. *Too emotional.*

"Come mourn with us…" Strike. *Too hokey.*

The clock behind me ticks; my fingers type, then erase, type then erase until only whiteness remains. I walk around the kitchen, which takes two seconds, before sitting back down. I feel a sense of urgency to answer people's questions now so I won't have to answer them over and over again in the days ahead.

Do I declare him a stillbirth because it will explain that he didn't survive outside the womb? Will it beg the question, "Did they know he'd died before they gave birth, or did he die while being birthed?"

Thirty minutes into my quandary, I've pieced words next to words in order to create an announcement for next week's church bulletin. "It is with great sorrow that Dennis, Kimber, and Eden Del Valle announce the in-utero loss of their baby boy, Long Beach, on June 29th. A service of lamentation will be held in the chapel today, July 9th, at 4 pm. All are welcome to attend."

I hit send.

I go outside to the backyard with a box of tissues to smell the heirloom climbing roses called "Sky's the Limit."

<div align="center">~~~</div>

In grief, so many questions go unanswered.

Do I return the baby cereal a friend gave me just last week since I won't use it? Do I take back the stroller the junior high basketball team gave me as a thank you for being a volunteer coach? Do I give back the Baby Gap gift card my boss gave me now that I don't have a baby to dress? Do I return the brand-new Pack 'n Play by the back door?

I go to the internet for answers. I open my email first. "I'm so sorry," hits me once in the subject line. Then, "We are so saddened." Followed by, "We are so sorry." I open this one to see what the onslaught of personal messages is about. I scroll to see the thread and it seems they are all sending their sympathy in response to Dennis' earlier email that I hadn't read until now,

This month marked the eighth month of Kimber's pregnancy with our second child. On June 28th, Kimber went to the hospital because she was feeling anxious about a lack of movement in the baby. The doctors did an ultrasound only to discover the baby was no longer alive. The baby was delivered the next evening, he was 2.5 pounds, 15 inches long. Kimber and I were still working on the baby's name, but our daughter Eden had long ago named him Baby Long Beach, so we thought we would honor Eden's contribution. A memorial service will be held for Baby Long Beach on Sunday. Dennis Del Valle

I check my emails. I'm hit in the gut by a subject line reading Babies-R-Us—a diaper coupon.

I grab the tissues as the next email says my baby shower is officially cancelled. Blurry eyes, I click on the screen intending to scroll to the next. Bam! At the top of the pop-up ad, in bold letters, "Congratulations! Your baby is full term."

I'm not sure I can feel my toes. I wiggle them to make sure they're connected.

I watch a Douglas squirrel run across the electrical lines.

I close my laptop and go outside to smell the basil and mint grow-ing in my backyard until my heart stops racing.

~~~

I'm not sure that we can pull our marriage up from the grave. Funny how I didn't even know it was there until we faced placing our son in one. We will be burying him in August, on his due date. Bury-ing him with my grandparents, my great-grandparents, and eventually, my parents. In the family plot in Washington. Dennis and I have talked only briefly about where we will be buried. Now I won-der if it will be together. I want to hope so. I want something to rise out of this ash, something to be beautiful again. I want to go on dates that include make-out sessions in Laguna Beach or Ragtime at the Ahmanson or Ben and Jerry's ice cream in the park, all events from our dating past. I want us to communicate only with our eyes: "I could look at you forever. You're mine. We belong together." We used to gaze at each other like that. I used to laugh as he told me stories about his middle school special education students whom he adored. That was before he taught high school and stopped telling me sto-ries—or maybe I stopped listening.

It's hard not to think about feeling ignored when he went home to sleep and never came back. My resentments could eat me up from the inside. At my worst, I want to devour him in anger. Yet, I don't want another death. I don't want to fragment this family. I want to get to the other side of resentment to hope, to love.

I look around at all the condolence bouquets in our living room, most past their prime—droopy, dry around the edges, and emitting an odor, sweet and tangy. At first the sweetness draws me in, but as I breathe more deeply something else lingers: a hint of rot.

~~~

I dream that Eden and I are at an art fair. I'm sitting on a bench, and she asks if she can go get a drink at the water fountain. "Sure, Honey, I'll wait for you right here where I can see you."

Two men dressed in dark attire get in line behind her at the fountain. Something about them makes my heart race and my stomach clench. I jump up off the park bench and rush toward them.

"Noooo!" I scream as I watch them grab her and drag her away from me, into the crowd.

"Mommy! Mommy!" she yells as she twists her neck in my direction.

Screams stick in my throat as I thrust my body in her direction, feeling as if my feet have turned to cement. Fear stuns me. I find my voice as the distance between us expands. "Help! Help! Someone help me! Stop those men!" I yell as I point them out while chasing them. "They have my daughter. Please help me!"

I lose sight of Eden until I see them through the crowd. They're 30 yards away from me.

"Help! Help!" I continue screaming as my eyes dart between people's faces and Eden. They are now heading toward the bridge where I know there's a boat dock and no one is helping me.

My stomach clenches again as her screams ring out. "Mommy! Mommy! Help!"

I save my breath for running.

I hear a motor start.

I pump my arms faster. My chest aches, like it could explode. I can see their faces now, scruffy beards. But the boat driver, hand on the gear shift has been waiting for me to see his smirk and then the hand pushes up, and the jet stream of water trails behind them as they move away from the dock.

She's gone.

I hold my arms out to her as they speed away. Her screams ring in my ears. Her strained face and panicked eyes are the last things I see.

My knees buckle as I stumble onto the dock. *Too late. Too late.* I fall to the ground as if I've been shot.

Suddenly I realize I'm lying down, surrounded by soft bedding. I open my eyes to see I'm not at a dock, and it's not daytime. I'm in my bed, with Eden and Dennis. My heart continues pounding against my chest. My body seems like its recovering from a workout—I'm so stiff. I listen to their breathing for hours before my dreams return.

~~~

I hold my bottle of little white pills over the black garbage can. Half full. I've duct taped the lid as I read I'm supposed to do. Flushing them down the toilet is no longer recommended. We're leaving. Our neighbors will take our garbage out to the curb. It's the only way to say good-bye.

Good-bye, numb. I love you. I love how groggy my mind can be. There are no sharp, blindsiding stabs of "he's dead" when you're inside of me. The fire in my nipples is gone. There is no cramping. I forget about my pudgy stomach. Until you wear off. Until I can't listen to Eden's day without having my mind long to go back to sleep—where I can sometimes meet him in my dreams. But he isn't coming home. Still, somewhere I'd hoped he would.
~~~

Questions That No Longer Have Easy Answers

How many children do you have?

How old are your children?

Are you done having children?

Resting In Others

It's mid-afternoon and we're headed to Santa Barbara to visit family over the Fourth of July holiday. Sharon has driven back to Phoenix and will return for the memorial service in five days. Upon our arrival, we anticipate cocktails, along with permission to abandon most responsibilities. Two massages are booked for tomorrow, compliments of a good friend, Janine. In the backseat, Eden reads one of her shark books.

Isaac Slade's solemn cords and rugged voice interrupt my silence. *"Between the lines of fear and blame. You begin to wonder why you came. Where did I go wrong? I lost a friend. Somewhere along in the bitterness."*

New tears form. *How to save a life... I lost a friend...I would have stayed up with you all night. Had I known how to save a life.* Images crowd into my mind of Dennis in his bed while I labored and me riding home from the hospital with his mother, not him. How easily the hurt still slices into me. I feel the singer's sorrow at having let down his friend. I imagine Dennis will feel bad, too, once we talk about it.

Combustion simmers just below the surface. I want to create a scene, some excuse to run off to my hometown where there are no stoplights or billboards, only 360 degrees of mountaintops.

Eden's sweet, high-pitched voice is singing along with the radio. Listening to her and to the tires hum on the cement, my muscles start to relax. Rotating around to Eden, I ask, "You're excited to see your cousins, aren't you?"

"Uh-huh," she says with eagerness in her eyes. "I'm going to tell them about my brother. Maybe we'll draw him some pictures."

Tears well up. "I'm sure he'd love that."

Dennis squeezes my hand as we pull into the driveway of my brother Brian's home. The front door swings open and a family of towheads races to greet us. The kids wave continuously until we open our doors. Then they jump around together, talking all at once. For us parents, though we have smiles on our faces, I see sadness mirrored back to me and hear sniffles I know aren't from allergies. My sister-in-law Kennan's arms enfold me like a ribbon on a package, squeezing me tight. I take in the message of her hug: "Welcome. You're safe. I'm going to take care of things."

My brother's huge hug is more like a linebacker-style squeeze. He releases me and holds me at arm's length, as if inspecting me to make sure I'm in one piece. I see tears in the ocean-blue eyes I've known for his entire life. "We're so sorry. We're shocked with you."

We walk through their familiar door and up the stairs to put away our luggage. I say to Brian, "I'm so sorry, but I need to lie down. My body hurts all over." I don't include, especially my breasts, full of un-tapped milk.

They both ask at once, "Can I get you anything?"

I turn to Kennan. "Ibuprofen?"

"Sure. Let me get it."

I confess to Kennan, "My breasts are killing me. They're getting worse. They're rock-hard and my nipples burn. It's been a week, and nothing seems to help."

"What have you tried?"

"Only wearing this nursing bra, which is elastic and comfortable."

"Okay. I'm going to call the local birthing center and a doula I know."

Lying back on the silky white comforter, I notice its butter-like softness against my skin. Dennis has already started playing with the kids in the backyard, as evidenced by the chatter and squeals drifting through the open windows.

"Uncle Dennis, catch me!" I hear growling. I imagine him with his arms out, Frankenstein style, running toward them with his mouth open and his eyes wide. They love it.

Kennan returns before I can go to sleep. "Soooo," she begins, pausing as if she doesn't want to hurt my feelings. "Looks like you're wearing the wrong bra. You need the tightest bra possible. Here's one for you."

I nod as a fuzzy memory of my discharge nurse telling me to wear the tightest bra I owned comes into focus. At the time I remember nodding my head automatically, just wishing she'd go away so I could go back to sleep, thinking I'd read the instructions she gave me later. I forgot I even had the paper until now.

"Did completely the opposite, didn't I?"

Kennan nods. "Ice packs will help, as will alcohol, which inhibits milk production. So, here's an ice pack"—she leans over to hand me one—"and I'm going to bring up a drink and keep them coming." We both laugh. I'm about as familiar with alcohol as an adolescent and she knows it. I suppose grief won't be the only thing I'll be feeling later.

<div style="text-align:center">~~~</div>

How am I going to get through a Fourth of July party?

Move mouth slightly upward when receiving condolences.

Move sound past lump in throat. "Thank you." "Yes, it was shocking." "We're hanging in there."

Don't stare at the walls while chatting.

Look at faces during conversations.

Act normal.

Remind self I have no normal.

Unclench jaw when people say, "I know families who have miscarried."

Nod a lot.

Say nothing while screaming in head, "I didn't have a miscarriage! I had a stillbirth!"

He was eight-and-a-half months old, gestation timeline.

If I had known that something was wrong, maybe we could've met each other.

Maybe I could've held him while he was alive.

Looked into his eyes.

Maybe he would've lived for a few hours.

A few days.

A few months.

A few years.

Until I died.

Nod. "Thank you for your kind words."

Remember not to stare at walls while chatting.

~~~

I like potatoes, especially mashed. We're back at home. Eden steers the conversation, "I love these biscuits! Mommy, where has Long Beach gone?"

I squish the potatoes between my tongue and the roof of my mouth, tasting the butter, salt, and a touch of something sweeter like mayonnaise, noticing a need to push past the overwhelm to answer, "He didn't develop properly, honey."

She jumps in, "Why did the doctors take him?"

"I love brownies!" She chatters on about how delightful the biscuits are but not the salad, the potatoes but not the chicken. She pops questions about Long Beach's death in between verbalizing her current delights and the anticipatory ones like the brownies for dessert and the play date with Mia.

"Where did they take him?" "Why isn't he in Mommy's tummy anymore?" "Why isn't he ever coming home?"
~~~

Squishing the potatoes between my tongue and the roof of my mouth, I cannot do it all—grieve, contain Eden's grief, rest, deal with Dennis, and observe proper social etiquette.

Dennis clears the table while Eden cajoles, "Mommy! Come draw with me."

I take a deep breath before moving around to her side of the table. I grab some paper and stare at the sixty-four-count pack of crayons.

A rush of questions hit me. What color do I start with? What do I want to draw? What can I draw—my stick figures are pathetic? My questions fade into, What? What? What? I close my eyes and grab in the direction of the crayon box—moss green.

I lift my head when Eden says, "Look, Mommy!" She's grinning as if she's holding a piece of candy. "I drew a picture of us all. We're all smiling because Baby Long Beach is here."

She has drawn us standing in a line—Dennis, me, Eden, and Baby Long Beach—with purple bodies. We're surrounded by red flowers and flying birds. She stares into my eyes and with an authoritative tone says, "I think Jesus is going to send Baby Long Beach back down to earth so we can smile again."

We sit silently together, my hand on hers, side by side. "Let's see your picture," she says, looking at a leafless tree, flying birds, and black mountains.

"Maybe you should put Baby Long Beach in your picture. You need some pretty colors."

~~~

Dennis and I have our notepads out on the dining room table, planning the memorial service. He looks at me with a raised eyebrow. I brace myself for a question. "So are we going to keep his name?"

"Baby Long Beach?"
~~~

"Yes."

"I think we can. Eden has been so confident in her name choice. She's introduced him to all of her friends at school." The reminder takes me back in time when I heard Eden declare her brother's name for the first time.

"Come! Come!" Eden says to her friend, Alyssa, on the playground of her preschool as she uses her hand to gesture. Eden waits for her to climb down from the sandbox, then grabs her hand and pulls her in my direction. "You need to meet my baby brother." Alyssa looks at Eden with wide eyes.

I try to hold back a smile as they both walk toward me near the gate. "Hi, Eden."

"Hi Mommy," she says. "I'm showing Alyssa my baby brother."

"Oh good," I smile at them both. "Hi Alyssa." She waves her hand, ducking her head just a bit. Eden stands in front of me, her ear on my belly. Their hands are joined, before she unlocks her fingers and places it on my belly next to her ear.

"Alyssa," she says. "This is my baby brother."

"Oooh." Alyssa says. "What's its name?"

"Baby Long Beach!" Eden replies as she lifts her ear off my belly, keeping her hand there.

I laugh. "Baby Long Beach?" Eden looks up at me.

"Yup. Baby Long Beach."

I continue what I assume is a game.

"Are we having a boy or a girl?"

Eden faces me, hands on her hips. "I don't know." I imagine she's thinking that's a dumb question. She starts jumping up and down as she does when she's excited. "It doesn't matter. Its name is Baby Long Beach."

"I think that could be a great nickname."

"No, Mommy. This is the name." Eden turns to Alyssa, "Come on. Let's go in the tunnel."

~~~

"They're out there, Mommy!"

I make my way from our bedroom to the living room window, shaking my body a bit to transition from my late nap. I stand next to Eden who is now sandwiched between me and Dennis.

The sky, the color of flames, catches my attention. As I enjoy the variation, my eye catches something closer - the "they're" settled on our front lawn in a standing circle, heads bowed. I recognize close friends, church members who we've more recently gotten to know, and our senior pastor.

Through the screen door, we hear the changing of voices as different people pray. We aren't close enough to hear words, only shifting pitches mixed with silence, filling the space of the people we can't hear at all.

Tears run down Dennis's face as I look over to him. It mirrors my own.

"What are they doin'?" Eden asks.

"Praying."

"Why?"

"I think they want us to know we aren't alone."

She pauses, as if really thinking about my words. "Let's go! We don't want them to be alone." She tugs on our arms like she's the rubber band and Dennis and I are the sling shot.

Dennis turns to the door while we both stack up behind him, "Well let's go be with them."

Tears are in the eyes of the women I hug, some running down their cheeks, some not. I'm aware I'm moving in and out of autopilot. My smile feels automatic. Stiff like soft plastic. My eyes looking at each face. But as I overhear someone saying, "Alicia, I love your new haircut," I didn't notice the three inches she's gotten cut off when we
~~~

looked at one another. When we spoke for several minutes.

Even my eyes aren't working well.

"I'm sorry it took me so long to write a card. I had no words when I first heard the news." The man who is known at our church for his thoughtfulness stands before me.

"I didn't think anything of your delay. I can understand not having words."

"Thank you. Sometimes it's hard not to put expectations on yourself over how to respond."

"I'd imagine there are a lot of expectations put on you as senior pastor."

He nods. Offers no words.

Alicia comes and gives me a side hug. "How's Eden doing?" We turn and watch her positioning herself at the base of the Liquidambar in what I know is her climbing position. I'm not sure how to answer, but she's the kind of friend who can wait until I find my words.

I look around for Dennis and see him greeting some of the men, palm slap to the chest, before going in for the hug, "Love you, brother," one after another.

I look back at Eden, farther up the tree. "She's navigating it. Having nightmares at night, but she's sleeping with us so that helps them be short-lived."

"Mommy, watch!" She's ducking in between the lower branches and leaves. I wave to her, so she knows I hear her.

"I'm so sorry. She's a trooper."

"She is. Thanks for being part of her parenting squad."

Alicia moves to stand in front of me and holds my hands. "I love her, and I can't wait to see her grow up." *If she doesn't fall out of that tree first and break her neck. Then die.*

We both wipe our eyes. Hug.

I wander over through groups of conversations, feeling the grass on my bare feet. I pause long enough to exchange a few words in response to comments. "We didn't know what else to do so we wanted to gather to pray at your house."

"I'm so grateful you did." My ears are on high alert. Noticing the leaves moving, rattling, as Eden climbs and pauses. Climbs and pauses.

"Wow! Eden," says one mom.

"You are an amazing climber," says another.

I locate Dennis and tune in to his conversation.

"I'm looking to you to know how to navigate this." I glimpse at Dennis to see how he responds. He nods and goes to the next guy.

I look back to Eden. She's so high now. Eight feet. *Feel your feet on the ground. She's done this hundreds of times. She's going to be okay.*

"Hi, Mommy," she waves. I wave biting back my response of "Be careful."

The sky is now the color of mushrooms. The object itself now hidden behind the west facing houses, behind the south bay coastline, behind the horizon, heating up Hawaii until it too will lose light and darkness sets in. I'm standing next to the tree now. Looking up at Eden, smiling and waving, while surrounded by a dozen or so of our dear friends and church family, makes me realize this will not be a grief handled alone. I hadn't imagined I'd ever really need a relational safety net. In fact, I prided myself in being self-sufficient and not needing anyone. I'd been short-sighted. This woven web of friends was superior to anything I could give myself.

A vigil.

A vigil for our son who never breathed a breath yet carried our dreams.

The Story of Us – Part VIII

I flop down on the bed. Covering my face with my hands. "I can't believe my luggage got stolen." I pause. "Why didn't God protect us? Or why didn't we do what those people in front of us did, take a taxi to the ship with our luggage in hand?" I resist the impulse to beat on the bed with my fists.

"Maybe it will turn up. This has never happened to my family, and we've taken lots of cruises."

"It's not going to turn up. It's already the second day, and we know it landed in Puerto Vallarta since we tagged it in the airport."

I turn to face away from him, giving in to the impulse of slamming a fist onto the bed. "It's our damn honeymoon. This isn't fair." I feel him sit down on the bed next to my leg. "We don't have money to replace all those clothes. And all those bridal shower gifts I've never even wore…" I trail off. I feel his warm hand on my shin. I whisper, "I can't believe I had my journal in there. It had all my reflections of our engagement, everything leading up to our wedding…" I feel tears come into my closed eyes.

Dennis matches my tone, "I'm sorry. This has been a disaster." I hear him take a deep breath. "You can cry about it, you know."

"Please," I say in a tone communicating scorn. "What good does that do? None of my things are recovered."

"Maybe it would help. We're still on a beautiful vacation and we could get some clothes."

I sit up in bed, scooting to the edge until my feet touch the floor. "Come on. Hugs and tears are overrated, let's go get me a bathing suit."

When Words Are Needed

How can Dennis be so engaged and present with Eden and her needs while so inconsistent with me? He shows up for her every day. He takes her on around-the-block walks. Goes on special trips to the bakery. Plays stuffies even first thing in the morning so I can get more sleep. So thoughtful. But then he does things like not leaving his phone on when I needed him in the hospital.

I sit on my bed, running through various openers to a conversation about my feeling abandoned. I imagine he hasn't thought about it once, but I can't stop reviewing his crimes. Where do I start with talking to him about it?

"Did you think of me when you went home and didn't come back? Did you get drunk? Is that why you slept so long and didn't call to check on me?" Too accusatory, perhaps.

"I'm devastated. You didn't come back for me. Your mother brought me home. How you could possibly have thought that was okay?" Maybe too hostile.

"Do you even love me?" Eww. Not what I'm going for, way too "Mommy Dearest."

I decide to start with what I hope will sound like a curious approach. I go out to the living room where Dennis is sitting on the couch. I sit in the chair so we have the end of the couch between us.

"Dennis, I'd like to talk to you about the hospital stay. Can we revisit that?"

"Sure. I've already apologized for shutting off the ringers on the phones. What do you want to talk about?"

What I want to say is, "I know you love me but I'm not quite sure how you expect me to know it when you leave and don't check in with me." Then my mouth moves and I'm not quite sure what it's saying. "Why didn't you hold me after our baby died? Why did you walk right by me on your way to and from the bathroom? Why did you ignore my early birth pangs? Why didn't you come back to the hospital to take me home?"

I see Dennis draw back into the couch and cross his arms.

I stop talking. Force myself to start counting to ten, make it to five before saying, "Erase those questions. Can you help me understand what your thoughts were the morning you left the hospital?"

He sighs. "I was thinking that I was exhausted and needed to sleep, so I turned off the ringers so I could sleep."

I feel the heat rush to my face. "Did you ever consider that *I* might need something?" *Haven't you acted like you don't need him for years? Maybe you don't want to face the fact that you might have sent the message that you didn't need him, that you could get along just fine without his help.*

But I'm not done with him.

"Why didn't you at least check in with me? Ask me how I was doing?"

Another sigh from him. "Well, I figured you'd call if you needed me."

"How could I call you if you turned off the ringers?"

"Good point. I guess I figured you'd call my mom since she was in town and could help you."

"Having your mom there isn't the same as having my husband!" *Unclench your jaw, Kimber.*

He looks angry back. "Look, Kimber. I was tired. I was in shock. I figured everything could wait until morning, and it was more important for me to get a good night's sleep. It wasn't my best thinking, but it all worked out okay. My mom was there, and everything got taken care of."

"It doesn't feel that way to me."

"What do you want me to say?"

"Look. I don't want to have to tell you what to say." *I want you to say, "I blew it. I abandoned you. I made myself more important than you, and I'm sorry."*

I remind myself of the ways Dennis *was* available—he held Long Beach, tried to find a nurse when I was screaming out in pain, let me squeeze his arm during labor, coached me through the pain as best he could without the epidural. But I wanted him to read my mind. I wanted him to know how to take care of me and this, I know, isn't fair. I didn't ask him to sit by me at the hospital. I didn't ask him to come back in the morning by 7:00, or at least call me. Instead, I built resentment and contempt toward him when he disappointed me.

As I gaze at him, it strikes me, though not for the first time, Dennis is not just my husband. He's a man grieving the loss of his son.

"Look, I'm sorry as well. I didn't tell you what I needed—what my expectations were. I would like to somehow start again." I think I see relief on his face, but I'm uncertain so I continue after seeing his nod. "I'm tired of living with blame and criticism so ready to be expressed inside of me. What I need from you is to not make assumptions about what's going to work for me. I need you to ask if you're unclear.

"I can do that," he says with pain in his voice. We nod—back and forth, he and I. Before I can say anything, he adds, "Or at least I will try."

I semi-smile, knowing he's asking for grace if he messes up. "Thank you. I'll try too." Something is here. A promise? A vow? A last piece of kindling dampened by worry that the fire won't restart after all?

I break off the last thought and move towards him. I get up, sit beside him, and take his hand. I lean my head on his shoulder. He puts his arm around me and pulls me close. There are tears on his cheeks. I wrap my arms around his waist, crawl onto his lap, and nuzzle my nose into his neck. No more words are needed. We have nothing to say. Our son is dead.

~~~

He has his recorder, like the good journalist he is, and sets it on the table right before he finds his seat. Our friend, Jeff Jensen, is no stranger. Yet, I find myself wondering if I can put my elbows on the table while he prepares to listen to our story so he can summarize it for the service—to be read by our friend, Keith.

"I want to get the story straight so I'm recording. Hope that's okay."

Dennis and I nod in agreement.

"Let's name that the obvious question, "Why?" has no answers, so let's move onto the next question, "What happened?"

"I called Dennis to tell him I was concerned and headed to the hospital. We'd joked that they would tell me I was some crazy mom and show me a picture of a perfectly healthy baby."

"When I got the news, I was at my office, and I felt like my life was suddenly hurtling down the wrong track. I just kept telling myself, 'This can't be happening. This can't be happening,' as I finished up some to dos before I rushed to the hospital to meet Kimber."

Detail after detail we spoke, not leaving anything out. I looked at my watch; twenty minutes had passed, and we'd only gotten to the evening we'd given birth.

Dennis was telling his side of the story: "I needed some conversation plus a meatball sandwich and a beer, so Steve and Matthew offered to come to the hospital. We found a nice spot outside, and we all talked and cried. I told them about doubting God's goodness.

I prayed for that baby every day, and what did it change? What was I praying for if God was not moved by my prayers? I've studied books. Studied the Bible. Studied philosophy. All of their ideas mean nothing to me right now. All of these ideas—they don't help. They just don't help. So I talked and they listened to me."
~~~

"Then there was the giving birth part. I knew it was going to be bad when I didn't get that epidural, so I prayed like David in the psalms. What was so clear, I needed the fortitude to endure the pain, not be delivered from it so when the pain got too bad, I kept saying over and over, 'Lord, be my strength, be my shield, be my comfort in this time.'"

"What was this time like for you, Dennis?"

"I felt more estranged from God than ever. I felt useless and powerless. I couldn't stop crying and I said, over and over, 'It wasn't supposed to be this way, it wasn't supposed to be this way...'

I jumped in. "We definitely felt separated from one another. His way of getting through the horror wasn't helping me."

"Yeah. We felt truly cursed, just like at the Garden of Eden at the fall. Pain. Death. Distance. Enmity."

Twenty more minutes passed as we talked back and forth about the details of the birth.

"What was it like to hold him?"

"It was confusing. He didn't have any obvious handicaps or physical abnormalities. They really don't know why he died. But the doctor said he'd go over the autopsy with me, with us, after the results are in."

"I thought when I saw Baby Long Beach, my grieving would have some sort of resolution. Instead, when I saw him and held him, I thought my grieving would never end."

"What is the last thing you remember about being with him?"

"I remember," Dennis pauses, wiping his eyes and covering his face for a moment, "I remember placing my finger." He takes a deep breath. "I remember placing my finger inside Long Beach's hand." He wipes his eyes some more. Taking a few more deep breaths. "I wanted desperately for him to squeeze it."

Around the tape recorder, we all wipe our eyes, dab our noses with tissues. I spoke next, "I just kept looking at his feet. I kept thinking of all the things he wasn't going to do." I take a deep breath. Look away, trying to gather my words. "I would never get to see him walk or run. His fingers would never hold my hand. Seeing him made clear what I was longing for: I can now visualize who he was," I pause. Wipe my nose. My eyes. "I wasn't longing to have a boy just to have a boy. What I was longing for was this person. My grief is for a life that was and should have been." Catching my breath one more time I whisper, "My grief is for Long Beach."

~~~

I'd done it, taken Dennis and Sharon's advice: "Get out of the house and do something normal." Their looks of hopefulness, as if this would improve my mood, *our* mood, had been too earnest to dismiss. But standing here now in front of these familiar rustic iron gates at The Dock Downtown, I'm reconsidering, though I say nothing out loud to Sharon.

Really, Kimber? Shopping?

Why not? There's no newborn at home to swaddle and feed.

But you're mourning. Hide.

I'm going in. I deserve to do something lighthearted.

As if reading my mind, Sharon says, "We don't have to go in if it's too much. We can go back home right now. Just let me know. My feelings won't be hurt no matter what you decide."

I stare into the warehouse, observing a small crowd of people mulling over furniture. "It's okay. Let's see what they have."

Stepping inside, I'm immediately drawn to a wall full of tall vases. A burnt orange vase with metallic glaze particularly catches my eye. Its curved glass body rising up from a chocolate brown base reminds me of a crooked tree reaching up from the earth. But I'm not sure where it would go in my house. It seems too tall for my
~~~

entertainment center, and too bulky for a table centerpiece. But maybe. Something to consider.

I make my way over to the bins and shelves of accessories and knick-knacks. Silk journals in hot pinks, bright greens, and turquoise tempt me. I pick one up.

You have a four-year supply of journals in a box at home.

Sigh. I place it back in the bin.

I wander aimlessly, adding a few picture frames to my cart, ignoring the voice that reminds me that *he* won't be included.

I spy some aprons hanging over a sawed-off wine barrel. I finger a peach and yellow apron, embroidered with daisies. *Is it okay to enjoy this apron? Should I really be buying anything?*

"Hello." I startle as I look toward the female voice. "I'm sorry. I didn't mean to scare you. Do you need help finding anything?" says a cheerful young woman wearing a tag that reads "Helen."

My brain is slow to register her question, so I don't answer, but she continues anyway. "We have some great inventory. The aprons you're holding were overstock from Anthropologie."

I mentally catch up at this mention of a favorite store, clinching the fate of the apron. As I place it in my basket, I angle my body away from Helen, but out of my peripheral vision I see that she hasn't moved on. The corners of my lips partially curl up in my polite "leave-me-alone" expression, but I play nice, "No wonder they're so cute. But I don't need any help. Thank you."

I look around her at the items on the surrounding shelves, purposefully avoiding eye contact. Dog food bowls. Dog blankets. Knitted dog clothes. *If only I had a dog.*

Why isn't she moving on?

My heart plummets when she looks at my stomach and her smile expands. "When is your due date?"

I wonder if all the blood has drained from my face. My chest feels like it's been stepped on, making it hard to breathe. I slowly shake my head, trying to blink back tears. I swallow, but my mouth is bone dry. My voice catches, but I force out a whisper. "I just lost my baby."

I look away. I don't want her pity. But I know I need to face her, not leave my words suspended in the air between us. I straighten my spine before rephrasing my answer. "My baby died a little over a week ago."

Helen's mouth drops open and her face expresses both horror and embarrassment. "I'm so sorry. I just thought... My best friend in Seattle lost her baby, too. I'm so sorry."

I nod my head, trying to breathe normally.

"What happened?" Helen asks, speeding up her words. "Do they know?" *Here we go.*

I become aware that my head is pounding. My legs feel weak. My stomach is knotting, making me feel nauseous. "We can't find a heartbeat" rings in my ears. Somehow I manage to say, "They don't know. They just don't know."

I don't hear her response; I only see her retreating. Hiding in the barrel next to me and weeping seems like a wonderful option.

As I move away, I catch my reflection in a huge floor-length mirror. Ponytail. Maternity shirt with embroidered flowers. Black stretch pants. And that belly, sagging over my waistline.

I should be home in bed. What a stupid idea to try to do something "normal," especially go shopping.

Once in the car, I close my eyes and let the tears drip down in silence.

"Do you want to talk about it?" Sharon asks quietly as we merge onto the freeway.

After we pass a couple of exits, I answer in my schooled calm tone, the one that masks the chaos raging underneath the surface, "The woman helping me in the store asked me when my baby was due."

I hear Sharon gasp, and I turn to look at her face. Her eyes mirror what's underneath my calm, and we are both suddenly tear-filled. "I'm so sorry," she says.

"Thanks." I whisper back as I look away out the window, "This is hard."

As we drive past the San Gabriel River and the Lakewood horse stables, I turn my attention to the relational God I believe in. I have a few silent words for him since he can read my mind. "You couldn't have kept me from this shocking pain today? You couldn't have stepped in just a little bit and have that woman not go there. Haven't I already experienced enough for now? I'm speechless. Why aren't you showing your face and your generous heart?"

Tears run down my cheeks, and I'm grateful for Sharon's quiet company—being with me, yet allowing me time to myself. It reminds me a bit of this God I'm struggling with. I've known His presence since I was 5 years old, when I knew in my gut that He's real, not just some made-up belief. I've held onto my faith when I felt suicidal, when I felt unwanted and not good enough, when I felt He didn't care for me. Since 14, I've poured my heart into my journals and prayers about these insecurities—eventually always feeling more at peace with myself.

So here I sit, a passenger, reminding myself that God is generous. Generous in this moment? Maybe. Maybe he's being generous because I'm rehearsing the victory and connection in my history. Maybe he's being generous in reminding me how faithful my friends are and that I could pick up the phone and people would spend the night every night if I needed them to do that for me. My people will sacrifice for me, just like God. And here I find his generosity, his faithfulness and take the deep breath I didn't know I was holding.

Held

Providence would take a child from his mother
We're asking why this happened.
Yet – this is the promise

This is what it means to be held:
Meals brought
Funeral foods made
Funeral program created
Scrapbook
Looking into faces of tears
Brownies
Cookie Dough
Purchasing bronzing kits
Offers to be available
Cards
Chocolates
Dropping everything to watch our daughter
Living in the ordinary with us

We are being held in every –
Tear
You aren' t alone
This totally sucks
Come here.
Tears are welcome.
Words unnecessary.

Inspired by Natalie Grant's Song "Held"

Memorial

I've delayed as much as I can. I've eaten chocolates, the size of his feet, four times now. I've cleaned. I've read. I've watched television. I've walked around the backyard three times. I've typed all the lyrics and copyright information and emailed them off to our friends to copy and deliver to the memorial service today. I can't avoid it anymore. It's a ceremonial good-bye. All the details are taken care of—the food for the reception, donated by church members and organized by Shelly, the programs printed, the chapel space provided, the music, rehearsed by our dear friends, and the announcement made in the church bulletin.

On the drive, I remain silent, but my mind jumps like a chickadee moving from limb to limb. Did we really need a service? Couldn't we grieve alone? Fears spring up. What if no one shows up? Who will? Is this a life worth celebrating, someone who didn't breathe one breath? Will only friends show? And of them, who? My stomach is anxious, bound up in phantom round balls, I'm aware I haven't eaten for hours. My jaw is tight, but I wish it wasn't so. I shake out my hands and lower my tongue from the roof of my mouth, hoping to send the message to my body, "I'm okay." I take a deep breath, "It's all going to be okay."

When we arrive at church, a place where I've come every Sunday for ten years, yet it feels as if I'm a visitor. I'm aware it's I who has changed, and yet I would swear it's the place itself. I wonder if this is a small slice of what soldiers feel when they return home after engaging in battle. Trauma changes the feel of ourselves to ourselves, making even the most familiar settings seem foreign.

Dennis, Eden, and I walk up the sidewalk lined in birds of paradise to the courtyard. Today, the fountains are off. I'm aware of an urge to hide, but the trees are skinny. I slip into mother mind as we walk into the foyer of the chapel, and I notice a poster board titled Embracing Eden in whimsical lettering which clues me in that her Aunt Rachael, an elementary school teacher, has put it together. Buttons, stickers, and feathers bring to life pages from different artists. There's an abstract bear with Picasso-like charm. One, stating "This is a picture of Disneyland for the whole family," has shapes in red markers that Freud would've enjoyed. Another paper has pink marker scenes with an arrow and adult writing, "pink ocean with waves" as if we couldn't identify it without this clue. Yet another, "Eden, I miss you so much! Jesus has your baby, and he is okay up there," signed Caleb.

"Eden, I pray that you can figure out what happened with L.B. (already a nickname) and keep this picture so you can think about the baby. Kylee." Still others, the neighbors, conveyed their grief, "We love you very much, Baby Long Beach. Love, Hailey." More explanations: "Jesus with Long Beach in heaven." "Long Beach saying, "Hi from heaven."

We're interrupted by little people hugging Eden, which at times requires a nearby adult to lend a hand for balance, lest they topple.

I slip away and move into the chapel. My turn to hold onto others. Hugging and aware of the ping pong between automated, "Thank you so much for coming," and taking in offerings of love and sorrow. As it happens, the sound person doesn't show. He's the only one with keys for the audio equipment room, so we can't play the music playlist I'd made in Santa Barbara with this very moment in mind. While people settle in the silence, thick with shed and unshed tears, an acoustic guitar breaks through the quiet. I look to the stage and see a brother of a former groomsman, who is here to perform later in the service, strumming. I take a deep breath, grateful he intuited it was okay to climb onto the stage and play.

I look around, the chapel benches filled with people, some I don't recognize. I find myself on the left-hand side of the front row. Eden sits on my lap. Dennis' left thigh touches my right one. I feel a hand on my shoulder, and turn. A friend, along with four more friends, who live 50 miles away, sitting behind me. They'd welcomed me into their artist community about three years ago.

On the opposite chapel benches I notice a whole group of family members attending from Ohio. They'd driven over from Phoenix with all of Dennis' siblings, who were also in attendance. My brother Brian and his wife Kennan, who drove from Santa Barbara, are sitting next to us.

Steve, our friend and the best man in our wedding, leads us in prayer, "We know not how to pray or what to say…" His voice fades into the background as I attune to the sniffles surrounding me, evidence that I'm not alone. A deep breath, almost a gasp, escapes from my mouth. Eden looks up with what feels like worry. I hug her closer, whispering in her ear, "It's okay, Eden. Mommy's just sad."

I feel her taking it in as she relaxes back against my chest. My friend, Maribeth, who'd invited me to join her in attending the artist group is up now to read. Her voice carries our sorrow as she reads a poem from John of Damascus:

Truly terrible is the mystery of death.
I lament at the sight of the beauty.
Created for us in the image of God.
Which lies now in the grave.
Without shape, without glory, without consideration.
What is this mystery that surrounds us?
Why are we delivered up to decay?
Why are we bound to death?"

Soon Beth, our worship pastor, goes to the piano and puts fingers to keys. I stroke Eden's hair, my hand shaking. I listen as voices of these friends and family sing around us, but my lips cannot move. I breathe deeply, listening to the words being sung on my behalf, "Come ye weary, heavy laden, lost and ruined by the fall…I will rise and go to Jesus. He will be my hope and stay." And then another song. "My help comes from you, maker of heaven."

My heart races in my chest. It's time for me to speak. I give Eden a hug and shift her over to her dad. On shaky legs, I make my way up to the podium. I hold my paper up slightly, but the rattles created from my shaking hands cause me to lay it flat before taking a deep breath. I begin.

"We wanted to take this time to share with you the meaning of our baby's name and share with you some of the events in our family before his birth." I continue reading, glancing up as I'm able, explaining how our baby was named Long Beach before sharing my feelings during my pregnancy. "This pregnancy was unremarkable. It seemed to be progressing along as expected but about two months ago I began to suspect that his movement was not strong. At my doctor's visits, the baby's heartbeat was normal, and I was measuring according to the expected growth. We discussed his movements, and it seemed like he was just less active than Eden but still within what would be considered normal. The reality that the baby never kicked, only swam and rolled made me begin to pray specifically to God for an openness and a loving heart for having a disabled baby. In my imagination, he was either laid back like his daddy, a good sleeper, or at the worst, he would have some type of disability. Sometimes, I would talk to him about needing to move more so I wouldn't be worried…I was diligent about counting movements since it was a concern. In his short life of 8 ½ months in my womb, he takes with him a part of my heart that is just for him."

Now Dennis gets up, and I place Eden back on my lap as I sit down. Dennis says,

My journey with Long Beach really started with the singing group,

Confetti Kids. Every Sunday evening last year, while Eden was practicing, Kimber and I had our first regular date nights since we became parents. One of those evenings, Kimber and I started discussing having a second child, and before too long we finally agreed we were ready. I also remember later in that week after a fight we had thinking, "Well, maybe we're not ready."

The crowd chuckles.

A couple months later Kimber came out of the bathroom and announced: "I'm pregnant!" It was around Christmas time, so we waited until Christmas to tell our family and friends. The greatest joy was telling our parents on Christmas day, they were ecstatic to have another grandchild.

Early in the pregnancy, Kimber and I shared a strong belief that this child would be a boy. I'm not sure how, but we knew that we were going to have a son. As we shared our feelings about a little boy running around the house, I became aware of some anxiety.

Now, I'll never know if my anxiety was a foreshadowing of things to come or if it was all just the things that I was consciously thinking of. The first thing I attributed my anxiety to was fearing that I wouldn't be able to offer a second child the kind of love that I had for Eden. After hearing from so many fathers that this was common and that your heart just grows when the child comes, that fear slipped away. Yet the anxiety persisted.

I shared my anxious thoughts with friends and mentors, and the only thing I could come up with was that I feared I wouldn't be a good father to a son. I know I'm a good father to a daughter, but I feared I wouldn't be a good father to a son. I feared that I would pass on to him all of my brokenness, pathology, my sin. I've been weeping that I'm not ever going to know what kind of father I would've been to him.

Dennis sits down. I squeeze his thigh and rest my hand there as his hand covers mine. I relax, knowing I'm not up to speak until after Keith, Dennis's supervisor and our friend, reads the story Jeff wrote on our behalf. He has the type of voice that carries without being strained. I try to stay tuned into his words, but I drift, listening instead to the soft sounds and gasps coming from my friends behind me as Keith reads. I'd already lived the scenes. But reliving it now through my friends behind me—their wordless sounds carrying weight in the tones, varying with different sections, gives me comfort. I'm not alone. My recollection that this has been one nightmare after another, validated through their sounds.

Keith sits and another former groomsman, Ken, stands at the podium to deliver his section of scripture.

Like a bird alone in the desert
Or an Owl in a ruined house
I lie awake and I groan,
Like a sparrow lost on a roof.
Ashes are the bread that I eat,
I mingle tears with my drink. (Psalm 102)

He pauses. His eyes meet Dennis's.

From the depths I cry to, O Lord,
Give head to my lament. (Psalm 130)

His voice picks up speed, getting a bit louder.

Does the grave declare your great love?
Is your truth proclaimed in the tombs?
Are your wonders admired in the dark
Or your mercy where all is forgotten (Psalm 88)

The angst in his voice is palpable as he continues.

Why do you turn away?
Why do you hide your face?
I wait for you, my soul waits,
And in your word I hope. (Psalm 130)

He pauses again. Makes eye contact with his wife in the second row.

Restore me, O God my Savior. (Psalm 85)

I take a deep breath. Hug Eden. Lean on Dennis' shoulder.

In all our afflictions he is afflicted,
And the angel of his presence saves us:
In his love and pity he redeems us;
He lifts us up and carries us all our days. (Isaiah 63:9)

I want this to be true, Lord. I want to feel carried.

He bears our griefs
And carries our sorrows;
By his wound we are healed. (Isaiah 53:4,5)

As Ken sits down, the brothers, Matthew and Mark go onstage for their performance. Mark strums his acoustic guitar while Matthew takes the microphone and begins, *Now is the Time for Tears,* by Charlie Peacock. I let the words wash over me, "Don't speak. Save your words. There is nothing you can say, to take this pain away." I silently hope this song immediately transforms anyone who wants to tell us it's okay. More sung words linger, "Silence the lips of all of the people with answers." *Yes, Lord.*

Pastor Eric stands at the podium, with his words transitioning us back into more sharing from Dennis and then myself, with a passage from Ecclesiastes. "It is better to go to a house of mourning then to go to a house of feasting, for death is the destiny of every man; the living should take this to heart. Sorrow is better than laughter because a sad face is good for the heart. The heart of the wise is in the house of mourning, but the heart of fools is in the house of pleasure."

I squeeze Dennis's hand before he takes his from my leg. He wipes his eyes and nose again as he walks. He looks around as if he's looking into everyone's eyes. He begins,

We've titled this, "Where is the blessing?" For me it is right here, and it is all of you and the love that you've showered on us.

The last 12 days, the house of mourning has broken down my defenses, my walls, that protect me from: pain, hurt, love. I was overwhelmed and I needed you, I needed your love and I've found that you love me, and you desperately want to show me your love. In the house of mourning I can love and receive love without fear (it's more accurate to say I'm Less Afraid).

Dennis takes a deep breath. Wipes his nose again with his tissue before continuing,

What I've written here explains what I mean: Its title is "The House of Mourning." Last week was the worst week of my life, my darkest hours AND it might be the days where I have felt the most alive, where I have felt loved like I've never experienced love before.

I've found in the house of mourning that it is easy to love and be loved. I've felt closer to Kimber and felt love for her that I didn't know existed, and I didn't realize how much I was loved by my neighbors, my church, my friends, even my family.

I watch as Dennis once again looks around at every row, every pair of eyes and emphasizes,

In the house of mourning, everyone is family. In the house of mourning, I have felt loved and have had the experience of really being held, all of me held: all my feelings, all my thoughts, all my needs. I cry; you have cried with me. I laugh; you laugh with me. When I'm angry or short, you give me grace, and if I don't want to feel anything, you have given me space. In the house of mourning everyone is my best friend.

Every day, for the last 12 days I've had no less than ten offers a day: "If you want to talk, or just hang out call me. I'm here for you." In the house of mourning, I never have to be alone. I've seen that in the house of mourning no one is too busy, everyone makes time, and my needs are celebrated. I've felt cherished by you as you've begged me to share a need. And then when I'm able to share a need, my heart has burst with love as I've watched you become delighted, and you've felt privileged because you get to put your love into action for us.

I recognize the sadness in Dennis' voice. We're both devastated and sad. This is our common ground right now.

In the house of mourning no feeling is wrong, no thought is condemned. I've shared my anger at God, I confess my difficulty praying, and everyone understands no one Judges in the house of God. The house of mourning has no judgment or maybe it does it's just that judgment and judges can't last long here because like everything else judgment is accepted and in the face of grace judgment dissipates.

In the house of mourning, you haven't worried about fixing me, correcting me, or even helping me, because there is no help for me, instead you have just tried to be with me, sit with me, understand me, love me.

Dennis pauses. Wipes his nose. Struggles to find his voice. Eden wiggles off my lap and puts her body on the church pew and lays her head in my lap. I stroke her hair. He continues taking a breath deep enough for all of us to see his chest move,

Lastly, I don't want to be here, I wish we were here to dedicate a healthy Long Beach to the Lord, AND yet I want to hold on to the blessing I've found here. I've found clarity. At times I've described my mourning as feeling like I'm in a fog and yet in that fog of mourning I've found a clarity of sight that has allowed me to see life and myself clearly. I've found it easy in the house of mourning to see what's important and what's meaningless. My grandfather used to say to me, "Dennis, don't sweat the small stuff (that's the p.g. version)."

The audience chuckles as he pauses with a smile, like he's hearing his grandfather speak. Dennis continues,

Unfortunately, I too often live life upside down, where the unimportant things get my focus, my anxiety and energy and the really important things I miss. I've found in the house of mourning, that it's just easier to focus on what's important, to focus on the present. I've found it easier to be in the present while I'm in the house of mourning.
Long Beach's death has jarred me to the reality that all die and that living can only be done in the present. I have no promise for tomorrow, I only have right now, this minute."

Dennis pauses and wipes his nose. I notice a feeling of pride as I hear his confession, holding a psychological complexity when bad things happen. It can't be easy. As a whole, Christians don't always appreciate people with doubts. They usually try to talk them out of them or eventually shun them. In the church, love isn't necessarily what abounds.

Dennis continues with his voice softer as if he doesn't trust the words will come out,

Long Beach's death has been like a slap across my face waking me up, 'pay attention you only have right now.'

Another pause. He wipes his eyes. He's unable to speak for several minutes. Then Steve gets up and stands next to him, hand on his shoulder. Words come,

I heard him saying to me yesterday, "Look around daddy, because you are loved!"

We're all wiping our faces. I glance around seeing teary faces and hearing the continued sniffles and the sound of scraping that tissues make as they slide out of the box. Dennis has gathered his papers by the time I look back at the podium.

Dennis wipes his eyes as he returns to his seat. I finish wiping mine as our hands find one another. I squeeze then turn and give his arm a squeeze as I stand to speak.

This is the darkest hour of my life. I can't help but wonder, "God, will this ever end? Will my longing for my little boy lessen? Will my longing to hold him at my breast go away? Will I ever stop hungering to nur-ture him, bathe him, change his diapers?" I'm left empty handed.

My voice picks up volume.

So, I wait. I grieve. I cry. I feel indescribable feelings that my dry eyes can't begin to express. Yet, I remind myself: I have not been abandoned.

I look around, letting Eden know I see her before reciting Psalm 139 verses seven to ten.

I pause, take a breath, continue,

> *I am being held with His right hand.*
> *Whether it be with your prayers,*
> *Whether it be in your weeping,*
> *Whether it be in your company with silence or with words,*
> *Whether it be with the Jesus believing nurse who received us into the labor and delivery unit who comfortably sat with us for an hour and gently asked, "Do you want to hold the baby after you deliver?" prompting us to make one of the best decisions of our grief...holding Baby Long Beach.*
> *Whether it be with meals being brought, programs being made, copies, offers and receiving of help. Whether it's in his still strong voice, urging me to pray, to focus on only His still but not silent voice in the midst of unbearable pain,*
> *I am being held.*

Eden has slipped down from the bench and is sitting on the floor looking up at me. I look at her. I see her eyes round, fingers touching her mouth but not in them, and her arms are around her Daddy's legs. I pause long enough to know she knows I see her and then I continue,

> *David continues in his psalm,*
> *If I say, "Surely the darkness will hide me*
> *And the light become night around me,"*
> *Even the darkness will not be dark to you;*
> *The night will shine like the day,*
> *For darkness is as light to you.*

I glance up from my paper. Stating the next words to my people, the ones in the pews.

We're being held.
I serve a God who makes order out of chaos.
Who speaks and the heavens and the earth were made.
Who lost his Son...
Before raising him on the third day.
Who left his Spirit so I do not cry out, "My God, My God why have you forsaken me?" Because he hasn't and never will.
He lives within me.
My spirit dances with His Spirit
Jesus sits at the throne and intercedes even when I don't have the words, or even know how to pray
And I know that my heavenly father reigns.

I pause again, making eye contact with my neighbors, my girlfriends called the Graces, family members. I see pain in their eyes. I see them listening. Really listening with their eyes and the wiping of their tears. Then I continue,

This is the God I serve.
This is the God I worship.
My grief will not be in vain.
I am already being transformed, changed by this little boy's life who lived 8 ½ months inside me.
His life was not in vain.
But when it all feels like too much,
Jesus has taught me to pray,
"My Father,
Who art in heaven
Hallowed be thy name
Thy kingdom come,
Thy will be done

On earth as it is in heaven
Give us this day,
Our daily bread
Forgive us our debts, as we also have forgiven our debtors
Lead us not into temptation
But deliver us from Evil for thine is the kingdom and the power for-
ever. Amen."
To God be the glory.

As I gather my papers to sit down, I take a deep breath. Somehow I feel lighter. I no longer feel like hiding and powering through this ceremony. I don't feel shame or fear that I'm to blame for Baby Long Beach's death. I want to be here, with these people. Shame has been replaced by love through what people are offering: sympathy in their gasps as they hear our story, noses being blown from grief, reverence as they hold a heavy mood in this space.

As I sit, Dennis gives my hand a squeeze. I squeeze back. Trusting that even though we've been emotionally distant in the recent past, even at the hospital, we can find our way.

To something.

We can call home.

The Story of Us – Part IX

In the shade of the house, which is the backyard as the sun travels west, I lean over to the realtor, "This is it! This house is what I've been waiting for, open floor plan, bright, wood floors—it's perfect."

He smiles. "Let's bring Dennis over here right after he's done with school. As you know, the market is hot so if we want to put a bid on it we'll need to do it tonight."

In the sunlight fading as it falls below the horizon, Dennis and I pull up to the curb with the realtor behind us. "I think you'll love it. "Come on," I gesture as I hurry out of the car.

I walk up the sidewalk to the front door as I go up the steps, a man is coming out of the house. "Hi."

"Hi, I'm the owner. Sorry I'm running just a bit behind to get out of your way." He starts walking down the steps before turning back to me, "I'm finishing up the floors."

"Oh my goodness. I love them. Absolutely stunning color—that warm honey. You nailed it."

He smiles. "Thanks."

I watch him go to his car. I shout before he gets inside. "You'll be hearing from us."

He chuckles loud enough for me to hear. "I hope so."

I turn to Dennis, "What do you think?"

He grabs me for a hug. "I think I love you."

"You do? What do you think about making this permanent?"

"I thought we did that at the altar." He moves away and grabs my hand, "What do you love about this home? It's hard for me to get over the last two homes we got outbid. So I'm seeing that this one is a bit smaller than the others."

"It is. But look at how bright it is. It's so simple in the layout—these three rooms run together without major walls and the kitchen, though small isn't blocked in with walls. It only has the half wall for the refrigerator."

"I can see that. It is bright and I know that's important to you."

"It is. And look," I point to the windows facing the sunset, "it's right out our front and dining room windows. We can see it every night."

"We can." He nods and moves around the house, first looking at the two bedrooms where he holds out his arms and touches each door simultaneously. I laugh and shrug my shoulders. He moves back into the room to the garage door. Opening it he says, "Our attached garage might be able to be turned into another room or space we can use."

"Exactly." He's facing me and we smile at each other across the room.

"Let's do it."

I laugh and repeat after him, "Let's do it."

In the sunshine of the next day, the realtor calls me, "Get that champagne. The owner has two bids and he picked you. He told his realtor you guys had a good feel about you. I laugh before squealing.

"Yes! How great is it that we ran into him?"

He chuckles. "Turns out it was really great. Welcome home."

"Thank you. Thank you so much."

After we hang up, I sit down at a nearby bench. I look to the sky. Tears flowing down my cheeks as I feel the relief relax my muscles from my chest to my toes. "Thank you, Lord. Thank you."

Being Held, With Comfort and Without

Hugging. I hug and hug so many bodies hearing words like, "Wow. Thank you." Sometimes hugging bodies without words, only tear-filled faces. My legs are getting a little tired. My stomach rumbling louder and more frequently.

Outside, I notice it isn't yet dark. The pinks and oranges haven't begun to show though the sun isn't visible over the houses. The Graces are waiting for me.

"Oh friend, that was so special and honoring," Shannon says, as she pulls me into a hug.

"That was beautiful, Kimber," says Mandy as she hugs me, "especially how Dennis shared so honestly about wrestling with God."

Amy gathers me tightly, "You have such a way with words. I'm way beyond misty."

Then it's Alicia's turn and she hugs and kisses my cheek before whispering face to face, "We're with you, friend. Just let us know what you need." I nod my head. My tears flowing again.

How I wish they were all at my house welcoming *him* home. But we aren't at my house. Yet, I'm leaving here today with the absolute knowledge I'm going to be okay. I'm not alone. We aren't alone.

As we enter the social hall filled with food and friends, I wish we were here celebrating rather than grieving. I would suggest moving the tables to the side and having a dance. I take a deep breath as I take a moment to observe the lively conversation and notice so many of my friends greeting my brother, Brian, who has known many of them from his high school days of visiting me during his spring break. I would have never guessed my community would still be in place from my college years over a decade ago.

I hear snippets of conversation, "How do you know Kimber and Dennis?" "Do you live in Long Beach?" "Oh my goodness, I haven't seen you since we graduated college!" A growl from my stomach reminds me I haven't eaten anything for hours so I smile, touching people's arms and shoulders as I walk past them, thanking them for coming if I haven't greeted them already before stopping next to Amy and Jeff, "Can I cut in line with you?"

"Absolutely," Amy says before Jeff adds, "How are you holding up?"

"Good. Can you believe how many people are here?"

"Well, you are both loved," says Amy with a twinkle in her eye.

I laugh. "True," I say as I stack my plate with sandwich fixings and salad. "I definitely feel loved today."

They both nod before Amy adds, "We are sitting over here. I'm sure we could make room if you want to sit with us."

"Thank you! I'm going to take that corner table just to buy myself a little quiet." Jeff adds, "if you change your mind, you know where to find us."

"Thanks."

I sit, but to my disappointment the food is tasteless, something I've noticed since his death. I notice a headache has started. I hope food will help take it away, but I make a mental note to ask someone for aspirin. Half my sandwich is gone before I notice Annie, one of Dennis' relatives, approaching the table. "Thanks so much for coming," I automatically say.

"Thank you," she replies. She leans closer to me, bending at the waist before saying in a quiet voice, "I'm not sure how to ask this..." My body tightens not sure what's coming next. "I know it's a service and all, but..." She pauses, looks down and then speaks very fast, "I love your purse. Where did you get it?"

I nod. Then, to buy time, I glance down at my camel-colored faux leather purse, rectangular with buckled pockets at both ends. I have no memory of purchasing this purse. I don't even know how many years or months I've had it. The thought that is clearest in this moment is get out of this conversation. I imagine crying. Then in the next second she's feeling bad and comforting me. I imagine being angry then I imagine the awkwardness that would linger. I imagine making nice and something about that feels inauthentic, so I compromise as I look to her, forcing a smile. "Oh my goodness, this seems like the perfect opportunity to ask about a purse." I look to see if she's registering my sarcasm but there seems to be none. So I continue, creating a story, "You know, this old thing I had no idea it was still fashionable with these buckles and all. I've had it for years and simply have no idea where I got it. But thank you."

She laughs softly, "Well it was worth a try, I've been looking for one just like that."

She scans the room and recognizes someone. Glancing back at me, she says, "It's good to see you. See you around." She takes a few steps before turning back. "And I'm so sorry. It's such an awful thing to have happen."

My racing heart reassures me that wasn't a pleasant conversation. It's only a few minutes before my friend, Sheri, comes over and I stop staring at the wall.

"You look like you could use a hug or a moment of silence. Let's pretend we're talking so you can have a minute to eat. I've noticed you've been talking nonstop."

I nod as tears well up. I have no words, but for a different reason. Good friends are why insane conversations about shopping at my son's memorial won't keep me in despair.

Still. I tell no one of the large bloody something that lands in the toilet on a trip to the bathroom. I'm hoping it, like that conversation, is something that will quickly pass.

~~~
~~~

I'm going to die. My body looks normal enough two weeks after a pregnancy, saggy stomach, still bulging over any pants waistline yet today I've ejected two golf ball-sized clots—one at the service and one sitting in the toilet now around 6 pm. I've also saturated a maxi super pad with blood, and I shouldn't be bleeding. The other item in the toilet, as I bend to exam my stool, seems to also have blood on it.

I haven't eaten beets or anything else red. Why else would there have blood in my poop unless I really was on my way to an early death? Maybe I have cancer. Maybe I'm bleeding out after my botched pregnancy and delivery piece by piece. That's it; I'm hemorrhaging. I'm going to lose all my blood and be unconscious by the time I get to the hospital. I need to go to the hospital. I need to be saved.

I sit down again. Heart racing, jaw tight. Headache back and in full force. Oh my goodness. I'm really going to die.

Dear God. How dare you take my life! Don't do this! Don't let me die. Don't let Eden be both brotherless and motherless. Don't bring another tragedy on this family. Will you really do this—let me die?

I look up to the ceiling as if God is there. *Are you going to allow this?*

I throw my hands in the air. Gesturing. Big. Big hand movement. *Really? Really, God?*

I finish gesturing at the ceiling. Determined, I stand. Flush. Point at myself in the mirror as if I'm preparing for an athletic competition.

I walk right up to Dennis. "I think I'm dying."

Dennis looks up. Sits up straighter. "Okay. Why do you think that?"

"I'm bleeding. I've been bleeding. I'm still bleeding."

"Did you call the nurse?"

"No."

"Why don't we start there. Here let me bring you the phone. I'll get the number."

I take his place on the couch, my heart still racing.

The combination of blood and recent pregnancy has the nurse sending me to the hospital. Now, Dennis and I are waiting for Sharon to drive the short distance from her hotel to watch Eden.

I sit, moving my leg up and down before facing Dennis at the other end of the couch. "What if…" *how do I say this?* "What if I don't come back, or am in the hospital for a long time?"

I can see he might be trying not to smile. "How 'bout we deal with that as it comes? Let's get you to the hospital to find out what's going on."

"Should I wake Eden up and tell her I love her, so she has this last possible moment, last memory with me?"

"Let's not wake her. I promise we'll bring her to you if it comes to that."

I nod, trying to force a breath out of me, but my chest is too tight to breathe deeply.

I see headlights turn into the driveway and race to the car, leaving Dennis to interact with his mom.

Soon we're driving north. "Okay. So this is going to be weird, but I need you to go with it." I stay looking straight ahead and take Dennis' pause as agreement. I want you to know that I want you to remarry. Eden needs a Mom."

I glance at him, choosing to ignore a partial smile that may or may not have flashed across his face. "Do you have someone in mind?"

"I don't but she needs to be screened and approved by the Graces."

"Okay. I can do that." He nods a bit. At a red light, he turns to me, grabs my hand off my leg and gives it a squeeze, "Hey, it's going to be alright." I nod, wishing I could believe him and feeling proud I'm not yet hysterically crying.

The hospital, it turns out, takes bleeding after recent delivery seriously. We bypass the Emergency Room waiting area and are led back to a bed in a triage room. When the doctor comes in, his words float, and I can't put them together as I wonder if he'll be the last professional I'll see before I die. I register a few words being spoken between Dennis, the doctor, and the nurse, "anxiety, standing, overdid it," intermingled with my own inner dialogue, Does Dennis know where my memorial service plans are? Should I be calling friends, writing anything down? How is it going to feel to die? Will it hurt?

After I see the doctor exit out through curtain, it finally registers that he told me, "I'll be back."

I lift the sheets and look in between my legs for blood. None. For the first time since I filled a pad with blood, I consider the possibility that I might live. I notice that Dennis isn't wringing his hands or praying without ceasing. He sits next to me, looking calm, available for eye contact and occasionally patting my leg. It hits me—we're alone. Surely someone who is hours from dying isn't left alone. My heart takes off again because I'm now certain it's the patient left alone who will die first.

I look around for the call button but before more panic settles in, a nurse comes in and attaches a new tube to the IV port. "I'm going to give you something to help you relax, a combination of anti-anxiety and pain meds." She's coaxing me as one might do a scared dog under a porch.

"Will this take away the bleeding?"

"You'll need to talk to the doctor about that, but you should be fine." Hum. I look at her skeptically. She's not answering my questions so it must be bad. I look at Dennis. He seems unfazed. Maybe he's hoping I die.

When she leaves, I stop recounting where I wish I'd traveled and begin scanning my muscles, noticing how relaxed my body is becoming. I've made it from my jaw to my shins when I hear the doctor's voice as he pulls aside the soft yellow and white patterned curtain.

"How are you feeling?" he asks, looking into my eyes. I notice he's calm and has a license to maintain. Certainly he doesn't have some agenda to let me die.

"Much better. Thanks. Who knew I was so anxious?"

"Well, you had a big day. I think you overdid it, which caused some bleeding—probably from standing too long and possibly not eating or drinking enough."

I nod. "I can see that."

"I'm going to get you hydrated with some saline, and then you can go. But you need to rest."

The reality of living longer washes over me like a gentle wave and tears fill my eyes but don't fall. "Thank you," I say.

"You're welcome," he answers with a genuine tone. As he turns to leave, he looks over his shoulder and adds, "You're safe. You're going to be okay."

"Did you hear that?" I turn to Dennis.

He smiles, "I did. Looks like I don't need to look for a new wife today."

"Good thing."

We wait in silence for my IV to drain into my veins.

Disturbing God

It is better to hit a pillow than a wall,
but you can still break something,
like you did in 1989,
not bothering to cover your thumb.

There were no echoes or cries.
like in Coyote Gulch,
five months before a finished birth.
Thump, thump--a steady rhythm

like an axe chopping wood.
Give him back, I screamed
like I'd done a thousand times.
I hate you.

Night Terrors Even Wide Awake

In my dream, I'm cold and wet. I can't get to Eden. She's leaned too far over the side of our red kayak to look at fish and she's fallen. With the wind at our backs, we're getting farther apart, but I can see she's sliced her arm. There's blood in the water, running down her arm as she gives me the universal "Help!" wave. She's now swimming toward me but getting farther away because the kayak is moving quickly. I try to reverse and paddle toward her, but my muscles are losing strength, my panic rising. For every three paddles forward, the wind pushes me five strokes back. I scan the shore, seeing no one to help.

"Mommy! Mommy!" I hear her yell over the wind.

I paddle furiously, getting nowhere close to her. I see her head afloat, grateful for her life jacket. Maintaining a visual of her as I try to figure out how I'm going to reach her, I almost come out of my seat as I see a dorsal fin ten feet from her. It's a shark. It has to be a shark!

My eyes freeze on her. "Not her, too! No! Not her, too!" I scream to no one but the wind and God.

Adrenaline gives me another boost as I put renewed effort into paddling. I yell back to her, "Kick, Eden, kick!" But I see her go under.

I jolt awake, my pulse pounding, and my body feels wet everywhere. It takes a moment to realize I'm lying in a pool of sweat.

The night terrors are frequent. What's more frequent is slipping my arm out of Eden's grip who is still sleeping with us, replacing it with a pillow, and sneaking out of bed with a sloth-like pace in order to avoid waking her and Dennis. During my nightly wanderings I have no agenda. There's nothing I want to do, nothing I'm hoping to accomplish when I'm up. Yet I'm besieged by restlessness. The entertainment center is three steps away from the bedroom door and no one can sleep through the beep when the TV powers on or off.

I wander into the kitchen and eat chocolate, a habit that produces guilt alongside comfort. I remember my therapist giving me "permission" to eat chocolate while I wrote my dissertation. I wonder what he'd think if he saw me now. I can't get enough of chocolate creams, truffles, mints, peanut butter cups, and chocolate-covered almonds and pretzels—but I know they're only numbing solutions that for now, fill a void—for a few minutes anyway. Maybe I'll bring it up in session with him in two days.

I still wish I could calm my restlessness with sleeping pills, but I haven't gotten a new prescription after throwing them away. Eden's death. When the sun's up, the fear of her death is as persistent as my grief. Almost daily I'm reminded of what could happen to her.

I wish she didn't need to ask me questions like, "Why can't Jesus send Baby Long Beach back to us? Why did he steal him? If God loves us, why did he take our baby?"

I settle on the couch, horizontal, wrapping myself in a faux fur blanket the color of a gazelle and pray,

God, your Word says that you are our refuge, our shelter in the storms of life. Be with us now. Deliver us from this despair, from this anxiety. Give us real answers.

I get up, turn off the living room lights, and get in bed on Dennis' side, nudging him over with my body. I grab his arm and pull it around me, in his sleep he snuggles against me. I sink into his warmth until my muscles relax and my breathing slows.

<div align="center">~~~</div>

Some days it stalks me. I regret every day I skipped my prenatal vitamins. Did I ever skip two days in a row? (Probably.) Did I ever take medicine I shouldn't have before I knew I was pregnant? (Maybe.) Did I turn on my back during my sleep? (Most likely.)

Wasn't I happy enough about having a second child? (I thought I was.) I'd had some dark days, exhausted and wondering how I was going to create emotional space for a baby. There were times when it seemed overwhelming just to get dinner on the table. I know in those moments I'd wanted only relief.

Even though I really don't believe it could, I ask myself over and over, did my sense of ambivalence rob me of my baby? And how will I ever be at peace with my body—the one that couldn't hold a baby—again? And my breasts. I want to cut them off. They're on fire, like they're being scorched by the sun's heat through a magnifying glass. I'm ingesting Ibuprofen by the fives, but it barely touches the pain.

How can this be possible? It's been a bit over two weeks. Lying here now, alone in the house as Dennis and Eden have gone to Disneyland with the family members who came out for the service, I admit to only myself, I regret getting pregnant. I regret every moment of inconvenience for blood tests, the ones my doctor said were unnecessary, but I insisted upon since I'd had gestational diabetes with Eden. Back and forth I'd driven, an hour round trip, only to keep getting the news: borderline high but not diabetic. What a waste of time. It didn't make a difference; something else would kill him.

<div style="text-align:center">~~~</div>

His greeting doesn't surprise me when he opens the door to the waiting room. I can hear the floor creak, hear the faint sound of the previous client turning the doorknob of the other door, the one leading to the hallway. "Kimber," he says in his Armenian accent. "Come in."

I walk through the doorway and into his open arms. He's solid and patient, not hurrying me out of his embrace. I stay until I take a deep breath before taking a step back and moving to the cognac-colored leather couch where I've found so many parts of myself over the last seven years. "Thank you. I needed that."

"Tell me…" he says as he sits in his leather chair located an arm's length away from the couch. I know this because he has to lean slightly sideways to hand me the tissues when I need them.

I take a deep breath. "I don't know what happened. At dinner I'd felt him move and then the next day sometime in the morning, I'd realized I hadn't felt him move much so I got worried. I went in and there was no heartbeat."

"I see. How are your dreams?"

"I keep dreaming of death. Not mine but of the people I love. I wake up in a panic and worry all day that Eden will die. Several people have offered to have her over on playdates. I'm too terrified to let her out of my sight."

"You should journal about death."

"Why would I do that?"

"It will take the power out of it."

"How?"

"Suicidal people are terrified of death."

"I thought they weren't afraid. I wasn't."

"You were terrified of the unpredictability of life. Most are. So they focus on what they can control—the timing of their death."

"I can see that."

"The scariness of life is what needs to be faced. Right now, death is scary to you. Journal about that for the next week."

I nod. Look at his bookshelf full of Bion, Klein, and Freud. "I can do that."

"Good. We're all going to die."

We sit there in silence, listening to the delivery truck's back-end slide down to close. There's a shout but the words are indistinguishable.

"Okay," he says.

I grab my purse and a tissue to go. "I'll see you next week."

~~~

My stomach bulges over my pants like soft dough before it rises. My belly button is hiding, squished by the excess flesh.

I knead the chunks, reviewing the reality, "My body couldn't hold a baby. It couldn't nurture a baby. It killed it. Denied the baby something he needed."

Stupid body.

Burning nipples.

My body is slow to catch on.

No milk needed.

I hate you.
~~~

The Story of Us – Part X

Shadows pass across Dennis's face as porch lights come and go, our legs transporting us closer to the ice cream shop. "So…" his voice trails off.

I watch him out of the corner of my eye. Even though I think I know what's coming my heart picks up speed and a ball forms in my gut.

"Tonight I want to talk about having children."

I smile. "Let's do it." I glance over at him. "Lately I've noticed how much we discuss our nieces and nephew and have been sitting with when we, or more specifically me, would be ready." He nods. I continue, "It has been five years of only us."

He chuckles. "So weird to think about. Well where are you at?"

We wave to a neighbor driving by before I continue, "I actually spoke to my research advisors last week, and they think I can get my dissertation done in less than a year."

"What does that mean?"

"We can start trying, and I'll be able to graduate before having a baby."

He stops in the sidewalk as he puts his arm and hand out like he's stopping me from walking into an oncoming car. "Whoa. Are you serious?" He belly laughs but I'm not sure what's so funny.

"What?" I ask as we continue walking.

He shakes his head. "Nothing."

"No. Tell me."

He laughs. I jab him with my elbow, but not hard enough to hurt. "You're a planner. And I'm so not. It's funny to me that you would ask your advisors, so you make sure you graduate before delivering."

I laugh with him. "Well. You know me—stress management is a forte."

"It is." Dennis opens the door, looking me in the eyes with a smile, "I love your planning."

I smile back and shiver as the air conditioning hits my warm body. "This might be the most monumental date night ever."

He grabs my hand, bringing it to his lips. "And it's going to include a lot more than ice cream."

Adult Gymnastics

"I'm waiting to hear from you," I say as I push the red hang up button on my phone. I'm sitting on a bench cushion, newly acquired from a neighbor's garage sale, butt indention included, but anything is better than the aluminum bench with no give. We, parents, caregivers, siblings, and a smattering of grandparents if hair color is any indication, aren't allowed to go down onto the main floor. Instead, we're perched above our children shouting phrases like, "Good job," "I see you," "Fantastic!" "Pay attention to your teacher."

As I wave at Eden who has popped out from the wall so I can see her, I feel my aluminum bench shake. I look to the left and see a parent from Eden's school, Evan's mom.

"Hello," I say as I force a smile.

"Hello. I didn't know Eden went here, too. We just changed our class to 3:30. Guess we'll be here at the same time."

"We will."

She looks at me with an expression that has my body tightening. As if I know what's coming next but I don't know how it will be delivered. "I wanted to say I'm so sorry about your baby."

I force a deep breath. I sit up straighter. *Yup. Thought we were going here.*

"Thank you." I glance back to the gymnastics floor beneath us, hoping to see Eden.

"Do they know what happened?"

"They don't. We have an autopsy appointment in a couple of weeks, but they don't think we will find anything out."

"How many weeks?"

"Almost 34."

"Wow." She shakes her head. "So horrible, isn't it?"

I glance back at her. She's still facing me, in an angle bodied kind of way, as if she's not going to change the subject. "It is." I look away. *How can I get out of this conversation? Could I pull out my book? Would that be rude? Do I care?*

"You must think about this," she pauses. "I even hesitate to bring it up. But don't you think if they could have only known something was wrong, they might have been able to save your baby?"

I nod. Unsure within myself whether this gesture is for self-comfort or to just make it seem like I'm agreeing so she'll stop talking sooner. She continues in a whisper, "He was old enough to live outside the womb."

"He was." I stand and look between parents to see if I can see Eden yet. No luck.

"I think that's the most horrible. That he could be saved."

"It's a hard pill to swallow," I say as I feel the relief of seeing Eden's face turn up to find me. She waves. I wave back to her. She now has my full attention. I'm not sure what apparatus her class will start on; I don't care. I stand again to yell, "You got this, Eden!"

She waves at me again. I wave as if I haven't seen her in a month. With that much enthusiasm. What I want to say, but don't say to the woman next to me, "What's most horrible is my baby is dead." In between waves and cheers (I can't remember when I've ever cheered louder), I admit to myself, "I wish this woman could have processed her condolences differently with me, but I'm grateful I've done the internal work in previous years, so I don't need her to show up as anyone but herself."

I give an internal cheer to myself remembering the words of Dr. P in a session several years ago, "True maturity means you don't need people to be different than who they are. They can show up as themselves and you're able to navigate it without judgment or feeling done to."

I take a deep breath. I look at the woman next to me before standing to say, "It's great to see you. I'm going to stretch my legs."

As I walked away, what I wanted to say but didn't say, is, "Thank you for the opportunity to see my emotional growth. I can't wait to be celebrated with my therapist."

<center>~~~</center>

I can barely put words together to make sentences. So as much as I hold excitement of going to church this morning, I already feel dread in my stomach. I don't want to retell my story, yet I know I'll be asked. We're curious creatures who often don't know what well-meaning questions do to nervous systems—the shaking and dissociation that shows up in the answerer as we recount our traumas. I already have an index card full of such questions.

"When did you know something was wrong?"

"Were you counting movements?"

"When do they think he died?"

"What if you'd gone in while he was still alive? Maybe they could have saved him?"

"Do you think you ate something or took some medicine you weren't supposed to?"

There's nothing routine about pulling into the parking lot on 36th Street, the ball of anxiety in my stomach has grown with each minute since leaving our house. I turn around in my seat so I can see Eden. "Eden, are you excited to see your friends?" I ask.

"Yes! I brought Uncle Kerby with me (her pink stuffed bear, which she holds up and shows me). We're going to tell our friends about Baby Long Beach and fairyland."

My eyes fill with tears, but I face forward, take a breath before answering, "That's great, honey. I'm sure they'll want to know." What will their parents think?

By the time I tug on the door handle and get out of the car, my entire body is screaming, "It's unsafe. Run! Run! Run! Don't go in there." Heat hits me—bouncing off the blacktop. I force myself to take a deep breath and put my hand out for Eden before turning towards the children's ministry classrooms. I'm aware fear is driving me so I force my mind to focus on my five senses. *Feel Eden's small hand touching your palm. Notice the coolness of her touch then her warmth as our palms come together. Notice your feet touching the ground – notice all four corners. You're safe. You're walking. Hear the bird. Notice the palm trees. You're supported.*

I somewhat believe my thoughts as I swing open the door and am blasted by cold air. Aww. A deep breath rises from my belly as I see my friend, Alicia, and she pulls me in for a hug. "Hi, friend. So good to see you." I let myself be hugged and nod against her cheek. Tears well up again. "Thank you. Good to see you." I feel my jaw loosen and I intentionally remove my tongue from the roof of my mouth.

We are greeted by friends one after the other, like hotel concierges, slowly moving us down the hall towards the sanctuary for the start of the service.

Notes from the piano fill the space between us and we all stand, well versed in the rhythms of the service. *Do I look like a mother who caused her baby's death by forgetting her prenatal vitamins?* I look around, feeling my forehead scrunched together like I used to do while thinking. *Am I smiling too much? Too little? How am I supposed to look after losing a baby?* I'd like to crawl in a box, pretend I'm not here, in this place I know it's important for me to be because I'm part of this community.

I'm standing in the middle. Half the seats behind me. Half ahead of me. Head bowed, I reconsider my outfit, a sleeveless salmon maternity top with grass green skirt. *Too cheery? Why didn't I sit in the back corner?* I dread the next part—greetings. I know everyone, but my friends are next to me, not behind or in front of me. I've stood too close to the aisle. I'm fair game for anyone. Just a hug grab away. My lips don't move with the singing. *Can we all pretend you didn't read the announcement in the bulletin last week? Can we pretend you didn't bring food to feed our bellies? Can we pretend you didn't bring your bodies to fill the pews and cry with us as you heard our story read over you?*

Can we pretend to be strangers?

We cannot.

I turn to greet someone but there are people by the aisle immediately and I'm swept up in hug after hug until the voices in my head are low. No need to be strangers as I receive grace after grace—not treated like the freak I'm feeling like. As people leave one after the other to go back to their seats before the scripture reader pulls us all back together, I talk with the person sitting behind me wondering if I have a shirt on that says, "I'm Kind. Speak Your Mind." This man, who I've known for almost ten years, shares with me his relief that my baby has died because modern medicine can keep so many babies alive that would've never made it before. This, according to him, is good news. My baby's survival would've been a burden in another way—as so many babies who can live with today's interventions are.

I'm a frozen nodder, a person who cannot stop nodding. I don't know what I'm supposed to say to this man who has no verbal filter. I don't know how to show up in this moment besides saying in my head, "Get behind me, Satan." The cluelessness that I'm hearing needs much more help than I could utter in response. So I end the monologue immediately as I hear a hush going over the crowd as a woman walks to the pulpit to transition us, "Thank you for sharing your hope with me," I say and remain standing for the reading of God's word.

"Count it all joy, my brothers and sisters, when you meet trials of various kinds."

I take a deep breath. *Wow. A lecture from God?* "For you know that the testing of your faith produces steadfastness." I take another deep breath this time feeling my feet on the floor, loosening my hands. I know sermons are determined months ahead of time. "And let steadfastness have its full effect, that you may be perfect and complete, lacking in nothing."

My empty arms, hanging at my sides feel burdened with their lack of fullness in the form of a baby's body. I take my tongue off the roof of my mouth. The God I believe in is sovereign. I don't understand this sovereignty. I've accepted my human mind cannot possibly do so. I recount Jesus' questioning God's sovereign will.

"Take this cup from me," Jesus says in the garden of Gethsemane before Judas gives him a kiss that will start it all in motion. His death. It leads to being treated as a slave might've been with the worst sort of master who claims to believe in God while punishing with a physicality that if weren't so measured, so precise, would otherwise lead to death. This was Jesus's fate. He forgave a fellow cross hanger before accusing God of his abandonment. "Why have you forsaken me?"

God answered. Eventually. In the form of complete darkness though it was day. In the ripping of the temple curtain. In the rumbling of heaven meeting earth. I imagine Jesus was unsatisfied; after all, He was dead.

In the same way, I'm unsatisfied. Left wondering as the pastor's voice is background noise, how my perseverance will in fact turn my empty crib into something more.

More complete than the life I yearned to have with this small person.

How does God do that? How does He complete tragedy with spiritual perfection in a way that my joy propels me to steadfastness?

How do I believe He cares when the sun still rises though I long for the dark? How do I believe when a curtain hasn't been torn?

I stand to sing, the service transitioning with its regular rhythm. Singing after sermon. As if the last time I was here isn't different than this time. As if everything is unchanged. As if nothing has changed. As if worshiping God can be done when my lips don't move.

We exit. Empathic glances and waves from afar as we all funnel through the doors into the foyer. Somehow, they help me feel more stable, less like a freak whose baby died because she did something wrong.

~~~

"How are you doing today?" asks the college-aged girl with the ponytail while she swipes my groceries in the checkout line.

My anger boils below the surface. I want to scream at her, just to let loose. My hair is in a messy bun. I have dark circles under my eyes. I'm wearing black sweatpants and an oversized maternity black sleeveless top.

"Fine, how are you?"

"I'm doing good. I'm going out tonight with my boyfriend when I get off. And you?"

I'm going home to be with my three-year-old who thinks the doctor stole her brother. That is, if I don't wreck while sobbing and driving because your next customer is obviously pregnant.

Out loud I say, "Oh, casual night at home eating ice cream. Hoping to beat some of this heat." I look only at her, not the woman behind me who, with eye contact and her own belly enthusiasm, may ask me when I'm due.

"Sounds like a good plan. I love Moose Tracks, too."

As she hands me my bag, she says brightly, "Have a good one."

"You, too."
~~~

Things that Make Me Cry

1. Passing the neighbor who bought us your stroller
2. Hearing an ambulance siren
3. Seeing a balloon
4. Every car seat being lugged around
5. Every baby carrier with a grapefruit-sized head poking out
6. Mini Chocolates, the size of your feet

Apologies: Stated or Dying On Lips Without Vocals

The right thing would be to apologize. I'm in my bedroom— shades drawn. I turn to notice the other in the room, next to me in the bed. Breathing mostly shallow so I know he's awake. "Hey," I say, looking over my shoulder, not quite into his eyes. I force the words out as if I'm a stranger asking him on a first date, "Would you like to come to my side of the bed and snuggle in this ninety-degree heat?"

I shift my gaze to meet his, tremble slightly. He answers in a soft voice, "That'd be nice."

My heart races as I feel his body heat coming closer to my back. Will I cringe? Relax? Melt together as we once did? He stops to place his hand on my shoulder, leaving room between us. I'm aware of the gap and am surprised it doesn't feel like a relief that he hasn't snuggled closer.

Five minutes pass before I bring myself to scoot toward him. I feel comforted as he wraps his arms around me. The sense of familiarity is like the beam of a lighthouse drawing a ship safe into harbor. Snuggled into him, it takes me another five minutes to say the words, "I'm really sorry for how angry I've been. I don't want to talk about it now because I'm exhausted. But in the near future I want to hear what it's been like for you to be married to an angry person. I want to do better."

I hear him take in a breath before pausing to blow it out. He squeezes me even closer despite the sweat pooling between us in the July heat stagnant in the house. "Thanks for saying that. I look forward to talking."

"It's a start," I thought.

~~~

The moon is a sliver shining through my curtainless kitchen window—waxing or waning, irrelevant. The secret is to keep clicking. Don't stop or a general malaise might call you back to bed. Click on a sleeveless shirt, three more suggestions pop up along with some pants, accessories, and shoes. I'm not sure of my sizing, still full of baby fat without the baby, still waiting for something magical to happen around my waist. Still, it's irrelevant. Free Shipping. Free Return Shipping. It's all part of the dopamine rush package. No achievement necessary. No real tactile pleasure. Only a plastic card to accompany the gambling—like sensation I've been fostering every night this last week.

Suddenly, my cutlery comes to mind. I wouldn't choose this pattern if I were getting married today—too dull. Click. A new set of 12 is on their way. The rug I've always wanted, but couldn't afford. Who cares? Click and it will be delivered in three weeks, right before we travel to Washington and take *his* urn. New pants that stretch and move; let's get all three colors.

The blue light coming from my computer begins to hurt my eyes after about thirty minutes. I feel the tension at the back of my eyeball. Still, I press on. I'm in need of beauty supplies, new candles, and the latest mug by Kate Spade. The stuffed fullness of my cupboards and drawers, irrelevant. I look around, noticing the vase from my grandma's collection—crystal but only medium height. Wouldn't a ceramic go better with my shabby chic décor? Crystal doesn't mix well, at least according to Debbie Diana's website offering free decorating advice that I've just clicked on while searching crystal décor and decorating styles.

I click on my local library website. I won't spend here. This brings a deep breath that I hadn't noticed I was holding. I click on 13 new books even though I know I'll never read most of them. Still, I don't care. It's the touching of something new. The holding of it. I try to be
~~~

the first one to check out a book, to hear that crack as the book gets held open. I put three new poetry books in my cart. Two more before I reach my twenty-five maximum.

What I avoid is searching grief stories. I've tried five of them and there aren't any chapters covering what to do when you want to throw out the crib your son was supposed to sleep in, or what's the reason you give the cashier for returning the brand-new stroller, or what to do when breakfast, lunch, and dinner are chocolates, the size of his feet. Or even what to say or where to look or not look, as your dear friends breastfeed in front of you, not out of spite or insensitivity but because we are at the bay together and their sons are hungry.

~~~

I'm carrying my lavender yoga mat into the studio I've been going to on Main Street in Huntington Beach. Mandy sometimes comes with me on Monday but not today. My heart pounds as if I'm new. My hands clutch my mat. My jaw clenches so I drop my tongue off the roof of my mouth and move it in between the teeth. I can feel the start of a headache.

Should I have come? Is it too soon? I wanted to come. Be brave. I wanted to hear a response from our instructor whose due date was a week after mine. I stand by the door, intentionally holding my head up, preparing for bodies to exit their class while I enter mine.

"You've had your baby."

I hear delight in her voice but haven't yet turned to see who's speaking. I take a deep breath, feeling the tears come. I turn knowing it's a familiar face. I'm greeted with a grin. Then another from this woman's friend. Rose and Clare. They come together and they've been so excited for me as they've watched my belly grow. I shake my head slowly. They are quick to catch on. Rose's hand reaches for my arm.
~~~

"I..." I try again. "The baby died. They don't know why. He just died."

"Oh, honey," Rose says. They shake their heads as their eyes turn sad.

"Does Angie know?"

I shrug my shoulders. "I emailed her, but I haven't heard anything back."

"Oh dear. I'm just so sorry. Good for you to come back."

I nod, "I had to get out and do something." We start moving forward as bodies move past us. "Thank you." I head for the far corner.

I grab my props: 2 wooden blocks, a purple band for stretching, and two Mexican blankets. I close my eyes as I sit in Sukhasana. I hear movement around me, still I dare not look. *Release your jaw. Release your hands.* I turn them so they're facing up, imagining the Holy Spirit's energy filling them.

I hear the instructor's greeting. I know right away it isn't Angie. Part of me feels relieved, part feels disappointed I can't share my pain in the same way she's tended to me in our simultaneous pregnancies. Over the next hour, it's impossible to keep my mind on the mat. I keep going to my grief—tears running down my cheeks. It takes everything in me not to curl up and weep, so I deny that image. Listen only to the instructions and do exactly what she says. It feels like a five-hour class.

As I exit, I'm aware of another loss, one I can control—I will never return to this studio.

<div style="text-align: center">~~~</div>

Dennis and I stand on the water. With other people. Watching a parade of pairs: dolphins, whales, sharks of all kinds. Eden is with a family we don't know, behind us somewhere. I don't know why she isn't with us, and suddenly, I don't want her to be with them. I want her with us. So I get her from them, parting the crowd until I see her eyes meeting mine. She looks distressed as I come to her—arms stretched out, like she would run towards me if the mother weren't holding her shoulder so she can't move. The teenage son stands next to her. I don't like him—the look in his eye, the semi-smirk that sends shivers down my spine. There are other younger children, but I do not care.

Eden and I go back to the parade. More dolphins, now some porpoises and manatees swim by us. She clings to me. I cling back, holding her in my arms. My brain gets foggy. I'm confused. Eden has ended up back with Dennis without me. But when I find him through the parade crowds, she isn't there. He reports with excitement, "I took her back to that family to play with the other kids."

I run to try to find her. Over and over again I fail. I'm enraged at Dennis. How dare he bring harm to our daughter! How dare he not know there was a predator in the form of a teenage boy! I find them after what feels like an unthinkable amount of time when a three-year-old is stuck to defend herself against that which I don't want to imagine.

She's upset. Crying. I'm crying, too. She is using the word "penis," something I've taught her to tell me about if she ever sees one when I'm not with her. I can't stop shaking. I want to punch the boy who isn't nearby. I want to punch Dennis who I trusted. I want to punch myself for leaving her with Dennis. I want to lay on this "water ground" and scream, "She lost her innocence. It's not supposed to be this way."

Instead, I shake and shake as I look into her eyes. I think I'm screaming until I wake up in my bed. Trembling.

I see the dark room. Notice I'm alone in my bed. The light comes in around the blackout shades. It's daytime.

I place my face into my hands.

"It's not real. That wasn't real." I whisper to the air.

One arm into one sleeve then the other before it's over my head. One leg into each pant leg and then it's pulled up to my waist.

I open the bedroom door pretending I don't feel like Eden has been abused by the babysitter.

And it's Dennis's fault.

~~~

I'm alone in the house, dressed in the clothes I wore yesterday. Maybe the day before too. Dennis and Eden have gone to the bakery on Spring Street.

I'm sitting on our leather couch. My chin in my left hand. Tea would be lovely. Smell good. Taste good.

But I don't have it in me to grab the tea kettle on the stove. Go to the sink. Turn on the faucet. Fill with water. Walk back to the stove. Turn the dial on the gas stove's left burner to 9. Go to the cupboard, opposite the stove, above the dishwasher. Grab the sage green teacup, the one my grandma used for her morning Folgers. Grab my favorite ginger-peach. Scoop tea into the strainer. Hook onto the side of the cup. Walk back to stove. Pick up kettle. Pour water. Steep. Grab matching small plate in case cup gets too hot.

I gaze ahead to the dining room table. A white plate from last night's snack remains at Eden's place. A blob, like something sticky, shines where I ate dinner last night. In the middle of the table rests a bouquet of flowers. Hot pink Gerber daisies bend at the waist. Sunflower petals are turning brown; they match the color of the water. I rehearse getting rid of the flowers.

Then I wait.

For the front door to open.
~~~

Wearing Envy

She's outside.

Walking on the sidewalk in her raspberry-colored shirt.

The maternity one with the baby underneath.

She doesn't see me staring out the window wanting to knock her down.

Rip off her shirt.

Do unthinkable things to her belly.

Steal her baby.

Make him mine.

Death and Grief Dug and Buried

"You told me to write about death. So I did."

"And?"

"And nothing. I think about it all the time."

"Where is its power?"

"It can happen at any time. Anywhere."

"You hate pain."

"Doesn't everyone?"

"Pain is unavoidable. It's the one thing life offers to transform a person."

"That sounds awful."

"Your mind is thinking about death all the time, fearing pain, and more than that, thinking about how unfair it is that you have pain when you think no one else does." He pauses, "That sounds awful to me."

"I suppose."

"Your imagination hasn't thought about all the time wasted on "why me?" instead of "why not me.""

"True."

"I grew up in a country ruined by war. In my youth, the oceans I surfed and swam were pristine, beautiful, peaceful. Then war happened. Beaches ruined. Humans destroyed. It can never be undone."

"You've made your point. It's helpful."

"Read me some of your journal."

"Okay," I begin, "I didn't realize how much I anticipate death—almost like I want to outsmart it. So I don't let it out of my mind so I can predict when it will be happening."

He interrupts, "I can predict it, too. In the future. Always."

I look over at him and mirror the sparkle in his eye. He continues, "You can survive this thing you're fearing. You've done it for five weeks."

"I have."

"You don't want to be obsessed with death?"

"No."

"Then live. Otherwise, you'll keep seeing death everywhere until you aren't wrong. And then, you'll have something worse than grief. Regret. Because you didn't live. You feared."

I nod. "I feel that. I regret not being more present while my baby was alive inside of me. I regret not enjoying more his swimming patterns. The ways he snuggled against my ribs or bladder. I complained. Now, I'd do anything to have him snuggle and make me uncomfortable—just one more time."

"You'd enjoy it now, this pain."

I nod as I look at him.

"Okay. I'll see you next week."

"I'll see you next week." I lean down and grab my purse, leaving behind a burden and taking with me something not yet formed inside of me.

~~~

She sounds like a bean-filled rattle climbing our Liquidamber tree. I watch from the front porch as my bare feet push against concrete, as the old-fashioned rocking chair springs back then forward until I propel it again with my push. Eden's in the tree. I'm accompanied by another, a knot. In my stomach. There without my permission. The shape of grief.

I'd like to kill it, send it off for an hour. Hell, I'd take 15 minutes without it just to enjoy life without interference. As the mourning doves, finches, and hummingbirds dart past towards the bottlebrush
~~~

trees and power lines, I'm reminded of being at a conference where I was the last speaker. I'd had a pit in my stomach then, too, tainting my enjoyment of others' material. It left once I started speaking. I suppose that's part of what makes this knot so difficult, living with the question, "For how long will you be here in my gut, nestling me?"

It's like this. Every morning I wake up with a sunken feeling in my gut that something has gone very, very wrong. It shapes itself into a golf ball right where he used to snuggle under my ribs. By mid-morning, it's grown into a tennis ball and has embedded itself under my lungs, squishing my breath as the cues that *he's* not here hit. The glances at the Gap bag with his backseat driver onesie. The unopened baby food brought by Grace, our neighbor, sitting next to my morning cereal. I see Eden's old bouncer sitting on the desk waiting. Empty.

By mid-afternoon, like now, I've encountered more reminders. The unopened bassinet next to the dryer. The empty stroller in the garage. The brand-new pack 'n play next to the back door. These cues grow the grief to the size of a balloon. Deep breaths are hard. By tonight, if it's like the past five nights, grief will embody all of me. Its weight crushing. Unsmiling my eyes as I press my face into my pillow. Hollowing my cheeks as I lie there. Tightening my jaw as silence speaks.

What's there to say, really?

It turns down the corners of my mouth. Creates a shallow breath. Instills an energy I can only describe "as not knowing what to do." Eventually, I'll close my eyes with the hope I won't be crushed as if by a boulder.

For now, the sun is too high in the sky, and my knot has yet to reach maximum size. Instead, listening to the rhythmic thud of wood contacting cement, I wait for Eden to appear as I rock back and forth. As we've done hundreds of times before, I know her head will pop through the leaves very soon.

The branch shakes. *Here she comes.*

"Mommy! Look! Look how high I am!"

"Wow! You're so high! I can't see you because the clouds are in the way."

She giggles as one who knows the punch line, yet still wants to hear the joke, "Mommy! I'm not that high. You can too see me. I can see you."

I laugh with her. Today it's not as loud. Not the usual. Not normal. But it's ours. It's our afternoon playtime shtick. Our television opener. Our, "I know what comes next." Our grounder when life throws a hurricane at us.

"Come sit by me. I want to rock with you."

"No, thanks. I want to climb."

And so she grows. Independent.

~~~

In three vehicles we arrive—my three brothers, their wives, my parents, my husband, and me.

Car doors open simultaneously. Bodies straighten with purpose. We're also burying my grandmother who died 18 months ago. We've brought the necessities. My mom's good with details and organization. Tissue boxes, four of them. Shovels, three, with steel blades. Camera, owner unknown. At the back end of the minivan, my dad turns to me, "Your grandpa had this digging bar made for me when I was fifteen. I never imagined I'd use it to bury my mother." His voice carries sadness enunciated by the pause and unspoken words "or my grandson."

~~~

Honeybees darting on the purple alfalfa buds. Robins bounding on the grass. Finches dancing among the aspens. Azaleas and gladiolas bordering the cemetery fence. In the distance, a snowless Mt. Gardner towers above the surrounding Cascade peaks. I'm delivering my son here, on his due date, in the shape of a brown pottery urn the size of a football.

We are the only living people in the cemetery this morning. No one speaks. My dad walks slightly ahead of us, his digging bar thrown over his shoulder like a rifle reminding me of the infinite amount of times I'd seen the same prop during my childhood. The cemetery caretaker has given my dad the instructions. I have nothing to worry about; he knows how to dig holes.

We're headed for the poplar tree, the middle one in the back of the cemetery. Dennis and I are arm in arm keeping pace with the rest of the family. I recognize names on tombstones. We pass the Boesels, Dorothy and Vic, whose waves and smiles I'd come to expect on my way to town. We grew together—they with their weathered faces and me shifting from passenger to driver's seat. Glimpses of the past come into my senses. Taste as we pass the Whites, whose apples were sweet with a deep flavor as if part of the earth was inside. Sound and sight with the Badgers; Warren's teasing voice talking about my grandpa's golf game, and Lois's chip shot, which kept her handicap low. I'm fully planted back into my childhood, where neighbors became family in crises.

When we get to our family plot, my dad gets right to work. Up go his shoulders, down goes the bar as he releases it. Thunk. Thunk. Ping. He's hit a rock. He picks it up, tosses it thirty feet over the cemetery fence into the sagebrush. Thunk. Thunk. Thunk. The dirt mixes with the grass as the digging bar's pointed tip breaks up the ground into an earth soup.

Not five minutes later, or maybe it was only three, he says, "That should do it," looking over to the hillside before meeting my eyes.

My brothers, Kerby and Bryce step out and give Dennis and me shovels. We hold each other's eyes before placing a foot on each shovel's edge and stepping down into the soil. I tip forward but catch myself before toppling. I don't want to try again. I don't want to dig a grave for him.

I bow my head. Tears come like a storm burst. My shoulders shake. Someone touches me, but I don't turn around to see who it is. Someone removes the shovel from my hand. Eventually I look up to see one brother has taken the shovel from Dennis and another has joined so now they dig together. My three brothers. His uncles.

I get down on my knees in the grass as I once did to accept Christ in the front of our Methodist church. Unlike that day, filled with excitement and anticipation, I feel only dread. I can't believe he's never going to do life with us. No new memories together, only the months in my womb and memories of his death. Will I get to visit him in my dreams?

Next to me, the pottery urn created by the Almquists who lived in the middle of the hill we're on—we'd passed their house with extra-large agave-colored vases drying on the porch. I'd bought the urn because I loved the swirled dark and milk chocolate browns created by the glaze and heat. It reminded me of mountain dirt, something I didn't see often in Long Beach. None of that matters now, as it won't be going home with me. It's come full circle and going into the ground. I kiss it as though it feels like kissing him. Dennis takes him, places him next to my grandma. Someone snaps pictures, the clicks mingling with the birdsong.

Following Dennis's lead, I grab a handful of dirt and we throw them in the hole. Dirt and pebbles clink against the pottery. I silently wonder if I can take all the shovels my brothers are holding and replace them with teaspoons so we can stay here all afternoon, delaying the time it would take to cover him. Such a different picture than covering his sleeping body with a blanket.

Dennis and I still stand shoulder to shoulder. I can feel his breath through his muscle vibrations from our closeness. A deep breath comes for both of us, and I make eye contact with my brothers and dad, nodding. They need no words but step up alongside us and dig.

We take turns filling the hole. It's a moment from a small-town cemetery—no one supervising. Only our family to say a ritual good-bye. Images flash through my mind of my male kin and I together—digging ditches for a fairway sprinkler system, sifting sand to put on tees, fixing a leak in the irrigation system, which let itself be known by the bulging grass, like a boil, on the otherwise smooth surface. So many memories of digging together—something that never happens now that we have our own families.

Today I was supposed to endure labor of a different kind. Instead I'm delivering him to God.

<div align="center">~~~</div>

My taste buds are numb, and I can't get enough moisture in my mouth to feel confident I won't choke. I skip the salad, imagining the roughage caught in my throat. I fix a sandwich on a hoagie roll—mustard and mayonnaise on the bread, fresh beefsteak tomato slices from the outside planter along with a few slices of freestone peaches on chicken lunchmeat. I sit at the kitchen table watching others go through the lunch line before taking a bite. After each swallow, I say a prayer it won't get stuck.

Barb and Kathy, two of my mother's best friends, sit down across from me. Craig, a neighbor whose wave from his pasture was as consistent as the setting sun, sits to my right. Barb and Craig have lived years with a son's death.

I've lost words for the moment. We all have.

The line at the kitchen counter has cleared out. I find words, "Over the years I've dug quite a few ditches on the golf course and dug for worms at the creek, but nothing's like digging the dirt where your son's ashes will stay."

Dennis adds, "And to hear the sound of those first few shovelfuls of dirt hitting the ceramic urn." He chokes up, tears falling from his eyes, "It's a ping I don't think I'll forget."

Heads nod and after several breaths, Craig adds, "I don't ever ride my horse without wearing Adam's cowboy hat. It keeps him close." He pauses before adding, "I feel he's with me."

"Thank you for sharing. When I see you wearing his hat, I'll think of you and him and his son who never met him."

Very few eyes are free of tears around the adults' table.

Around us, the sing song voices of the five and under kids, along with Kerby and Anna, carry tunes about carrots and the deliciousness of milk in between bites of lunch. I loosen my jaw, soften my hands, and feel grief and joy swirling together in the kitchen.

Grief, Cat Style, Or For Some, Catty

Grief.
One of life's staples.
Yet, kicking and screaming, I resist.
Pretending I can decide,
Grieve today
Or grieve tomorrow.
Please.

As if anyone can avoid the transforming power of grief.
A minister's wife refuses to pray in public after her son dies at 20.
A man who drinks alone in silence every night after work since his wife
died

15 years ago.

A girl who becomes a doctor after her mother died in the hands of one
when she was four.
A woman becomes a well-loved funeral home director after her mom
commits suicide.

Grief.
It yowls.
It waits.
It pounces and then settles.
Leaving in its own time.

It's chattering at me.
I'm not going to be angry with my body for poorly keeping my son
alive.
I would never, ever, ever consider starving it as punishment.
I would never, ever consider sticking a finger down my throat in retali-
ation.

Or would I?

I tell myself,

I want to celebrate (yay! yay! yay!) with those women who haven't had
to deliver a death from their body.
I would never want to glare or stick out my tongue in their direction.
I would never (no! no! no!) consider stealing their baby,

Just borrowing him for a little while.

I would never, ever think "why me and why not them."

Or would I?

I'd never (no! no! no!) snub them, if one should be conversational.
I'd never be superficial or catty behind their back.

Or would I?

I'm just saying,
If I had a choice,
I'd want my friends to have more issues than me.

Grief.
It snarls.
It purrs.
It pounces,
Then transforms,

For better or worse.

Part Three

Making A Whole

It's Been Three Months

I have a pit in my stomach that burns. As we pass each stoplight getting closer to Eden's school, it grows bigger and bigger. The last time I'd seen the other parents, I was pregnant—really pregnant. Can I sign her in fast enough to avoid talking to any of them? Can I give a brief wave to her teacher of three years?

"I can't wait to go to school! How much longer?" Eden's voice from the backseat stops my imagined exit plans.

"Probably two more songs."

"Do you think Alex will be there? Alisa?"

"I don't know, honey. I think so, but it's hard to say who's coming back."

I take my tongue off the roof of my mouth. Loosen my jaw. Stop gripping the steering wheel, shaking one hand out, then the other.

"What are you doing, Mommy?"

"Just letting my muscles relax. Reminding them to be calm."

"Why?"

"Sometimes I grip the steering wheel too hard when I'm feeling a lot of feelings. I'm sad to drop you off. I liked playing with you all summer."

"It's okay, Mommy. We can play when I'm done."

I chuckle. "Yes. Yes, we can. Thanks for that reminder."

Walking through the school gates, one of the moms flashes me a big smile. "Is your baby at home?" Shit. Already a curve ball when I don't even feel suited up.

I stop. Shake my head, regrouping as I think of what to say. Shit. Why hadn't I thought of this and rehearsed words. "No. He." I trail off before taking a deep breath and looking her in the eye, "He died."

I see her embarrassment, spreading up her cheeks, a bubble gum color. "I'm so sorry," she stumbles over what to say next. I step in and rescue her.

"It's sweet of you to ask. Of course, you didn't know."

She nods her head. Reaches out and touches my arm as she moves toward the gate. "Again, I'm so sorry."

I pick up my speed. Give Eden a hug outside the classroom door. "I'll see you after school."

She opens the door, barely looking at me as she responds, "Okay, Mom."

I rush in behind her, not lifting my head except to locate the sign in clipboard. I hear her with back turned, "Alisa!" A chorus of squeals lingers as I shut the door.

As if one strike isn't enough, on my way back to the parking lot, Ruth's mom is coming in the gate carrying her newborn. "Hi!" I say, maybe a bit too enthusiastically, but I'm not taking any chances of receiving empathy from her. I avoid looking at her infant carrier as I pass her going out of the gate. My arms have never felt emptier.

The gates close as her reply hits my brain, "Hi." I keep walking, head down. I can't get to my car fast enough. I drive a block. Pull over and sob. I use my shirt as a tissue, wondering only once if I'm flashing the middle school kids walking past as they walk across the busy street to their school.

By the time I pull away from the curb, there are no more tweens walking on the sidewalk. The bells have rung. They're in class. Everything in me wants to rehearse pick up—how to get in and out as quickly as possible. How to avoid more meltdowns. How to act enthusiastic. But as I recall my insufficient preparedness coming to school, I turn up KROQ and drive home.

~~~
~~~

"Just as I thought, there's nothing discovered in the autopsy. Everything inconclusive."

Dennis is quicker than I, "What does this mean for future pregnancies?"

"You should be fine. Kimber is in an age bracket considered higher risk, but plenty of women have successful pregnancies at her age."

Finding my voice, "Do you know why we didn't know something was wrong?"

"I saw in your chart you didn't have an amniocentesis."

"I didn't. We didn't see the point given we wouldn't do anything with a result indicating birth defects."

"I understand. You can always do one next time if you want to be reassured for your next pregnancy."

I nod because I don't really want to get into the discussion of why I wouldn't be getting one next time either. My opinion hasn't changed with our outcome.

"Anything we should know before trying again?" Dennis is speaking this time.

"As far as I can tell, you're in the clear."

"Thanks so much for taking the time to meet with us," I say.

"Absolutely. I really want you to feel as good as you can going into your next pregnancy."

"Thank you. This has helped. It's good to know that there wasn't something obvious in the report to impact future pregnancies."

Dennis adds, "We really appreciate it. It's been hard."

Dr. Greene nods with empathy in his eyes. "I see no reason you can't start trying whenever you're ready."

"Thanks for the reassurance. I want my body to recover a bit more before I can even wrap my head around being pregnant again."

"Everyone needs their own timeline. You'll know when you're ready."

As I push the button in the elevator for floor one, I feel disappointed. I wanted answers. I wanted a prescription. More than anything, I wanted guarantees.

Turns out, the universe is still the same. There are no guarantees.

~~~

I find myself playing with stuffies for the fifth time this morning. My ankles hurt so I've moved two small pillows under them as I sit cross legged. "Okay, Eden. Who do you want me to be?"

She hands me her stuffed Siamese cat, shaped like a real kitten unlike the overstuffed, ill-shaped versions along with a small, silk feeling pink bear named after the uncle who gave it to her, Uncle Kerby. "You be Siamese Kitty and Uncle Kerby."

She grabs her stuffed puppy sized golden lab and small giraffe. "I be Raven and Giraffey."

"Okay."

"I be the doctor and you be the Mommy and Daddy." I nod. "Come see the doctor," Eden demands as she sets her animals in place.

I take a deep breath. "Hi, Doctor. We are here today to get help."

"I need you to go in that room and lay down." Eden points to our mini doll bed with the giraffe. I play walk over with Siamese Kitty and cover her up.

Eden looks at me. "Mommy, you stay here." She puts her hand out and turns her back. She talks to her stuffies, "While she's laying down. You grab her baby. Okay?" She starts bouncing up and down as she gives a conversational pause. "Take it to the other room so she can't find it."

I cringe but keep play talking between the animals I'm in charge of. "It's okay, honey," I say as I move Uncle Kerby talking to Siamese Kitty.

I hear Eden's muffled voice saying, "Go now."
~~~

She play-grabs the blanket from the kitty and before she runs away she says, "Mommy, cry. Siamese Kitty needs to cry. Her baby just got stolen."

I nod and make a crying noise.

"Louder, Mommy."

I obey and raise my voice, pretending to cry as she leaves her bedroom, back hunched over as she acts out the scene.

Alone in her room, I stop play crying, wondering when Eden will get tired of doctors stealing babies.

The Worm

The worm writhed on the dry, cold pavement.
I perceived it as helpless and played Shepherd.
Bringing it forth onto green-bladed pastures
I ran on – smiling only with my eyes
To do otherwise would have exaggerated my feeling
Today a worm lay dead on the dry, cold pavement.
Doubt clouded my mind
Had I been moved by compassion or moved by power
Helper or Disabler
Playing God or Moved by God

I looked for a worm today.

Whose Office Can I Hide In? And Other Strategies for Empowerment

As I walk up the stairs from the parking garage to the cinder block building where I work, my attention turns to the ping of my soles connecting to the steel anti-slip strips on the concrete, and I'm once again faced with the real fear, "Am I going to fall apart on my first day back at work?" My mind flips through a number of scenarios: find a colleague and start weeping then need to go home, skip through the hallways like Mary Poppins to let everyone know I'm not depressed, suck my thumb and curl up in a ball on the floor of my office so they admit me to the psychiatric ward, put a sign on my door, "not in," or create a receiving line so I simply can get that awkward "first time greeting after a tragedy" done all at once.

I open the heavy glass and metal and force a deep breath through my tight chest as I walk up the walnut wooden stairs. I feel like I have a scarlet letter only mine says "former intern and post doc with baby birthed still."

My first visit is to the front desk, which I navigate without any awkward exchange because the person is new and has no history with me. I find my new office, grateful to be in a section with fewer people before walking myself to the director's office because I don't want to be anxious wondering how we will greet each other.

"Hey, Liz." I immediately relax as I see the compassion in her brown eyes.

"Hi there," she gets up and gives me a hug. "We are here for you. Whatever you need."

"Thank you. I feel that."

"I'm so grateful..." My eyes fill. I swallow, "I love it here. Grateful to have this work."

She nods her head. "Just let us know."

"I will."

Returning to my office, I relax my jaw, noticing my heartbeat isn't quite as fast.

One down. Twenty to go.

You can do this, Kimber. There's no reason to fear making others uncomfortable.

In the lunchroom, when I enter, they all stand up and give me a hug. One at a time. These women are both mothers and yet to be mothers. I knew many of them when I'd been an intern six years prior.

When I leave, I feel full with more than food.

~~~

I haven't made an appointment. My first stop is in the basement to request my records of my hospitalization. I want to see how they documented my delivery, so I fill out the proper form. They will be ready in two to three weeks.

I have another stop. My heart races as I walk down the hall and into the next building. I'm greeted in a perfunctory manner by the front desk clerk, "Can I help you?"

"Yes. I'd like to file a complaint."

Her face changes and she sits taller as if bracing for a fight. "What exactly is it for?"

"I want to discuss how I was treated during my stillbirth."

She seems to brace even more and responds without softening. "I'm sorry for your loss." I nod wanting to get our social exchange over. She stands up and continues, "Okay, how about you come right in here and I'll get a manager for you."

I wait in a gray fabric cubicle. No pictures hang on the walls. No personal touches in the space. "Hello. I hear you have some
~~~

complaints," says a sandy blonde man dressed in a white button down and beige slacks as he slides into the chair behind the desk.

"I do. I hope my complaints might help others who are in my same situation."

"What situation is that?"

I can't tell if he's being coy or truly doesn't know why I'm here, so I continue, "I had a stillbirth and the nursing staff wasn't prepared for my medical needs."

He nods. "I'm sorry."

"Thank you. My second issue is I also wasn't properly cared for while giving birth."

"What do you mean properly cared for?"

"I was left alone for too long."

"Often times a mother is left for long periods of time until the labor is harder."

"I didn't get my epidural."

"That can happen."

"I ordered it two hours ahead of time."

"If there are a lot of women needing them…"

"My nurse said I couldn't get it because I needed more fluids. She adjusted the drip that she'd attached to me several hours prior on her way out."

"I imagine you're in a lot of pain. Sometimes we need to find someone to blame."

Gaslighting. Something I happen to be experienced with. I lean forward. Look in his eyes. "I had severe pain. I was physically traumatized. All because of human error."

"I see."

"I'm not really sure you do. I'm a psychologist. I know who can help me process trauma, but others won't be so fortunate.

"I will look into this for you."

I pause. I don't believe him. He's not even taking notes. Sitting here makes me realize I don't have the fight in me to hold him accountable or take it up with the state nursing board.

I lean back. Take a deep breath. "You know what, let's move on to my second complaint."

"When I was moved out of labor and delivery, I wasn't given any supplies like pads and the special underwear, so I made several big messes."

"So you're saying the nurses didn't take care of you?"

"No. I'm saying the nurses on the post op floor didn't have the supplies to give me. They had to figure out where to get them."

"Did you eventually get them?"

"Yes. But"

He interrupts me, "So what would be the problem?"

I feel my jaw lock in. Adrenaline is now coursing through my body. If we were in a boxing ring, I'd go in for a knockout. I lean forward. "Neither the nurses nor I should have to figure out where to get more supplies when they are standard procedure for the postdelivery ward."

"So you're filing a complaint against the floor 7 nurses?"

"No. I'm filing a complaint against the labor and delivery nurses for not giving me the right supplies."

He pulls out a pen and takes a few notes on the pad of paper in front of him.

"Listen. I'm not blaming anyone. But your hospital needs work. I want stillbirth patients to be better cared for. It's an easy solution." He looks up from his writing. "I want you to create stillbirth supply kits and give them to the patients who aren't moving to the postdelivery ward."

"That's a great idea. I will pass it along to our quality control team."

I stand up. He stands up. "I'm sorry about your loss."

"Thanks. I appreciate that."

I turn to leave but pause. "I hope you follow through on my suggestion because losing a baby is devastating, and no one should have to feel like a burden because the hospital has failed to prepare for something that is fairly common."

Walking to the car, my body still feels alive with adrenaline. I want to get angry. I want to blame. I want to scream out loud, "What the fuck! Why am I being treated as if I have a mental problem?" As I drive away, I soften my hands. I loosen my jaw. I take a deep breath before silently giving myself permission to "let it all go."

I don't want this battle.

Then again, no one ever does.

~~~

"It's not fair that Ruth has a baby brother, and I don't." Eden and I are sitting on the front porch, rocking in our chair the color of a red delicious. "Ruth shows him off at lunch time by sitting next to him in his car seat."

I nod, imagining how difficult it is for Eden when Ruth's mom, an assistant at Eden's school, brings her baby to work every day. Due a week apart, we'd compared bellies until school let out in mid-June. "You're right. It's not fair."

"How come they got to keep their baby?"

"Their baby was able to grow all the parts he needed. Is it hard to see Ruth's brother?"

She nods and leans her head on my shoulder.

"I'm sorry, Eden. Sometimes people get to have things we want."

"I want a baby brother." She pauses, "Can I have another one?"

"I'm not sure," I pause. "We'll have to see."

She crawls down from the chair, faces me, and leans on my legs. I feel as if she's studying my face.
~~~

"Will he die too?"

I glance at the jasmine vine, leaning over to smell the flowers next to my head while buying time to respond. "I don't know that. I hope not." I look at her, "Many babies don't die. You didn't."

"I hate waiting!" She crosses her arms and stomps her foot.

"I know you want a baby brother so much. I wish he was here, too." I stand up and grab her hand, "We can go visit some of our friend's babies. They'll let us treat him like a baby brother."

"Could we bring 'em home?"

"I think they would be missed, but I'm sure we can go play with 'em."

"Let's do that, Mommy," wiggling off the chair and heading to the screen door, "Come on!" she says as she glances back at me.

I stay and rock for a few more minutes. Sometimes, baby brothers don't need to be brought home from the hospital to be family.

The Story of Us – Part XI

The sunburn on my face no longer hurts. The only pain I feel is coming from below my waist.

"You can push, Kimber. You can do it!"

I'm squeezing Dennis' hand, while Abby, my doula, puts a hand on my back and shoulder. "For pushing purposes," she'd said when we started 30 minutes ago.

Tears flow down my face. "It hurts so much. I don't have much more strength," I say as the contraction subsides though the pain never fully eases. "I don't know. I'm getting dizzy."

As if the walls have ears, a nurse comes to my side and holds up an oxygen mask. "Here you go, honey. Let's give you a boost. You're almost there." She pats my hand as she moves away. I feel the pain increase. I know it will be time to push in moments.

The team of nurses and a midwife are at my feet. "You can do this, Kimber" I hear someone, "Bare down, you got this."

Beside me, Dennis squeezes my hand before he coaches, "You're strong. Come on! You got this!"

I move my body more upright, yell, like an Olympic weightlifter, trying to zone in with my mind and body on the right muscle groups. I don't feel anything move even as the contraction dies down. I lean back, taking in the oxygen through the mask. Abby wipes my forehead. The midwife looks at me. "Your baby is almost here. These next two contractions I want you to really focus on baring down. Give it all you've got."

I nod but she seems too optimistic. I close my eyes, feel the tears running down my cheeks. Dennis brings his face close to mine, "Look at me." I focus my eyes on his. "Two more. That's it. Just like in the weight room. Come on. You're a rock star."

I nod, feeling the pain build again. I wait until I'm ready to push before yelling. I imagine lifting those last two reps where my arms want to give out. "One two three four," I hear Dennis saying. This push, I feel burning and yell out in pain.

"That's it," I hear the midwife's tone of excitement. "We've got a head."

I want to sob in relief. I feel weaker than I've ever felt before. Spent. I hear Dennis as if in a tunnel, "Keep going. You got this." I keep yelling and pushing. I close my eyes, breathe in the oxygen. I want to stay alert. I feel the relief as the contractions lessen. I'm on autopilot—pain, push, yell then breathe.

More tears come. I hear the cheering as if I'm not quite in the room. I haven't floated away; I'm weak but not in a scary way. I paste a smile on my face because I'm done. I wait for the rest of my body to feel it.

Then, a new weight. Six pounds even to be exact gets placed on my chest. I feel my smile for real and it's only her and I. "Hey Eden. I'm your mama. It's so good to meet you."

She's on her belly. Her head is bobbing as she tries to push up. I hear a voice to the right of me. "Look at her, she's already pushing up. She's strong."

Louder and nearer, a voice says, "You need to pat her a bit more. Let's get her lungs going a bit. It's good to work them."

A squeak, like a mouse, follows. I look up at Dennis. "Do you hear her?" He wipes his eyes, nodding. "We got ourselves a squeaker."

I turn my voice down a volume for only Eden. "You're already perfect. Just how you are."

Comfort With Words, Then Bam! Hit Over the Head

"I haven't seen you, yet. I was out of the country." I look up to see my former supervisor in my doorway. I see tears in his eyes as he moves in to give me a hug. "I'm so sorry. I get it. My first love died of AIDS."

I shake my head. "What a tragic loss. I'm so sorry with you."

His eyes shift as if he's in a memory but looks back at me before speaking, "And then so many of our friends—same fate."

I gasp. Put my hand over my heart and keep shaking my head. I have no words.

"It went on and on, funeral after funeral until we found better treatments." The tears remain in his eyes.

"I'm so glad you're here with us, with me. You've been with so many people in their grief and pain."

"It's been a huge focus of mine, grieving." We keep one another's gaze before he says, "This all sucks. It's horrible. Somehow we make it through and find life again."

"I believe you. I love your husband, Bob, and your amazing life."

He nods in agreement, wiping his eyes. "Me too. Come by my office anytime. I get it."

"I feel that from you." Tears enter my eyes again. "I may just take you up on that offer."

"Countin' on it. I can always use a good cry."

~~~

For seven years we've been meeting once a month, yet I'm carry-ing an unusual burn in my stomach, like I'm anxious. Heart beating
~~~

out of my chest, I drive the familiar route to Amy's house where the Graces are meeting.

Turning right onto Palo Verde Avenue, I notice my jaws gripping each other. I relax and soften my tongue. I loosen my palms on the steering wheel, noticing the sweat on the black faux leather.

I let myself in and move into the kitchen. "Hey!" says Amy as if I was the guest of honor. She gives me a hug, followed by Mandy, Alicia, and Shannon, who are also in the kitchen pouring themselves some kind of white wine mixture. Alicia hands me one and we sit down at the table, eating Amy's staple—a Barefoot Contessa signature, cabbage salad with smoked salmon and grilled zucchini. We are shoulder to shoulder around the rectangular dinner table when Alicia drops her fork mid bite and says, "This is awful."

Amy's look of shock mirrors my own as we stare at Alicia, who continues, 'Why can't you be here with your baby!? I hate this silence, no coos or watchful eyes looking at us."

My eyes fill but I can see she's crying, not bothering to wipe her eyes, letting the tears run freely over her cheeks onto her avocado-colored shirt.

I whisper, "I wish I would've invited you all to come and meet him."

I hear several answers of "I would've liked that." My eyes are too full to register Amy left the table until she returns with tissues. We pass them around, finding more words.

"I'm so sad that Baby Long Beach won't be playing with Ian. I imagined them being best friends."

Nods. We look at Mandy whose face communicates her ongoing pain of the past four years. Today it's all unspoken. We lean in and squeeze her hands. Rub her back.

After dinner we go into the living room for our circle time, hot tea in our hands.

I start. "I know it might seem like I need much of the sharing time, but I don't. I really want to escape in your lives and care for you."

"Are you sure? We'd love to give you the time." Shannon sits next to me on the clean lined, beige fabric couch, close enough to put her hand on my knee.

"I'm sure."

We take turns speaking around the circle.

"I'm lonely. It's hard being home with a six-month-old."

"I lost it yesterday when the juice box got dumped out in the back seat."

"I'm struggling to find time for dance. It's a part of me and yet, it seems like I'm exhausted all the time and don't do it."

"I just got offered a job at the community college by my house!" We start cheering, which turns into clapping and hollering.

"I want to give a toast," Amy says in a volume that can be heard over ours, "to dreams coming true and lives being changed!"

We raise our glasses, and our voices mix together in a cheer until, like corn popping, the word "eyes" rings out. It's our celebration ritual, started four years ago when Alicia asked us to really look into one another's eyes as our glasses clink together.

Three hours together and then we say good-bye. On the way home, I'm struck with an unfamiliar feeling, calm. My imagination places me in a boat with stormy waves, crashing against the wood but I'm unafraid of the uncertainty that life brings. We all have waves crashing against our boats, not just me with my grief. Somewhere that knowledge settles inside of me. I'm not alone.

<div align="center">~~~</div>

It came in the mail. I knew what it was by the large manilla envelope with the name of the hospital in the corner. My heart races almost to the speed of a month ago when I was in the building making my complaints. I rip open the letter hopeful for a positive response. *Will there be change?* "Thank you for bringing your concerns regarding the postnatal transfer policy in which you were transferred to the 7th floor without supplies, the quality of service you received from the 7th floor nursing staff, and also the quality of treatment you received from the nursing staff on the 7th floor in which you were not monitored or given postnatal discharge instructions during your inpatient... I sink into the kitchen chair next to me. *I was completely misrepresented.* I find myself wanting to send a basket of fruit to the 7th floor nurses because they did just fine. No mention of the labor and delivery unit where I didn't feel monitored and whose responsibility it was to send me upstairs with supplies.

I unlock my jaw, take a deep breath, and read the next paragraph. I skim as I assume this paragraph, unlike the one above it with subtle spelling errors, like "with out" and "post natal," has been used over and over in this particular template. It's the bottom sentence that says it all, "Please understand, however, that all such reviews are subject to statutory confidentiality and privacy considerations, and the results cannot be disclosed."

Of course. Par for the course. Everything feeling like I'm pushing a boulder up a hill, and it keeps rolling back down, making me start from the beginning.

I grab the tissues. *My effort led to nothing. My pain will not be turned into a better system, a better way to place women on a separate unit with a baggie of supplies that doesn't burden an unprepared nursing staff but rather allows for smooth transitions in an awful, shitty circumstance.*

I read the rest of the letter filled with next steps I can take if I'm not satisfied with the result. I fold it. Put it back in the envelope. Place it in the trash. I take my tongue off the roof of my mouth. I walk to the wooden rocking chair out on the porch and rock. Feet hitting floor then rock. Over and over until my heart stops racing. I imagine another woman on another day able to take up the torch for better aftercare for women suffering these types of losses. I bless her efforts, hoping these blessings will help her stay the course when up against medical systems with a long history of doing what's best for the medical professional, not the patient.

Then I get up. Grab my car keys. Drive down Iroquois to pick up Eden. I wave to Dorothy, who's out watering her roses. Left turn. I wave to Tricia, who's getting in her car. I call Shannon, who has a long history of hearing me.

"Hey Shannon, it's so good to hear your voice. I've had a doozy of a day. Can I tell you about it?"

I hang up ten minutes later. Feeling validated. Ready to enjoy my daughter.

~~~

"I'm going into the kitchen to grab a glass of water." As the water enters my glass cup, a thought hijacks my mind and my heart starts racing, "What if she dies?" Before the cup is full, I leave it on the counter and run the twelve feet back into the bathroom.

She has her eyes closed. She's laying on her back. The bath water waves over her body. "Oh my God, she's not breathing."

I bend over. Reach my hand to her arm and pull. Her eyes fly open. "Mommy!" she exclaims.

I let go. Sit on the closed toilet and sob. Eden sits up in a scramble and stands, looking back at the bath water as if there is something dangerous. I wave my hand, as if fanning my face. "It's. I catch my breath. It's okay, Eden." Her ocean blue eyes stare back at me—wide. I reach to pat her. "Mommy was having a moment. These are happy tears."

"I'm scared, Mommy."
~~~

"Makes sense. You were so calm, and I just came in and grabbed you."

"Why did you do that?"

"My mind was mixed up. I didn't pay attention. I'm sorry, sweetie. I didn't mean to scare you. How about I read you a story while you keep taking a bath?"

"No. I'm done."

More tears fall as I grab the towel. "Of course."

Trauma hits again.

~~~

Lumpy. Bumpy. Nothing smooth in the front. I look around the front room to see if any of the women are watching me, noticing the visible bulge from this slim fitting shirt. I'm suddenly warm and I watch the red move up my face. I realize I haven't really looked at my body for months. I haven't observed the changes—rounder face, dark circled eyes, flimsy arms. Bulgy. Thinking about it now, I'm not sure I even bother to turn on the lights most mornings to get dressed. I certainly don't lift the blackout shades since both our northern and eastern neighbors have six-foot fences where a naked body would be easy to spot through the windows.

I hurry back into the dressing area, hoping the home shopping host won't ask me, "How's that working for you?" I push, then pull, the shirt over my gut and broad shoulders. It seemed so much easier getting it on.

"Don't rip. Don't rip," I mouth to the air until it's over my head and off my body. I put three other tops to the side. No need to try them on, at least not in the size I grabbed off the rack. I hold up a long brown skirt, pulling to see if it's stretchy. A deep breath comes up. I didn't know I'd been holding it. I shake out my hands that want to wiggle my belly, pinch it until it hurts or hit it, as if that would make
~~~

it go away. A surge of adrenaline tempts me to do it. No one would hear me. No one would suspect the hitting I would do with my hands, or the mental shame I'd shout to only my mind. As much as I'd like to redo my late-night chocolates, I wouldn't want to redo how close it makes me feel to Baby Long Beach or how, for a moment, my grief gives way to tasting something good.

I know I have to return to "out there," to the women who are chatting, carrying on even though I feel like there is nothing to talk about in my grief bubble. I want to pretend as if my stomach isn't wearing my grief. As if I could feign excitement for another woman's career selling clothing. As if I could participate in getting my neighbor some free clothes from the commission made tonight.

I step out into the living room. Sit on the couch. Smile. *Where does one put her hands to avoid having her stomach noticed?*

Grief Concealments

1. Positive Thoughts – You're just fine. See – You're over ***it.***

2. Online shopping cart: 2 pairs of shoes – 8.5, 1 ring, 3 pants, 1 swimsuit

3. No appetite

4. Insatiable appetite

5. Mantra – Don't Think About IT. DON'T THINK ABOUT IT.

6. Staring at the television (volume irrelevant)

Crawling Along, Like a Sloth

*N*o, no, no. Stop, tears! I'm in my office with a student I've seen twice. I have no idea why I want to cry, but if grief could be described as clothing, she'd be outfitted in it. "I can't feel sad or cry. I just feel numb," she's telling me.

I take a deep breath, hoping I can keep any tears from coming. "When do you think this started, feeling numb rather than sad?"

She doesn't hesitate, "We couldn't cry in our family. When I was six, my bunny died, and I'd get sent to my room every time I'd start crying about it."

"What did your parents do when you cried?"

"They sent me to my room. They said, 'You can come out when you get yourself together. We don't cry in this family. Too much good here to cry. Sometimes I missed dinner."

I swallow the lump in my throat. *I'm not going to cry. I'm not going to cry.* "Wow. Sounds like you were smart not to cry. Were there any other times you wanted to cry but couldn't?"

"My boyfriend died in a car wreck last year, a month before graduation."

I feel pressure building behind my eyes. I look away, taking in the colors of my oil painting from Paris. She continues, "He was going to come to college with me."

"I'm so sorry."

She shrugs. "I think what made it worse is that my dad made me give back his letterman's jacket to his family."

I whisper, "Why?" unsure she'll hear me.

"He told me, 'It makes you cry all the time, give it back.'"

"How long had he been dead?"

"A week."

The tears come now, running down my cheeks. Now that they're here, I don't wipe. My client notices faster than her eyes could blink twice, "Oh my God, you're crying. Here. Take a tissue," thrusting the tissue box beside her at me.

"Thank you," I say allowing myself to really feel the wetness come down my cheeks. I lean forward, "Are you going to banish me?"

She laughs. "I wish."

"What's it like to see my tears?"

"Weird. I can't say I like it."

"It seems like you enjoyed being the one to hand me a tissue."

She laughs. "I did. How awkward. You didn't even know him."

I nod, absorbing her disgust but also realizing how good it feels to bring some sadness into the room. I look again at the painting across from me, taking in the umbrellas of the women walking the Parisian street. "I didn't. But I know you—even just a little bit. And it makes me sad that you didn't get comfort and that you had a very important person die."

We nod together, looking at each other. I notice her eyes are blue. I hadn't noticed that before. "Maybe we can work together to find a way for you to let in comfort. I'm not afraid of your sadness."

She nods.

"I can hold it until you're ready to take it back."

I can see her eyes—thinking. I follow hers, focusing on the water fountain I have in my office.

"I'll think about it."

"That's fair. We're out of time but I want you to expect you may feel a lot of sadness this week. You might not. But if you do, come in early. You don't need to be alone."

She nods, "See ya."

Will she come back? Were my tears too much?

I don't have to tell anyone, especially if she doesn't come back.

~~~

I stand in the shadows of the pine tree partially blocking my front window. Every evening at six, they pass by. Tonight they have on matching red shirts, his barely visible in the stroller. His big sister's shirt says just that "Big Sister." She's a year younger than Eden, and she's got a brother.

I don't know if he has blonde hair like his dad or brunette like his mom and sister.

I didn't show up on their doorstep with a plate full of cookies and a cheerful, "Congratulations" when he came home. Damn, I haven't even gone out to my porch in the three months since, to wave hello.

I can't recall his name. But his due date, two days after ours would've been, remains locked in my memory.

~~~

The return address of the white envelope read, "Los Angeles County Registrar-Recorder." I didn't need to open it to know what it was. It had been between my Southern California Edison bill and the fundraising letter of the Los Angeles Mission's Thanksgiving drive.

I sit down at the kitchen table. I'm tempted to grab the Sunset magazine, also in today's mail. Delay it a bit. Draw it out so I can savor the official proof my son lived. I imagine a curious relative two hundred years from now getting these records as she does a family tree.

I rip open the seam with my fingers, no letter opener for me. I take a deep breath. Pull out the white paper with its squares and rectangles. Last: Del Valle. Middle: Court. First: Long Beach. His name is official. Forever in the books. I glance over the day and time.

My palm is hitting the table before I can stop it. A fucking "F" trumpets off the page under gender.

One fucking letter.

It would have been more acceptable if the letter read "n" or "k." Typist error. Instead I have too many systems to blame. To point my finger at. The hospital. The coroner. The funeral home—did they even have a part in this? The county of Los Angeles.

Did I even get the right ashes?

I stop my thinking before I can even question that further. I take my tongue off the roof of my mouth. Rub my fingertips together so I can feel the grooves, their individual indentions—each finger with their own pattern.

A fucking paper.

Proof of life.

One more obstacle to overcome in the path of grieving.

One fucking paper—it could've been so easy.

Instead.

He doesn't exist.

Only she does.

<div align="center">~~~</div>

Feet pound on the floor as I startle awake. Before I can fully open my eyes, Eden jumps on our bed and grabs my arm, tucking it against her body before she closes her eyes. There's no need for words. She knows she can come in anytime and sleep with us as long as she starts out in her bed. I glance at the clock as I settle next to her, 1:34.

I stare at the dark ceiling trying to notice my body heavy on my bed. I close my eyes. I focus on my breath, but my ears won't tune out. I hear a car door closing somewhere on the street. I hear a dog barking in the distance. Farther away still are the sounds of cars driving. *Keep coming back to the breath.*

I notice the rise and fall of my chest before sneaking a peak at the clock again. 1:54. I push a deep breath out of my nose, loosen my jaw and close my eyes again. *Feel the weight of your body on the mattress.* I start with my toes and heels. *Is Eden okay? Why did she get up?* I notice my calves against the mattress. *When is too long to let her sleep in our bed?* I imagine my supervisor saying to me, "I'm sure she won't be in your bed when she's in middle school. Just relax. Don't worry about it. See what happens with time."

I start again, forgetting where I was. Toes, heels, calves. I take a deep breath. I open my eyes and turn to the clock 2:19. I roll onto my side, put a pillow between my knees. *How am I going to get up at 5? Just close your eyes. Don't worry about it.* My forehead starts feeling achy, like it has its own pulse. I force a breath. I start counting backwards by 7s. *999. 992, no 993. 980—what? This is hard. [That's the point.] 985. 978.*

I jerk awake as the alarm goes off and lift my arm to find the off button. My body feels heavy and not in a good way. *Don't think about it.* I push myself up with my right arm and swing my legs over the side of the bed. "Upright," I tell myself without moving my lips, "One foot in front of the other."

I go into the bathroom. Take care of all the necessities, including splashing cold water on my face. I'm already dressed to leave--a trick I've used for these early mornings. I sit on the couch next to my tennis shoes and socks, putting them on. I grab my duffle bag and head for the car. To my knowledge, Dennis and Eden haven't heard a thing.

Two hours later, after a spin class and a hot shower, I drag my tired body up the stairs from the parking lot to the front door of work. I feel like I'm carrying a 60-pound backpack though I have only a small purse and lunch at my side. These mornings I enter the building wishing I drank coffee. I figure it's a habit for when I'm older— for now, I hope the method of distraction will eventually wake me.

Still gathering my post-doctoral hours to get licensed, supervision is the first thing on my schedule.

Rebecca's door is open, so I walk in and close the door. I don't waste any time sharing my burden of a sleepless night.

"Should I be at home and not working? Do you think that's why Eden keeps having nightmares?"

Rebecca pauses before answering, "You've mentioned she loves school and her teachers."

"She does. She cries on the weekend when she can't go. Still, what if I'm ruining her?"

Rebecca tilts her head, so her jet-black hair covers one eye briefly while half-smiling at me. "You're the attachment specialist, you tell me: Will she be ruined?"

I chuckle. "I think I feel mixed about it," I pause. "My attachment mentor suggests that twenty hours apart from Dennis or myself is just great. She feels safe and loved by her teachers. You can see it in her face when she talks about school. Still…"

I look away, examining Rebecca's red silk wall hanging with embroidered birds and a river running between two mountain ranges. I notice for the first time the varied blues in the water. Taking a deep breath, I continue, "I can't really say she's being ruined. Deep down, I guess I don't think she will be. I think this is about me."

Unwanted tears show up. I don't want to start the day crying. I see Rebecca nod, read compassion in her dark brown eyes. I'm struck with how much emotional space I'm being given.

Do I share just how crazy I feel?

I look away before diving in, "I cry every time I pass LAX on the way to work. It's not because I don't love my work, I do. But it's what's missing." I grab a tissue as the tears run down my face. "I should be home taking care of my son. I shouldn't be commuting." I look in her eyes and see unshed tears, "I just miss him."

I wipe my eyes and look around the room before whispering, "I wanted so badly to be his mother."

She nods. Her tears still in her eyes. "I'm so sorry. You love being a mother."

I nod. She grabs a tissue out the box next to her. Then she continues, "It all makes sense, these feelings you're feeling."

"It's awful."

She chuckles, accurately sensing a mood shift as I glance at the clock. Fifteen minutes before I have a client. I take an audible, deep breath. "I'm crying with clients. I now have a box of tissues by me and them."

"You know, Kimber," she pauses until I'm really looking at her with all of my eyes, not just looking in her direction as I can sometimes do when I'm overwhelmed with feelings, "I think you're learning how to be real with your clients. It's uncomfortable, for sure, but you're offering something that not every therapist feels free to share—your tears."

She leans closer to me and says, "I really want you to take this in. You could become one very powerful therapist because of what you've been through. Really. I get the sense you've been compassionate for a long time, but now you've been gifted with the experience of rawness."

I nod as new tears come and fall down my cheeks. "I can see that."

"It's made you vulnerable in a good way. So often we sit before our clients acting like we have it all together. Or we know it all. I think you're finding something more valuable to offer your clients—you."

~~~

"Do you want to start trying for another baby?" I ask. Dennis and I are lying next to each other in our bed. The room lit like a new moon night. Our shoulders touching. Nothing else.

"I wish I knew. But I think I'm not ready? How 'bout you?"
~~~

"I don't know. I'm anxious about my age. I'll be 37 in three months."

Dennis rolls to face me. I turn my head but not my body, barely making out his nose and eyes from the slit of light around the edges of our blackout shades from the distant streetlight. "Is our relationship ready for more stress?"

I whisper back, now looking at the ceiling. "I don't know. I don't want to cause more loss to Eden. I'm committed."

"I don't either. You know I'm going to be there for this next pregnancy, right?"

"Yes. I know you will be. I'm also going to be better about asking for my needs, so I don't get so resentful."

"You mean when I don't read your mind?"

I turn facing him, shoving his left shoulder with friendliness. "Hey!"

"Hey yourself."

We move into one another's arms, staying there with deeper breaths and our lips touching.

~~~

"Hand out the presents!" a choral demand of excitement comes from Eden and her three cousins, all under the age of six. They seem to be very done with the adults sitting around and talking. On the outskirts are two more younger cousins, whose eyes suggest they're taking in these older cousins.

Don't let your mind go to who's missing. I take a deep breath and refocus on Eden grabbing a cousin with excitement before turning around in a circle.

"Okay!" my mom, who Eden calls Mimi, yells over the excitement. "Find a seat with your parents and then we can get started."
~~~

I sit in a leopard print beanbag. Dennis is next to me in the navy blue one. Behind us through the window, snow covers the ground. It will be here for another two to three months. The sun is hidden from the low hanging clouds, also blocking the Cascade mountain range usually visible from these windows. Eden comes and sits in between us. Sometimes standing to jump with excitement, other times sitting and clapping her hands.

Each person opens a present. Then we go around again until they are all unwrapped. Squeals of delight and the donning of the hand-knit scarves, fingerless gloves, and beanies makes for a festive living room scene.

"We have one more gift," my mom tells the group. My dad, the assistant in all things Christmas related, hands out envelopes for each person in the family. As people go about opening their envelopes, my mom pulls me and my brother, Bryce, who had a miscarriage a year before Baby Long Beach, aside and hands us each a white envelope, "Here's for my angel grandbabies."

The three of us wipe our eyes as Bryce and I say our "thank yous." As I take out the check inside the envelope, the tears keep coming. I feel just how grateful I am that Long Beach is being seen on this special Christmas day. I allow myself to imagine him looking down on us, missing us as much as we miss him.

<div align="center">~~~</div>

"Is it hard for you that I'm pregnant?" My pregnant coworker and I are alone in the lunchroom.

Before answering I pause, taking in her face, which I read as being sensitive to my predicament, "You know, this summer I wouldn't have been able to stand it. I couldn't even attend a good friend's baby shower."

She nods. "I can understand that."

"Now, therapy has helped me make more peace with my loss, and I'm genuinely excited for you."

She looks down before looking back at me. "I want to be sensitive for what comes up in you."

"I'm glad you asked because I don't want you tip toeing around me, either."

"I appreciate that."

"Thank you."

~~~

"Your faith is amazing."

I look up from my computer to see my former supervisor, someone I'd spent four hours with every week six years ago, standing in my office doorway. "I'm curious why you say that."

"I see how your grief doesn't sweep you away. Such a tragedy, yet you have so much strength."

"I never thought of it that way."

"You're going to get through all this."

I tear up. "It's the people in my life, including so many here, that carry me through this all. My close friends know that loving Jesus means showing up, loving with action."

"I notice how you eat in the lunchroom every day. You don't isolate."

I wipe a tear escaping from my right eye. *Why are you crying? This is happy.* "It's one of the best things about being here. Connecting with great people."

"Do you think believing you'll see your son again in heaven helps?"

I look up to the ceiling not wanting to be distracted by her facial expressions as I gather my thoughts. "You know, for me, it's that I'm
~~~

not alone. In that hospital. It was awful. But it could have been worse."

"How so?"

"I wouldn't have had an admitting nurse who asked if I wanted to hold my baby. I was in complete shock. I'm embarrassed to say I would have never thought of that possibility without her."

Liz shakes her head. I see the compassion in her eyes. "It's impossible to think in shock."

"Then there was the doctor who told me exactly how my induction meds would work. I knew I wouldn't be getting a break from pain once I started labor."

I wipe both eyes now. I see tears in her eyes as I continue, "That was key to making it through my pain mentally. If I would've been looking for a break..."

"It would have changed everything in how you could focus." I nod at her words.

"In my faith, I don't believe that was coincidence. I believe it was God's mercy being with me in a horrific event, something he didn't choose to stop but instead was with me."

"Well, whatever it is—your faith brings out a strength inside of you that's remarkable."

"Thank you. I receive your words."

Sometimes faith can be seen, not heard.

Make Me A Poet

Make me a poet
So I might find my way to the countryside
In the presence of an ash blonde daughter's pigtails whose
eyes take me back to the summer sky where I drove a tractor
round and round the field, cutting grass

Make me a poet
So I would not miss the eye twinkle connected to the smiled,
curved lips
As my 7-month-old giggles in anticipation of another round
of peek a boo

Make me a poet
So a day of bad physical pain can be overthrown by the won-
der and mystery all around me
Like the pair of golden eagles landing in a nearby tree
And the meadow flowers filling my visual pockets, empty
from living in concrete known as the city

Make me a poet
So I may live.

The Grind of a Woman

The toilet water is red. Not pink. But red. Again.

What's going on?

What the fuck is going on?

Fucking body. Fucking aging body that just won't stop showing me it's headed towards death.

Will Eden be motherless at age four?

~~~

"I'm sorry to say that this vaginal bleeding needs to clear up before you can try to get pregnant."

"How long is that going to take?" I ask Dr. Jones, an Ob-gyn who is new to me.

"I'm not sure. I suspect your bleeding is at ovulation and this sort of thing clears up when you take it easy, and your body is able to heal."

"What can I do?"

"I would take it easy on those spin classes. Rigorous exercise stresses out the body, taking important healing properties away from an injury because it's always trying to heal the broken-down muscles."

I nod. Take a deep breath. "It's my only consistent stress release."

"Try walking. Your body needs healing. Think of it as a season of rest."

What I don't say but want to say, "I've been in a fucking season of rest called debilitating grief. I'm sick of it. I don't want any more fucking rest."

Out loud I say, "I'll try it."
~~~

~~~

"I don't want you to go to work, Mommy!"

"You don't? Tell me about it." I kneel down next to her after I grab my camel-colored work bag.

She crosses her arms in front of her chest, scrunching her eyebrows. "I want to stay home and play stuffies with you. I don't wanna do circle time or take a nap."

"I wish I could stay home. I love playing together."

Eden stomps her foot while scrunching her eyebrows. "Then do it, Mommy!"

"Well, I need to go to work because I've told them I would be there, and your teachers are waiting for you."

She grabs my arm and pulls it close to her chest. "But I don't want to go anymore. I want to stay home."

"I hear you. You'd love to stay at home." She nods. "Are you afraid?"

Tears fill Eden's eyes as she nods again. "What if you leave like Baby Long Beach?"

I wrap her in a hug. "Oh honey. I don't plan on going anywhere. But you know what, you will never be alone. I can promise you that."

In the hug, I wait for her to take a deep breath, the type that signals her body has relaxed.

I hold her at arms-length. "Why don't you set up the stuffies so when I get home we can jump right in. Okay?" She gives me a quick hug before going into her bedroom.

As I back out of the driveway I whisper to myself, "She'll be okay. She's going to be okay."

~~~

Today will be the last day I pour my thoughts onto the pages of my Crane and Company navy blue journal with a gold border. Two weeks shy of eight years is when I started this journal according to the front cover I title every journal. This one's name is "Another Angle to Living." According to the entries, I journaled daily for three months then dropped off to once or twice a week which then turned into once every two months, then three, then twice a year until I've hobbled along filling it in sporadically.

A lot happened over those years—graduating with my doctorate, birthing two babies, nine years of marriage, buying a house, passing one clinical psychology licensing exam, finishing my internship, and starting my post-doctoral work at UCLA with a number of years in between, and wanting to leave my marriage 2,483 times. The latter, I suspect, kept me away from the journal. After all, how many times could I write, "This isn't working?"

As embarrassing as it is to name it, my baby dying is what I needed to find another angle to living—to stop obsessing on all that was wrong with my life, including my marriage, and get focused on what's here in this life I've built.

I've been journaling every day since the new year—seven weeks. On these pages, I've found the dismissed little girl inside of me who'd carry a metal folding chair, her journal, and a pen a quarter of a mile up the 45-degree slope out the front door. She wasn't worried about the bullsnakes she'd encounter or how much her lungs and quads would hurt near the top. She just did it because she needed to get away from a noisy house of three younger brothers. In the late spring, the views held the glory of a fifty-mile-wide golden blanket of sunflowers and blooming bitter brush.

I've also recovered the teenager inside of me who drove around and around the golf course cutting the fairway grass on the 1950s Ford tractor, sitting on top of a pillow and Sears catalog to see the golf balls and trees in the fairway. She had a lot of time to think. I haven't given myself thinking time as I've aged until now.

My work situation, being invited to do a part-time post-doctoral internship, something the center has never done before, gives me a boost of hope. I'm giving birth to my career as a licensed professional, something I wouldn't have been able to do if my son would have lived because I wouldn't have felt comfortable leaving him 30 hours a week. Now, I'm going to finish all my hours by June. I can be licensed soon afterwards. I didn't know how it was going to be possible. I've been given a way.

I close my eyes. Warmth spreads from head to toe as I feel the sun's heat on my cheekbones, eyelids, nose, and lips. A breath I hadn't known I was holding fills my lungs but doesn't go into my belly. It's a part of my body, my core, my womb, that I still seem to avoid. It doesn't seem to have thawed yet. I shake out my right hand, tired from gripping the pen. I'm at the end of the page. The last page. I take another deep breath before ending with one last line, "Birthday Wish #1--another baby."

<center>~~~</center>

We're walking on the beach path we traveled daily at sunset during his summers off as a teacher and weekly the rest of the year. We'd lived two blocks from the beach—an upstairs apartment on 2nd and Esperanza.

In that first year, we'd spoken of how many kids we wanted.

10 (my answer). "Okay," with a bit of sarcasm that had no bite (his answer).

Where we wanted to live.

Somewhere more rural with more trees (my answer). By our community of friends (his answer).

What we wanted to do professionally.

Work with people in recovery and the shelter challenged population (my answer).

Get hours to complete his master's in clinical psychology (his answer).

Today, almost nine years later, the wind is gentle and cool, a welcome reprieve from today's unseasonably warm day of 91 in March. Off in the distance, we can see a marine layer coming in off the ocean, making good on the weather forecast to drop twenty-five degrees tomorrow.

"So I wanted to talk again about having a baby. As I told you last week, my doctor has cleared us to start trying." I don't look at Dennis, only straight ahead. "Where you at?" I turn to look at him while I keep walking forward on the paved beach path.

He looks at me, "Where you at?"

I nod. "I know there are concerns about how stressful our marriage dynamic has been these last few years. I think the hospital disconnection highlighted that."

Dennis nods at me, looking into my eyes, while we both made our way towards Shoreline Village where we'd turn around. We pass a couple pushing a stroller. "I think we've been doing better at being less angry, do you?" he asks me.

"Yes, but as we know from the research a baby adds stress to any marriage no matter how good."

"True. I'm not getting any younger and pregnancy doesn't give me a glow. It messes with a lot of things, including my insulin levels."

"I hear you—that's a concern."

"Yes. Also, I know no matter what the stress, I don't want a divorce—ever. I don't want to bring that kind of sorrow to Eden. Or me for that matter."

"Me either. We can always go to therapy and get support."

"I think we need to get a couples group together made up of our friends from church. Let's be more intentional of being supported."

"That's a great idea."

A solo jogger passes us on the left. The sky pink and purple as the sun closes the day.

"Let's turn around so we're back before it's dark."

"Hey," Dennis pulls me off the path so we're standing in the sand nearer the water. He hugs me before whispering in my ear, "I want to get old together. I want to know you. To watch our family grow into something more than we had."

I nod my head into his shoulder before leaning back to speak, "Does that mean you're ready?"

"Yes. Yes, I want to try for another baby with you."

I smile then use the bottom of Dennis's t-shirt as a tissue. I pull him closer to the beach, away from the beach path. "I'm sorry for being so angry and not asking for my needs—resenting you for not meeting them. Will you forgive me?"

"I will. Will you forgive me for not doing a better job of helping, including at the hospital?" I nod. Dennis pulls me in for a hug, "I want to be close. You're the most important person in the world to me."

I wipe my eyes on his shirt, taking care to do it somewhere other than where I wiped my nose. "Thank you. I receive your words. I forgive you."

We walk closer to the water, kissing like it was that first year of marriage. When we were giddy in love. Before the cracks became large between us and barrenness started to be the only thing that thrived.

Could it be?

Waking up at 5 am, I feel a bit queasy in my stomach. Mild. *I must be hungry.* Not enough to stop me from driving up to work early to do my spin class. My eyes feel heavy and tired even though I've gotten nine hours of sleep, having gone to bed at the same time as Eden. *Odd.*

As I open the front door to head into darkness out to the car, it dawns on me—God could be answering our prayers already with a yes.

I set my red duffle bag down and tiptoe back into the bathroom and grab the pregnancy test box. I open and take one out, sticking it in my beltline for later since every minute I wait to leave delays me two minutes given how early morning traffic hours work up the 405 to the west side. Besides, I've already emptied my bladder when I woke up.

Two hours later, I walk into my building and head to the down-stairs bathroom, the one that seems to be rarely used since only the conference room is nearby. I pee on the stick, sitting on the toilet—not wanting to assume no one would come in.

One line. I stare a couple minutes longer just in case the second line takes longer to make.

I really thought I was pregnant.

It's okay.

You'll be okay.

I practice smiling in the mirror a couple times, hoping by the time I interact with my coworkers, it will look real on my lips.

Longings…

Unfulfilled

Fingers tenderly touching my belly
Circling. Massaging.
Willing.
A bump to form.

1489 days and counting

Intimate caress jaded
Touches not for pleasure, now for a purpose
Willing the blood flow to stay away
As cramps rise again
Month after month

The house gets quieter
As longings grow deeper
Until the muscle dragon grinds his teeth
Then tears flow
Along with blood

Basketballs, footballs, volleyballs, alike
Disappear under t-shirts in private moments
To practice positive thinking
Of cradling the softness of flesh delivered out of my uterus

Moments of fantasy bumps in the mirror
Leave an ache
As one line never becomes two

As plastic sticks are thrown away

Baby Pinks and Blues come and go
At parties in the honor of another
Blessed One. Normal One.
Someone who most deserves one

For how long will I be out of the club?

1489 days and counting…

Sticks and Stones

We are in balancing stick pose for the second time. Five more poses before I get to be in corpse—a position I'm unsure I'll get out of this morning. I don't feel myself. I'm counting each breath as a way to not flee this hot 100-degree room.

Do I need to throw up?

Do I need to lie down?

Did I eat enough yesterday?

Did I drink enough?

Am I going to pass out?

Should I already be in corpse pose?

Should I be cooling myself down outside the room?

My breasts ached when I did eagle pose. Am I going to start my period during class?

Why am I dizzy?

"Keep your mind on your breath. Don't worry about what's coming next," says Nicole, our instructor.

Three more poses until I can play dead.

~~~

I'm holding a stick with a line. I grab the box and pull out the instructions. I skim to the diagram. Pregnant. Not pregnant. *Shit. I'm an idiot.*

Pregnant. *Just like earlier this week.*

I'd imagined jumping up and down with elation or shouting with joy maybe even doing a jig. But none of those impulses are present now. The stick feels heavy in my hand. I sit on the toilet, elbows touching knees, face covered by hands, as tears fall down my face. I
~~~

take an internal scan, I find feelings of relief, fear, joy, terror, uncertainty all balled up inside of me like they're pushing to get under my ribs. Will I really be able to live my life as a more fully present human being? Will this new responsibility throw me back into my rushed life where I'm onto the next thing in my mind but doing the present thing in autopilot? Flashes of the past ten and a half months momentarily illicit pain—the backseat without a car seat.

Feel your feet. I count to ten. I identify all the colors in this tiny space--lamb's ear green, gold, silver, spring green, white, moss green and charcoal gray, aspen trunk gray. A breath emerges along with tingles coming out my fingers.

An unwelcome tremor enters my body, and my hands shake so I do a self-hug—straight-jacket tight. I squeeze and move my toes back and forth until I find a calm, discharging a breath once again. It feels different this time around.

I focus my ears on Eden's squeals of delight as she and Dennis play stuffed animals in the living room. After my hands stop shaking and my body gets warm, I know it's time to leave these four walls. I flush, pull up my pants, and while washing my hands I feel the groves of my fingertips. Then, I breathe in, "You're pregnant." Exhaling, "You're having a baby." I get a tingle of giddy as I start imagining how I'm going to tell Dennis and Eden.

I relapse into wishing I'm someone I'm not—that I'd had a pre-made plan for this moment, like a t-shirt reading, "Baby #3 now on board" or a poem with lines like, "I want to puke and it's your fault but don't worry sex won't stop—at least for eight more months." I've done none of these, but I do know how to wing it. Looking pupil to pupil in my mirror reflection, I mentally cheerlead, "You've got this. It's all good."

I take a deep breath and sit down between Dennis and Eden as they finish the story line of the stuffies barely escaping a mountain lion chasing them on their hike. It occurs to me we may have been too transparent about the reason for the mountain lion signs on our Malibu hike last Saturday. Giraffee is now positioned in front of the pink bear, Uncle Kerby, Raven, who isn't a raven but a golden retriever, and Siamese kitty like she's about to give a speech. I pick up Giraffee and take the lead. "Family," I say with a pregnant pause. "It would seem that we will be growing by one. A baby giraffe is growing inside of me. The pregnancy test, too gross to bring out, is in the bathroom as evidence."

I think I see joy and confusion flash across Dennis' face before he whispers, "Really?" I nod slightly, knowing he catches my message. Eden, too precocious for her own good, sits back, and looks at me as if I've told her she can eat a chocolate cake for dinner. "Mommy. Is this true? Are you pregnant?"

The game is up. Tears flow down my cheeks as I nod then say, "It's true." Eden squeals before leaping into my arms with a force that would've knocked me over had Dennis not put his hand up to brace me upright. He moves close as tears move down our cheeks. The warmth of our bodies moves through me filling my joy and taking away some of the fear.

"I hope this baby doesn't die," Eden whispers.

<div align="center">~~~</div>

Day five of pregnant, and my calm hasn't been found. I hear voices berating me when I imagine eating cookie dough ice cream. It says, "Stay away from sugar or your baby will die." There's also another bothersome voice, showing up every few hours to go through a current checklist of symptoms. *"Nauseous? Cravings? Tired? Am I tired enough for the baby's development? Headache? Swollen Feet?"*

This question gives me pause before another voice disputes the fear, "Already swollen at five weeks?" Still, the questions keep coming, building a ball of anxiety in my stomach that spreads throughout my limbs before my whole body starts shaking at her conclusion, "*Oh my goodness, the baby has already died. We haven't even made it to the doctor, and you killed him.*"

Three hours according to the clock, I watch as I lay in bed before I sit up after my body stops shaking and my breathing returns to normal. I prepare to join the family for dinner by washing my face with cold water in the bathroom. I roll my shoulders out a bit—tight from fear.

After greeting Dennis and Eden, I sit down, eyeing the salad with chicken on top. I take a bite. I nod my head at Eden's story about lunch today.

Before I realize, I'm having my own conversation without moving my lips.

I think talking myself out of extra monitoring may have cost Baby Long Beach his life.

~~~

Tears fill her eyes. "I'm 30 weeks and I can't even imagine losing my baby at this point."

I nod as I allow my eyes to mirror hers, feeling my feet on the ground, wiggling my toes, as the tears fill my eyes. "It was devastating. Completely unexpected."

She nods. "Earlier in my pregnancy, I was sad with you but now..." she tears up. "I can really imagine it."

"Thank you." I place a hand on my heart, and avoid looking at her bulging belly, ripe with baby. "I really feel your empathy. It's a gift."

She nods. "You're welcome. I really felt it this week and wanted you to know."

Walking back to my office, I count my steps. Feeling from heel to toe on each step. I check my computer screen and see my client has
~~~

arrived. I rub my fingertips together, feeling their ridges, until the urge to sob melts back into my body.

The Story of Us – Part XII

"When did you drink the water?" the ultrasound glances at me as she runs her wand on my belly.

"I waited until 15 minutes before, then slammed it down." I look up at her with a cringe not knowing how she'll respond to my confession. "It's not exactly by the book but this isn't my first rodeo as they say."

She laughs. "There's plenty of fluid here to take some pictures." She's looking at the screen while she continues moving her wand through the gel on my stomach.

Dennis puts a hand on my shoulder, moving his body against the bed. "Can you tell what gender the baby is?"

She glances at him before reangling the wand down by my waistline. "I'm trying. I keep going at it with different angles but whoever this person is, there's no cooperation."

Still looking at the screen, "Mom, why don't you shift over a bit and let's see if we can get this person to move so we can get a peek."

I feel like I'm moving in the same manner as a seal—taut, uncoordinated on land, and jerky. "While we're waiting, I'll say unofficially your baby looks healthy. Of course, the doctor will take a look and give you a call but there isn't anything I see of concern. Fluid is good. Measurements are good." She turns to smile at us as she wipes her wand. "I'm going to give it a few minutes before trying again but we may be out of luck."

"I can't believe I don't have gestational diabetes this time where I'd get ultrasounds regularly to make sure the baby's developing."

Dennis laughs. "Well I suppose that's one downside. The other downside, the little one will be called Baby Long Beach for bit longer since we'll need to find two names rather than just one!"

We laugh together as I rub my belly. "Eden is going to love that! Now we've gotta get a move on, I don't know how much longer I can hold out from using the bathroom."

As if on cue, the technician returns. "Let's try this one more time." She moves the wand, pushes with a little prodding every few seconds. She shakes her head. "I think we have someone sleeping. There just isn't any movement changes here so I'm sorry to say that I can't get a clear view."

"Bummer." I take a deep breath. "I love to know these things."

Dennis chuckles as he helps me to the edge of the bed. "Already taking on the personality of the mother."

I laugh. "Okay, pot calling the kettle black."

Terror, Sensationally

I'm still in therapy. Today, my mind is tricking me. I'm sitting in this familiar waiting room that smells of old leather and age, like the wooden homestead I grew up next to, yet I feel like I just got off a roller coaster and it wasn't pleasant. My ears are accustomed to the sounds of this place; after nine years, there's little strain as I wait for the familiar click of the exit door to know the patient before me has left and it will be less than a minute before I'm greeted and invited to come in.

As I walk in and lie down on his tobacco-colored leather couch, the tears come. He can't see them in his position behind my head, but he will hear them when I start talking. I suspect he can feel my sadness. I sniff before asking to have a tissue. I hear the soft, white paper tissue slide out of a box and show up above my head. He waits. I listen to the traffic sounds coming in from Wilshire boulevard, the honks, the slide of the metal doors in delivery trucks before a shout of "good-bye."

I take a deep breath, "I'm such a failure. I'm already ruining this baby. I can't calm down. I wake up in the middle of the night drenched in sweat. My heart feels like it's run a mile all the time now." I pause to consider if I really want to go there and do, "I'm not absorbing my food; it's running right through me, several times a day."

"Where has the excitement and joy from last week gone?" he asks.

"I don't know. I don't believe it now. I believe death is coming."

"It's easier to believe in fear and death. It's safer. Just like it's easier to be insane than sane. Pushing away the fear—that's harder. Your mind is attacking you."

I pause, tears continuing to roll down my face as I chew on his words, "Can you get it to stop?"

He chuckles at this. Then silence lands again. Comfortable.

He speaks behind me, "I think you need to sit up today. I think you really need to see me and know I'm with you."

I nod though I know he can't see me before I roll my right side and push myself up with my left hand. Immediately, sobs come out and I hiccup. I bend over and cover my face with my hands. *You aren't alone. He's here.*

My breathing starts slowing down. I look sideways, seeing him in my peripheral vision. I take my time wiping my nose, my eyes. Then as if my fears were a torrential storm, they've lifted. A belly laugh, one that surprises me, rises up as I look at Dr. P, "Is this what you had in mind? Me crying more hysterically after I sat up?"

He laughs and shrugs as if he knew what would happen. "Well. Finally you're here and see I'm in the room with you."

I nod. Look away and let a thought land that returns my anxiety to my stomach the size of a volleyball. I say it. "What if this baby dies?" A couple more breaths pass, "What if I kill this baby?"

He lets this float in the air a bit before saying, "Then we deal with it."

~~~

"Hmmm. I can't hear a heartbeat." My body goes dead still as if a mountain lion is smelling me. I'm not sure if I've been breathing until she says, "Let's turn you to the side to get a different angle." I no longer feel my body. It's as if I'm floating, watching the doctor move me to my side.

I force a breath in my lungs that feels like I'm expanding a balloon for the first time. It's stiff. Like I haven't been using my lungs in quite some time. I feel the apparatus getting colder as the doctor's
~~~

movements change from rushed to slow. She doesn't say a word of concern, but it's written all over her face. I look away, not wanting to see on her face the message my baby has already died. So I stare at the ceiling, feeling my body like it's floating. I didn't think my hands could shake more than they were while in the waiting room. Or my heart pound harder, but both rev up in speed. *I'm dying.*

Out of the corner of my eye, I notice the doctor fiddling with the monitor. I look back at the ceiling, willing myself not to look at her. My entire body jerks as the room explodes with a rapid *whoosh!* "There you are," she says with a smile. "Already hiding, are you?" A heartbeat.

<div align="center">~~~</div>

My body doesn't comprehend the sound, isn't reassured by her smile. Rather, it deflates like a pierced tire as sobs escape. I fan myself as if my hand will dry my tears, and we can pretend I'm not losing my proverbial shit while lying practically naked on the exam table. "I'm sorry," I somehow manage to say.

The doctor looks confused, but I can't speak, so I use my hand and gesture with my index finger to communicate I need a minute. Another part of me wants to gesture with the middle one, a better representation of how I'm actually feeling. Eventually I notice warmth on my leg. I look in that direction, Sharon's hand. I force my mind to notice the warmth as my body keeps shaking, and I've yet to stop crying. After what feels like hours but is probably only minutes, I turn to the doctor, fanning my face again but looking beyond her, avoiding her eyes. "I'm sorry. I just need a minute. In fact, I need to use the bathroom."

"Sure. Take your time. As you can hear, you have a healthy one here—heartbeat is going strong."

I try to breathe in the reassurance, but my mind is looping.

He or she could die.

You have a healthy baby.

He or she could die.

On shaky legs, I lock the bathroom door, I drag the garbage over, knowing I'm going to lose it. Out both ends. I take my time. I gather the parts of me I can find, feet walking me back into the room, legs carrying my weight, hands that open the door, and eyes redder than when I entered.

Driving away, I mentally regroup and throw away all fantasies that I can pick up, think positive thoughts, and everything will work out. *Fuck.*

~~~

"You're my favorite thing that has come out of my son dying," I look into the brown eyes of a colleague I've known for six years, having met on our mutual internships. I continue, "I would've never come back to work if he'd been born."

"That's right. It's always good to be with you. It's a treat."

We eat side by side as a handful of students walk by. *In some sense, how wonderful it would be living as a young student again.* "Who knew you'd be my supervisor? When we were in peer supervision all those years ago, I wouldn't have predicted that."

She laughs. "It's a challenge."

"I've made your spicy pumpkin soup four times in the last two weeks."

"It's a favorite. Finding good food I can eat has taken some work."

"I'm sorry you've had to change your whole diet and live with the knowledge that your symptoms will get worse over time."

She looks at me, head nodding. "Thanks. I'm doing anything to help what's ahead."
~~~

I nod back knowing her neurological condition is unpredictable in progression. "It seems like yesterday when we had a whole bunch of answers."

She finishes chewing her bite of beet salad, before saying. "Now we're learning how to sit in the uncertainty and questions."

~~~

The last time I'll see this office is four pm Thursday, after I've loaded my four-door sedan with my one box of office décor along with my various wall hangings. The last time I'll sit at this computer desk is also Thursday, after I've logged off, which will be after my charting is finalized.

My palms are sweaty as I walk downstairs to our staff meeting room. I know what I have to say to close this important chapter. I could get away with making private good-byes but I'm not one to shy away from group confessions.

If we were a church, the beginning of our meeting would be considered prayer requests. Today, someone shares he has leukemia—prognosis unknown. Another confides that his new husband has fallen into depression. Another's partner of ten years died unexpectedly of a heart attack three weeks ago and she's putting her grief in words, and yet another is transferring to a different university, closer to home. As the room fills with silence, adrenaline courses through my veins while I rehearse in my mind: "I'm having a baby. Due January 24th."

Finally, I take a deep breath and speak first to the wall before trying to make eye contact, "It goes without explaining that this has been a difficult season. I've felt nothing but love and support throughout this year. You've cared through your hugs and your words of all kinds, including "Grief sucks." You've shared with me your pain, your losses, and let me know I'm not alone. So it seems
~~~

fitting that as I'm finishing up my last week that I also tell you I'm twelve weeks pregnant. Due January 24th."

A collective cheer fills the room. If we were younger there's a vibe that suggests a section would be jumping up and down with a rhythmic word or two as fists are raised in a university fight song sort of way. I look around the room, taking in delight-filled faces and tears start to flow from my eyes as my happiness leaks out. Those close enough to me put their hands over mine or on my shoulder and arm as they tell me one at a time, "I'm so happy for you."

After the meeting, a line of congratulatory hugs wraps around me. I wear the feeling of being seen and joined in celebration as a smile.

My work is done.

~~~

Sitting on the exam table for my second appointment, swinging my legs I tell my doctor, "I'd like to get tested for gestational diabetes earlier than normal."

"Tell me more."

"I got it with my first baby, and it was serious, where I had to use insulin even though I was exercising daily and eating according to the diet."

"Alright. Not a problem. I'll write you an order to be in your digital chart. You can go anytime."

~~~

There is one balloon. Blue. It matches the color of the smog filled sky outside our dining room window. "Daddy! Tie this to the chair where Baby Long Beach would sit." Eden pushes the gold-colored string towards her dad, the balloon is slow to follow but eventually catches up.

I see him take a gulp as if swallowing his tears before getting out, "Okay." We all understand today isn't a day to fuss with manners.

"Eden," I say with a higher pitch than usual as I try to fake enthusiasm as we walk toward the kitchen, "Let's make the cake."

"Okay, Mom! I'll get my stool from the bathroom." She changes direction and runs through the living room. As I pull out the bowl and mixer, I hear the scraping of her plastic stool against the stone floor. I start unpacking the canvas grocery bag.

Two-layer devil's food cake mix.

Four serving-size package of Instant Chocolate Fudge Pudding mix.

One container of plain yogurt—cold to the touch.

I take a deep breath as I pull out the container with the baby's face on the label—laughing. *Prunes.*

He'd be eating baby food by now.

"I can't wait! I can't wait!" Eden repeats as she jumps beside the stool she's set next to the mixer.

"This is the best cake, isn't it? I say, trying, but missing the mark of child-like enthusiasm.

"Baby Long Beach would've loved this cake, Mom!"

I paste a smile up on my face, hoping it will help my words sound brighter. Lighter. "He would have." I open the cake mix, "Here. Pour this in the bowl."

She grabs it. Pouring with one hand on top and one on bottom—just like I'd taught her. She looks at me, "What's next?"

I hand her the pudding. "Open this with scissors, then pour it in."

She stands a bit taller, as if she knows she's been entrusted with a dangerous tool even though she's been using the rounded scissors for years now at Montessori. As she tries on her autonomy, I spray the metal Bundt cake pan with cooking oil and pour cocoa powder, before wiggling to coat the inside. "Great job," I say as she pours the pudding with minimal spillage over the side.

I hand her the plastic measuring cup. "Please get ½ cup of water for us." She gets off her stool and moves over to the sink.

"Do you think Baby Long Beach can see us?"

I take a deep breath. "I don't know, sweetie. I'm not sure how heaven works."

"I want him to."

"Me too." I crack the two eggs, one after the other. I loosen my jaw. Take my tongue off the roof of my mouth. I focus on loosening my forehead by relaxing the muscles.

"Is this good, Mom?"

"A little too much, I say as I place it on the counter. "Good try though. Can you get the chocolate chips?"

"Yup. I know where they are 'cause I'm big."

"You are big."

"I wish Baby Long Beach got big."

"I wish he did, too. You really wanted a little brother."

"There's a brother in your tummy."

"Do you think the baby is a boy?"

"Yup 'cause I talked to Jesus about it, and he said it's a boy."

~~~

Later, as Dennis, Eden and I sing "Happy Birthday" our voices echo in the room. I regret not having any friend's voices to join in. When I'd thought about this scene last week, it seemed too depressing to extend an invitation to them. After all, who are we fooling, having a birthday party with no little boy to receive it?

As the off-key singing continues, I'm struck by the thought this is a celebration of survival. Surviving a year without our little boy, and we couldn't have done it without our friends picking up the pieces with us through their conversations, meals, gardening, and all matter of mundane things that let us know we weren't alone.
~~~

As our song ends, Eden looks between Dennis and I, "Should we cut a piece for Baby Long Beach?"

I shrug, lifting my eyebrows to Dennis to indicate I had no idea. He looks at her, "What would you like to do?"

She says, "He should have one then when he looks down from heaven he won't feel left out."

"Perfect," I say. "Let's not leave him out."

The next morning the piece is gone.

I find it later in the garbage as I'm discarding the eggshells from breakfast.

I resist the urge to grab it and eat it, anything my mind can conjure up to feel closer to my son. Even if make believe.

~~~

Answering the phone, a nurse identifies herself as such.

"We got the results in for your diabetes bloodwork, and it was positive, so we'd like to set you up with the specialist doctor since it's so early in your pregnancy."

Relief floods me. My body going haywire—certainly a sign of good baby growth. "Great. Let's do it."
~~~

No Manual

There is no manual for visiting your son in the cemetery. I create one in my mind as Dennis and I drive up Rose's Hill, a country field away from the chain link fence we'll walk through.

1. Bring tissues.

2. Camera optional though necessary if remembering the length of grass against *his* stone from one year to the next.

3. Bring journal and pen so you're reminded of what you'd like to say.

4. A blanket for lying down, your head to *his* stone corner.

5. Bring tissues in case you've forgotten them since reading number one.

6. Touch someone's hand so you can imagine it's *his*. Then cry. Sob. Ache. And if you're lucky, hug someone next to you.

7. Take your shoes off so you can feel the energy of the earth, not because you're a self-prescribed hippie but because you live in a universe where the earth is alive with connections and it helps you remember you're not buried no matter how many times you wished you were to escape the devastating pain. *This is especially relevant if you have children still living because you don't want them to feel like they lost a sibling and a parent on the same day, unless tragically that is indeed their story.*

8. Resist the temptation to lie here all day and night, listening for a whisper in the wind or an owl on the tree who seems too close to not be *him*.

9. Visit the inscribed marble placeholders of friends, who were sons themselves, and remember other parents live with a "never to be whole again" kind of heart.

10. Say good-bye and wonder how much you should visit in order to be a good parent.

    There is no manual when visiting your son in the cemetery.

Bach Flowers, Panic Attacks and Names

My hands shaking. Palms sweaty. Four small bottles. Middle finger size. Dropper lids like baby bottle nipples. Side by side on my kitchen counter. Promises on labels. Bach's Rescue Remedy for stress. Hornbeam for weariness. Rock Rose for panic. Star of Bethlehem for terror.

A drop of each on my tongue.

Will this kill my baby or save it from my terror? Will this cause a death? Did I cause death? Damned if I do. Damned if I don't.

My TMJ and resting heart rate of 103 suggests I need some type of external intervention. Meditation and yoga practices aren't enough. Nothing is working. Desperation, a friend to sleeplessness, taunts me at the edges.

I say out loud to no one, "You don't fucking know what kills babies."

"Science or history can't help you."

"No control studies."

"Only guesses by a system run by other humans, which most prominently promotes the findings of European male minds."

My heart pounds on my chest muscles as if knocking to get out. I drop my tongue off the roof of my mouth. Loosen my jaw. A deep breath follows. I unscrew each lid, leaving them loose in the bottle. With shaky hands, I grab the far-left dropper, lift and squeeze. One. Swallow. Return to bottle and grab the next. Two. Swallow. Repeat. Three. Swallow. Repeat. Four. Swallow. Taking a deep breath, I notice my stomach hurts. It hasn't gotten the message it's okay. That I'm good with my decision.

I reach into my imagination and picture Jesus with me. I imagine Him at the counter putting an arm around my shoulder, comforting me, reassuring me I'm not an outcast. Reassuring me that no matter what happens next, He's with me.

My breathing feels deeper. I put my hand on my chest and my belly, noticing the rhythm of filling and deflating of my core as my breath moves in and out. I notice the tightness in my jaw and take the tongue off the roof of my mouth.

Before too long, I hear the birds outside the window. I go to the back porch and sit, feeling the sun on my face.

I pick up my phone.

Call a friend.

"Hey, do you have time to talk? I'm freaking out."

Much later, I get up after feeling the gurgling in my stomach. Make my way to the kitchen to satisfy something I haven't felt in several days. Hunger.

~~~

My heart is pounding, breathing shallow, sweaty palms and black spots are showing up in my vision. I've come to my bed, hoping the feel of the mattress underneath my entire body would calm me.

It doesn't. I deepen my breath. More black spots. I move the pillow under my head, so I'm no longer flat. I put my hands on my stomach. My heart races even more. *Is the baby moving? Shouldn't I be able to feel movement by now?*

He's died.

I know he's dead. Three weeks after I last heard a heartbeat at a doctor's appointment and death has struck.

Deep breath, Kimber.

Deep breath. You've felt nothing. He's too small.

Wiggling my toes now. Wiggling my legs. Wiggling my hands. Wiggling the little toe. Wiggling the big toe. Wiggling the legs like the waves at the bay.
~~~

He's dead. The baby is dead. Does he have a gender yet?

"Ripple. Be the ripple," I mumble as I move my arms above my body. I soften my tongue. Take it off the roof of my mouth.

Dead. The baby is dead.

I force a breath. It hurts to breathe.

I'm going to die. I'm going to leave my family.

I look at the bedside clock. I've been at this for 18 minutes and I'm not even close to a resting heartrate.

I get up. Slowly. Black dots swarm in front of my vision and my feet feel like lead. I stand until the dots dissipate, and with them my feet feel lighter. I find Dennis working in the garage.

"Dennis, I'm going to the hospital to get monitored."

He stops what he's doing and rushes towards me, "Is everything okay?"

"I'm panicking and I can't stop."

He nods and slows his pace until he wraps me in a hug. "That makes sense. Sounds like a good way to stop."

"What if they treat me like I'm foolish? Like I'm some neurotic person," I whisper?

"You'd hate that."

"I would."

"I don't think you're neurotic."

"You don't count."

He laughs. "Do you want me to come? I could try to find someone to watch Eden."

"No." I take a deep breath. "I just need to hear the baby."

"Okay." He pauses, "For what it's worth, I don't think you're crazy."

"Thanks. That's why I married you."

He pulls me closer and nuzzles my neck, "Whatever is happening with the baby, we're going to make it."

I squeeze harder. "We will."

~~~

The white walls remind me of every other hospital I've worked in or visited. What feels different is I've chosen a different hospital from where Baby Long Beach died. I have no bad memories here.

I take a deep breath as I walk up to the nurse's station counter. "Hello. I need to get monitored," I tell the dark-haired nurse.

"Hi there. Do you have any pain?"

"No."

"Did something happen to make you think something is going wrong?"

"I had a panic attack. Something just switched inside, and I can't tell if it's intuition or being triggered." I wipe my eyes, looking down at the counter. "I had a stillbirth last pregnancy. I need some reassurance right now."

"Of course," I hear compassion in her voice, so I look up at her. "Let's get you hooked up so you can relax."

The tears don't stop. She hands me tissues as she straps me into the monitoring system. As she turns the volume up, I jump at the whooshing sound coming out of the speakers.

"There you are," she says to the monitor. We meet eye to eye. She rubs my arm before turning to leave. As she opens the door she continues, "You take all the time you need. I'll be out here when you're finished."

~~~

"Are you finding out the gender?" the ultrasound technician asks us.

"We are," Dennis says smiling at me.

"Okay. Let's see if we can get this little one to cooperate."

"Our past children haven't been so cooperative so work your magic, please."

The tech smiles at me before she places the wand on my belly as I help her expose my belly by holding my waistband below my waistline. All eyes are on the screen, taking in the head, the body in the sideway angle. She moves the wand higher on my belly, giving us a better angle of the lower half. "Oh, there he is in all his glory."

"He?" Dennis asks.

"Yup. Do you see here, she points to the screen, tracing in the air, "This is his penis."

Unannounced, emotion unlocks the flood gates in my eyes and streaks down my cheeks. I grab Dennis hand and squeeze as we look at one another. "Oh, now you're going to make me cry," says the tech.

"Join us," Dennis says, "they're happy tears." After wiping his nose with a tissue he'd brought in his pocket he says, "We're having a son! I'm going to father a son."

I chuckle as I sit up and prepare to leave. "You are."

~~~

Taking a deep breath, I open my Bible to Second Kings chapter four. It's a spiritual rhythm I've done for years, continuously read through the Bible. As my eyes move across the page, tears come at the protests and indignation from the woman of Shunammite who faithfully served God with her hospitality toward Elisha. She was given a son as prophesized by Elisha despite her old age. She'd protested, told him not to get her hopes up, but nine months later she gave birth to a son.

Fast forward in the story, written here in black and white, this son dies before she does, and she's indignantly angry as am I thinking of Baby Long Beach and our joy, our anticipation—*why not keep our womb barren and give us grief of a different kind?*
~~~

She cries out as I have done so many times this past year, "Did I ask you for a son, my lord? Didn't I tell you, 'Don't raise my hopes.'?" I stop reading as the words are too blurry. I grab a tissue and take my time before returning to the page. Elisha responds by sending his servant with Elisha's staff. But it isn't enough, the boy doesn't awaken. So Elisha goes to the woman's house, shuts the door, and prays to the Lord. "Then he got on the bed and lay on the boy, mouth to mouth, eyes to eyes, his hands to his hands. And as he stretched himself out on him, the boy's body grew warm. Elisha turned away and walked back and forth in the room and then got on the bed and stretched out on him once more. The child sneezed seven times and opened his eyes."

Sobs emerge as they meld with goosebumps. Was this God giving me a promise that the death in my womb would be reborn? Would this son live? I can't quite allow myself to believe. It's too simple—too perfect in its story archetype. But I move ahead, grab my laptop, and type into my search engine, "Name Meaning of Elisha." There, on the screen, in several versions, "The Lord is my salvation."

The Lord has spoken. Our name found.

~~~

"Congratulations on finding out you're having a boy."

"Thank you," I say to a woman who's identified herself as my doctor's nurse. "Unfortunately, the ultrasound had something that requires your doctor to check you sooner than your next appointment."

My heart drops into my gut, forming a massive ball. "What do you mean?"

"Nothing that is immediately concerning for you or your baby, but the doctor would like to see you in the next few days. You haven't been bleeding, have you?"
~~~

I sit down in the chair right next to me. My stomach threatens to throw up my lunch. "No."

"Great! If that changes, come in right away to the labor and delivery unit."

"Is the baby going to be okay?"

"The doctor states no concerns about your baby. She just needs to check you and see if you might have placenta previa. "Again, it's not an emergency. Just something that needs to be checked out."

"Could this be why I'm feeling so much pressure on my pelvic area?"

"I can't really say. Definitely ask your doctor when you see her."

After hanging up, I go immediately into a grounding routine to keep anxiety from taking over. Put one hand on my chest, the other on my belly while I name 10 objects in the room out loud. "Jug, book, television, couch, chair, end table, dining room table, button fern, cat, pillow." There has been no deepening of my breath, so I start naming colors, "Camel, chocolate brown, pink, red, black, spring green, gold, orange, cherry wood, moss green."

"You're safe. The baby is safe. Breathe." Nothing moved. No release yet, no gurgling in my stomach, tingling, or breathing to indicate I've discharged my triggered anxiety. So I start naming textures, "fluffy, furry, shiny, glossy, rough, smooth." A deep breath starting in my belly, moves up my core, into my chest and out my mouth. *You've got this. This isn't an emergency. You'd know.*

I get up from my chair and head outside to smell the jasmine on my front porch before my brain can once again grab onto concern.

But doubt intermingles with the flowers.

But would I know?

Focus on the smell. Notice how sweet it is.

Would I really know?

Feel the leaf, how smooth it is. Dark green, white, ivory lattice, red chair...

~~~

I'm greeted by the female doctor I'd met last appointment. We go right into it. "What are you experiencing?"

"Pressure in my pelvis, some lower back pain." Soon afterwards, I find myself lying on the examination table with my feet in stirrups. I note I have lost any concern about exposure, how far I've come since my first pelvic exam at 18 in a freezing room like this one where my virginity and anxiety of being examined made it painful. I'm not a fan of how quickly my mind has gone to previous pain because I'm in a similar situation. My heartbeat picks up a notch and I feel like my hands are on the verge of shaking.

As I scramble up as graceful as a seal, she gives me feedback. "Everything looks good down there; however, your ultrasound shows you have complete placenta previa." My heart, which was already high, starts racing and it's hard to take a breath. I nod automatically hoping the information is all good on the internet because I can't make meaning out of the phrases I grab, "I don't think…adjustments. You're earlier…not as concerning." I catch myself in automatic mode, almost floating above my body but not quite. I stop my nodding hoping that will help lift the anxiety threatening to increase. "One in 200…" My focus attends to her tone, which is positive, but I'm not reassured. After all, statistics are never reassuring to those in the 1 percent category; 1 percent of all pregnancies end in stillbirth.

I'm lost wondering why I never invite Dennis to these appointments. Today's not the day to unpack this quandary I keep finding myself in—dysregulated when I know the science that says having another person with you helps stay calm. Why do I not even think about doing so? You'd think after tragedy struck, I'd be more cautious, yet here I am again—dazed, terrified and unable to comprehend much being said to me until a familiar phrase breaks through my cloudy thinking, "Do you have any questions?"
~~~

I start shaking my head before I catch myself and say, "Can you tell me that again? Why I shouldn't I be worried?"

She nods reassuringly, gives me a partial smile, and talks slower—starting now to take notes, "Sure. I'm going to write it down for you as well." I nod, grateful she's sensing my overwhelm. "You have it early, and it's your uterus measurements that is giving you this diagnosis rather than bleeding, so this is all good news. It will likely correct itself, so I'm not super concerned. We'll monitor your symptoms when you come in for your regularly scheduled appointment, but call us if you have excessive bleeding, or in your case, start bleeding at all."

I nod rhythmically before catching myself, flashing back to the ways some patients rocked themselves in their room on the psych ward I worked at after graduating college and wonder for a fleeting moment if this is the start of my psychological meltdown. Taking in that she hasn't seemed too concerned about my mental state the last few minutes I ask a question, "Could this condition be the pressure I'm feeling in my pelvic area. It's like I'm nine months pregnant and about to give birth. It seriously feels like I'm headed for labor."

"I would imagine it's because this is baby number three. Your body knows what to do and it's creating space in your pelvis. But let's keep monitoring to make sure everything's okay."

My heart continues to pound as nothing is reassuring about this visit so I try again to find answers that could lead to relief. "So you don't think I need to do bed rest or anything?"

"I wouldn't say so. I think your sensations are more related to carrying two children before this one. I don't think there's any reason for bed rest. Usually, we do that in the third trimester or when there's bleeding."

I nod over and over, but brain fog has settled in, and I focus on making it out of the office without sobbing or worse, curling up in a ball on the floor.

~~~

I've called Dennis on the way home, so I don't have to relive the news any longer than possible. He's sent the word to our friends, who I know will be praying for us. As I open the front door, I head straight for the bedroom in full "I trust my own intuition" mode. Dennis stops me in the living room with a hug. After taking a deep breath, I push away and say in a tone that matches my raised eyebrows, which clearly states don't question me, "I'm going on partial bed rest until I stop feeling the low pressure." I add over my shoulder, "Please bring me a margarita and keep them coming until this placenta previa clears up so I can stop panicking."

"No really. What can I bring you?"

I shrug. "Give me a minute after I'm laying down." I get under the covers and plump up my pillows against the wall to support my head and back as I recline at an angle. Through the door I yell, "Can you bring me some water and the Stress Remedy bottle on the counter, yellow label?"

"You got it," he says at a distance that suggests he's near the bedroom door.

I breathe in deeply, feeling alive and filled with gratitude in my gut over Dennis showing up for this crisis. Already, I have texts and voicemails telling me I'm being thought of and prayed for. I've got all the support I need. Now, if only my body would cooperate and grow this baby without any more complications.
~~~

The Story of Us – Part XIII

We are all outside, Dennis, Eden, and I. The temperature is 82, an outlier in January. My hands smell like lemons, the consequence of hand squeezing them for lemonade, which we are drinking.

"It's not fair. I don't have any brothers or sisters like my cousins."

I feel a heaviness in my chest. "You want siblings, don't you?" I take a deep breath and look at Dennis whose face looks empathic.

"I'm sorry, Eden," he says.

She crosses her arms and sits away from the table. "Are you going to give me some or what?"

I start writing down this conversation in my mind, already transferring it to the journal I keep on meaningful conversations between me and her. Yet, this mental image doesn't shift my mood. "I don't know, honey. We will need to wait and see."

"Why don't you know?"

"Well, sometimes our bodies can't grow babies." I look to Dennis, who's looking out into the yard, before returning my eyes back to Eden.

"You grew me."

"I did. And I'm so grateful. But it doesn't mean it can happen again."

"Why not?"

"Well, our body is always changing. So sometimes it just doesn't work like that." I take a slow drink of lemonade.

"It's not fair. I want people to play with that live in my house not across the street."

"You do," Dennis says. "You love playing with other people."

"Are you trying at least?"

I look at Dennis as he glances up at me still wearing sadness on his face. "We are, Eden. We are trying." What we don't say, but what we both know is Dennis and I have been talking about how much conflict we've had the last two years. We're hopeful we can work through it. We keep saying we're committed for the long haul yet we're not even sure what we're arguing about except we're both unhappy. Besides, my biological clock is ticking loudly these days. We've already waited three and a half years since having Eden and I'm more than halfway to forty.

I pull my eyes away from Dennis, back onto Eden who nods and un-crosses her arms, grabbing her yellow plastic cup of lemonade and bringing it to her mouth. "Aww," she says smacking her lips. "This is good stuff, Mommy." She nods and takes another drink. "Real good stuff."

Triggered and Tissues

I take a drink from my purple plastic water bottle, trying to cool down from September's 80-degree weather lingering in our bedroom all day long. I pull my laptop onto my pillow resting on my thighs. Day two of partial bed rest. I click on my "you've got mail" email service.

My back aches. My legs feel full of lead, and I can't seem to get rid of a metaphorical ball in my gut that's camped out in the uncertainty of whether Elisha will live. I'd thought it would lessen when I sent out the email last night asking for prayer. It hasn't. Instead, it's housed itself right below my ribs, stealing my appetite.

As I wait to connect, Dennis pokes his head into the bedroom. "Looks like someone delivered dinner for us. It was on the porch. There isn't a card or anything, just food."

"Fantastic! That is amazing."

My eyes move back to the computer screen. I click on the envelope with a red 53 next to it. Up pops a line-by-line listing of the unopened emails, a quick glance, tells me over half of them are in response to my prayer request. Unexpected is an email about one of my dad's good friends. I click on it first, skimming the content as my eyes fill with tears and the ball in my gut grows and feels as if it's reaching from stomach to back inside my rib cavity. I read again my dad's first words, *"How does anyone deal with the loss of not one but two sons in the matter of two short years?"* It hurts to breathe. *300 people at the prayer vigil. Unrelated deaths—one a teenager, the other a curious little boy.*

I move quickly to the toilet and lose the contents in my stomach. *No guarantees.* I take my tongue off the roof of my mouth. I feel the ache squeezing my temples together. I start again, reading the responses to my email.

"Believing with you."

"Praying. You aren't alone."

"I'm trusting with you and for you, committing to prayer on your behalf and on Elisha's! (love the name by the way.)"

"All I know anymore is that God is good…all the time…the rest is a mystery that I'll never get this side of Heaven."

"Shit. Are you kidding me? Praying for you now."

I read them over and over until the headache leaves, my stomach returns to normal. I get out paper and pen, writing my condolences to the couple who in two years find themselves without living sons.

It takes a village.

Dear Lord, bring us all a village so we can put one foot in front of the other.

I can't find a heartbeat

"How's your day going?"

I look up at the nurse whose age I'd guess to be early 20's. "Good. How about you?"

"Just fine. I'm going to put this wand on your belly. We like to get a heartbeat for the doctor."

"No problem."

She places the wand on my right side. Nothing has come out of the hand-held device. I go on high alert. I look at her face to watch for flashes of concern. The two sides of her brow get closer. Not looking up she says, "I can't find a heartbeat."

Crash—my gut explodes in panic. My breath stops. She moves the wand. *Whoosh* fills the room. "Oh, there it is," she says.

I'm already out to sea, pulled by a riptide, uncertain how I'm going to get back to shore. My cheeks turn red as I realize the gasping noise also in the room is from me. The nurse looks at me, wide-eyed.

"I'm sorry." I gasp. "I'm triggered." I take several shallow breaths as the nurse stares, still wide-eyed. "I had a stillbirth," I say noticing my heart racing even more.

"I'm so sorry." She starts looking at the apparatus she's still holding. "I don't know what happened."

I wave in her direction. "You didn't do anything wrong. I just need some time to calm my body down."

She nods at me, eyes still round.

"You don't need to stay in here. I'm a psychologist. I know how to do this. I'll come get you when I'm calm."

I wiggle my toes. Rub my fingers together to a count of "one and two and three and four and…" *You're safe. The baby is safe.* I rock my head to the rhythm of my fingers. When I'm confident I can stand, I start dancing in the room. I take my tongue off the roof of my mouth, soften my jaw. *Come Lord Jesus. You never leave me nor forsake me.*

"I'm safe," I say under my breath as I move to the right. To the left "Elisha is safe."

My feet feel more and more solid on the ground. My vision cleared. I open the door to find the nurse. "I'm okay." I practice under my breath, entering into a mental war over whether I should apologize for my uncontrolled response, which I'm perceiving ruined the nurse's day. Before I lose contact with my distress by focusing only on hers, I get ahold of myself.

Leave it. Haven't you had enough without bringing in some mental shitshow that will make you feel worse? Besides, when are you going to stop being Miss Independent and ask someone to come with you to these appointments, so you have support?

~~~

"Can I have the tissues?" I ask as I enter Dr. P's Beverly Hills office for possibly the last time.
~~~

Tears fall down my cheeks and my lips quiver as I imagine our good-bye planned for today's session. Our time together has spanned twelve years of my life. *Will I be back?*

He sits in his dark brown leather chair, and I sit up on his similarly toned leather couch. He waits for me. "For some reason it feels harder this time. I know we've stopped before, but my daily life is two hours away given the traffic and I don't imagine I will work near you again."

"You can come visit me. But, yes, it is different."

I look him in the eye so he can see I'm really taking him in. "You've changed my life. You've changed my kids' lives." I pause to wipe more tears away. My bottom lip is trembling as I find my voice again. "Thank you."

He nods. I can see in his eyes he's taking in my gratitude. I also see him agreeing with me, he has changed my life. What hits me in this moment is the lack of pride I see. It feels like it's more a demonstration of professional confidence, a taking up space that still allows for me to take up my own space.

I look down at my feet as my elbows rest on my knees. "I'm ready to meet this little guy, Elisha. You helped me let go of Baby Long Beach, so I won't be trying to make up…" My words drop.

He takes them up. "You've said good-bye. Look how present you are now." He pauses. "Do you remember when you first came—always racing off to this or that. The more the better to you."

I nod, remembering how relieving it felt to get off the production hamster wheel when I took a year off before my third year of graduate school. He continues, "You aren't afraid to stop. To feel." He leans forward in my direction, "To love."

I nod, whispering, "I remember."

"Remember how afraid you were of pain? You were so against it."

I laugh. "Oh my goodness. You were so in my face about it, too."

He laughs with me. "I had to shake you loose somehow. You were so wound up. Everything was so serious."

"I was." I look out the window, catching a pigeon flying past our fourth-floor window. "I despised pain and was so angry at the world every time I was in it." He nods, lifting his eyebrows in agreement. "And the blame...someone was to blame. If not me, then someone else."

"It spoiled the good inside you. Spoiled love. It was as if love couldn't exist if there was pain. But you've learned--they coexist. One is needed for the other."

"Yes. You've taught me, really showed me through your care, love, at least for me, is best internalized when I'm sitting in pain and helpless with nothing to offer."

"You didn't know how to be. Only do for others. Now, you know how to invite others in. You don't need to be alone."

"I have." The words linger as I take a deep breath.

"Your attacking mind is quieter. Not so much on the hunt anymore."

"She's not."

I look at him again. This time I whisper. "Who am I going to tell my hilarious vocabulary stories to?"

"What have you got?"

"Last night after her bath, Eden said we needed to "download the bathtub."

He laughs from his belly. "She's a smart one. You'll have your hands full with her."

He looks at me without any trace of playfulness, "I don't plan on going anywhere for quite a while. Come visit. Tell me your stories."

I nod.

"I'll try."

"Okay."

"Can I give you a hug?"

"Of course."

I squeeze him, reminding myself to breathe so my muscles are more relaxed, attempting to remember this sensation of his arms hugging me.

On the way to the elevator, I wonder to myself if I'll ever hear again what has become a familiar echo—my soles hitting the tiled floor in this office building on Bedford Avenue.

A Moment of Together

Sun streaming in through the window.

We sit in a circle.

All eyes seeing one another and being seen.

One of us has shared he has leukemia —

prognosis unknown.

Another's new husband has fallen into depression.

Another's lifelong partner died.

Heart Attack.

One day alive.

The next, dead before lunch.

We all come with something.

Spoken and Unspoken.

Fragile.

Tenuous.

Unbreakable.

As a Circle.

Day Five Hundred and Seventy-Four

Though I'm fifteen minutes early, I hurry as if there's nothing to enjoy, nothing to soak in on my way up the elevator to the second floor. The hallway to the baby monitoring room for high-risk pregnancies is unremarkable. I'd been here each week for the last three. I signed in as I usually do, my hand moving across the page but my mind worrying about what's to come. *Will I need to go to the bathroom once I get hooked up? What will I eat after I'm done? Will there be traffic on the way to pick up Eden from school?* So caught up in my thoughts I barely register the nurse looking over the clipboard. "Last one," she says, breaking into my thoughts as I write down my name next to the due date. January 24th, one week from today. I glance up as I take a breath that I must've been holding. "Let's hope so. I'm so ready to meet this guy."

She smiles and I follow her to the bed on the far side of the room. Two of the five beds are occupied, but neither mother faces mine. The sound of their babies' heartbeats reminds me once again that all babies don't die in the womb. I lie down and go through the motions of leaning my upper half back as the nurse wraps two bands near my underbelly before squirting gel on my abdomen. I find no comfort in the familiarity or having felt Elisha's kick minutes ago. My mind goes to tragedy again and again. *Breathe. Keep breathing.*

My belly expands as a deeper breath fills my center. I focus on the nurse's face as she looks at the monitor but realize within a few breaths I'm having difficulty breathing again because I'm anticipating something being wrong. I turn my head to focus on the walls thinking of the best word to describe the color, *oyster.* My breathing feels less trapped now that I'm not watching the nurse.

Though I'm trying to be mindful, I recognize I've been tight until I hear Elisha's heartbeat in the monitor. I try to push him away from my ribs because he's snuggling a bit too close for my comfort.

He's kicking me now, shifting closer to my hips. I close my eyes even though I can feel the nurse still at my monitor. *Feel your breath enter into your nostrils. One. Two. Three. Exit out your mouth. One. Two. Three.*

Her voice startles me, "Can you feel that?"

I open my eyes, finding her as if she held a life buoy and I'd just fallen overboard. I place my hand at my heart, trying to calm its heavy pounding. *Her face looks calm.* "Feel him moving?"

She looks at me briefly before pointing to the monitor. "See this line?" I nod. "This pattern is showing me you're having some contractions." She pauses, still watching the lines on the screen, "I'm surprised you aren't feeling it."

"What does this mean?"

"Well," she says as if describing the weather outside, "We might have a baby today."

"Really?"

She looks at me, turning her entire body to face mine as I continue laying on my side, "You're having contractions every five minutes. I'm going to call your doctor, and she'll come to see how dilated you are."

As I watch the monitor by myself, trying to feel the contractions but not having any luck, I'm reminded of yesterday's doctor's appointment where I learned I was three centimeters and 70 percent effaced.

Neither of us, however, expected this progress so soon.

<div align="center">~~~</div>

I whisper into the phone, "Hey. We might have a baby today."

"What?! No way."

"I know, right? I'm not even feeling the contractions, but the doctor is on her way down to check me."

"Oh my goodness. We were supposed to be at that Laker game tonight. Can you imagine?"

"That would have proven exciting!" I laugh. "I could've gotten on the big screen."

"So what do you want me to do?"

"Put people on standby—your mom to check flights for flying in, figure out who can get Eden from school…"

"I'm on it. Should I cancel clients?"

"I'll call you after I'm checked by the doctor."

"Love you."

"Love you, too."

I place my cell phone beside me as I look up at the doctor coming over to my bed. We get right to the business at hand.

"Well. How does having a baby today sound?" Dr. Kim asks.

"Sounds great," I say as I return her smile.

"I think we can make that happen. You're 4 centimeters and 80% effaced. Is there anything you'd like to do before getting admitted to the delivery unit?"

"Can I eat there?"

"You can't. You can eat afterwards but it's hard to say how long you'll be. Why don't you go grab some food and meet us in the delivery unit in 45 minutes?"

"Will I be okay? Like, I won't start having hard contractions while I'm gone, will I?" I give her a bit of a smirk, "This is my third. I've heard horror stories of car deliveries, you know.

Dr. Kim laughs. "You're not even feeling the contractions now, are you?"

"No," I say matching her lighthearted tone. My heart races as I have a flash of disappointment when imagining Dr. Kim saying no to my request. "Um. I have a question for you." My hands start shaking. I put them on my belly where I feel Elisha moving.

I sense her mood shifting to match my seriousness. "What is it?"

"I'm worried about my body freezing up during delivery. I had a really traumatic birth last time with the amount of pain my body had to endure. Given what I know about embodied trauma I don't trust it to not shut down."

"So what's your plan?"

"I'm wondering if I can have an epidural before the pain gets too intense."

"Do you think that will help?"

I take a deep breath. I can see in her eyes she's taking me seriously. "I do. In my professional research about trauma and the body I think I need that kind of support."

"Okay. Let's try it."

"Really?"

"Really. I'll write up the order when we get you admitted."

"I was thinking I'd have to give you my seven reasons why."

She grins. "This is your area of expertise. So I trust what your gut is telling you. From my perspective, your baby will be fine. You'll be fine. The downside, it may prolong labor, but we can address that should it happen." She stands up. I'll see you up there."

"I'll see you up there."

~~~

Hospital gown on, check in complete, I'm still feeling no pain but I'm counting breaths for a different reason. My nurse isn't crazy about my plan for an epidural. "It can stop labor altogether," she says, "making it much longer."

I nod, pausing my counts. "I know. But I think it's the least risky for my situation."
~~~

She doesn't have a scowl on her face but it's close. I continue, "I can't take the chance my body will freeze under labor pain, which could cause something worse like an emergency C section."

"Well. It's your call. Your doctor has given the okay. I still don't agree."

I want to gravel, make her agree, try to win her over somehow, but I realize collaboration comes in many forms. So I continue, "If my labor does stall out. Can I ask you for advice? Will you help me with all the tricks you know? You can tell me 'I told you so' after we're all done."

She laughs. "I'll help you. I think we're going to start prepping you now since we have everything ready but let's get you to your room and get you and the baby hooked up."

I feel how far Elisha's dropped, there's more pressure down below but I'm without pain. As I wait, I picture him resting on my chest, maybe helping him latch onto my breast, like Eden's birth. Then in the next breath, I flash to getting the news he's stuck in my birth canal.

"You're okay," I whisper while we wait for Dennis and my nurse. I continue rubbing my belly until my heart rate returns to normal.

Movement by the door draws my eyes. "Hey, hey!" Dennis says as he walks in. His smile fills his entire face. "We're meeting our son! We're doing it!"

When he reaches me, he leans down and pulls my head to his shoulder, "Are you ready?"

"I am."

He pulls back so we are looking each other in the eye, our breaths mingling. "I'm going to be here this time. Whatever you need--foot rub, back rub, taking over the labor...". He chuckles, backing away to stand, "Okay, not that but you get the idea."

I nod. "I know. I feel you're here already in a different way."

~~~

"Let's clean you up before we get you that epidural you ordered. I imagine things will progress quickly."

My bottom half is soaked from my water breaking just minutes before. "Okay. Let's do it."

"Your doctor will be in to check you."

As soon as I was back in my bed, Dr. Kim shows up. "Let's check you and see what's going on. What are your pain levels?"

"I'm about a five or a six."

"Okay. Good. You're dilated to eight and almost completely effaced. Let's get that epidural and we'll go from there."

"Sounds good."

We go over the usual, the anesthesiologist and I, along with my nurse and Dennis. "Medications you're allergic to." "Codeine, penicillin. Also, my body is sensitive to medicines so please go light."

"Well, I need to make sure it's working so let's see what we can do. I'll need you to sit up and hold still. Can you do that or should we wait for your next contraction?"

"They're manageable right now—painful, but I can do it."

"I'm going to clean the area and then you'll feel a poke," he says as I feel cold hitting my skin as a small section gets swabbed.

"Okay." I take a couple of breaths trying to relax my body, which seems to be on edge more than a moment ago when I was lying down.

"Uhhh. I can feel that going in. Should I feel like I'm going to faint because I'm feeling like I'm going to faint. I start to lean over on my right side, feeling the room get smaller. I can see in my peripheral vision the anesthesiologist picking up his speed and putting something new into my IV."

"That's not typical, but you should be feeling better in a few."
~~~

I close my eyes, as my head swims, trying to locate something solid. As I count my breathes, I get to twenty and open my eyes. The room has stopped spinning. "How are you feeling?" he asks.

"Better." I pause trying to really feel into my head, "Yup. It feels like I'm not going to faint."

"Tell me how much feeling you have in your legs. I want to make sure it's working."

"They feel really heavy. Like if I wanted to move them, I couldn't."

"Okay. Sounds like it's working. If anything changes, let your nurse know and I'll be back."

"Thanks."

I feel Dennis at my arm, rubbing it gently. "How you doing?"

"Okay. I think I'll just wait and rest here for a minute."

"Just let me know if you need anything."

I nod, right ear on the pillow.

I watch the clock. Ten minutes have passed. I take a shallow breath. "Dennis?"

"Yes?"

"Can you go get my nurse. I feel like I have bites all over my stomach. It's itchy. I'm wondering if this us normal."

"Sure thing."

Within a few minutes he returns with my nurse. "Hi. What's going on?"

"My entire belly feels itchy, like it's being bit by ants."

"Well. That can sometimes be a side effect to the epidural. It's rare but it can happen."

"Lucky me," I say with an upbeat tone as well as a layer of sarcasm. "I'm definitely one who likes to break those odds."

She chuckles with me. "Is there anything that can be done?" I ask.

"I'm afraid not. It should wear off over time."

I slowly rub my hands over my stomach. Soon it looks like a sunburned belly. I look up at Dennis who holds up some lotion. "Want to try?"

"Sure. Let's get that."

He starts standing. Then he sits, moving the chair over by the side of the bed. I'm reading a home décor magazine but keep getting pulled to the biting sensation that feels everywhere his hand isn't. The itching is relentless.

The contractions progress, feeling like muscle cramps in my pelvis area with brief periods of reprieve. I look at the clock, three hours since my water broke.

I start rocking to the sound of Elisha's heartbeat. Over and over again.

As the pressure increases, I wonder what the excitement is all about, getting an epidural. It's underdelivered. Traded one pain for another—biting fleas. Still, we continue to limp along to the finish line.

"Can you go get the nurse? It feels intense down there, so I'd like to be checked," I say through gripped teeth.

"Sure."

The television is on the basketball game – the one we were supposed to be attending.

"I'm feeling a burn and a lot of pressure. I think it's getting close."

"I'd say so. Don't push yet. Let me get your doctor." As she walks out the door, she turns back, "Your body moved along nicely. Great job."

"Thank you," feeling secure, not smug, about having a team player as my nurse. Tears spring up in my eyes. I catch Dennis eyes and he matches mine. Squeezes my hand. *This is happening. It's really happening. I'm going to meet my son. I'm really going to meet him.*

A team of people, another nurse, my nurse, along with my doctor enter the room. "It sounds like we're going to meet your son," Dr. Kim says as she sits on a wheeled stool at my feet.

"I hope so," I say through my discomfort. "I can't wait."

I hear Dennis near me along with female voices. "You got this, Kimber." As I'm bearing down, Sharon, my mother-in-law peeks in. She looks around and checks back in with me. I barely nod my head, but she knows it's an invitation to come in. She stands by my side, my right. She starts rubbing my arm. Her tears are close to the surface.

After a couple more contractions, I hear a collective "aww!" before he screams. It's jarring and I jolt. Crying first and then sobbing as my nurse places him on my chest. I notice he's lighter than my cat, Oedipus, who loves to sit in the same place.

I see only him. I know Dennis is right beside me along with Sharon, but my eyes move back and forth as I hear him scream. He looks blue. Or is it purple? *Isn't he supposed to look pink? Why does he have so much white film on him? Oh my God, no. Baby Long Beach had white, lots of white. He's dying. He must be dying. His cries will turn to silence. He's not going to last. He's so fragile.*

I force my hands to hold onto him. I feel them more than see them shake. There is a nurse near us, Elisha and me. I notice my entire body is starting to shake and my legs threaten to fall off the stirrups. *Why isn't she concerned about his color?*

I feel like my heart could run out of my chest. I start praying without moving my lips, "Please God. Please don't let him die."

I keep noticing my nurse isn't panicked. No one is panicked.

It occurs to me Elisha can't fall because he really can't move yet. I take a deep breath, noticing the fullness of it. I find my voice in whispers, not matching his screams. "It's okay. I'm here. I'm really here." His screams continue not missing a beat.

I watch Dennis cut the umbilical cord as I stroke Elisha's back. Sharon's hand on my shoulder feels warm as my body settles into shakiness as it discards the pain of childbirth. Tears flow down my cheeks as I look at Dennis and say, "We did it."

He smiles and nods. "We did it."

~~~

I hear her before I see her. "Come! Hurry! I'm meeting my brother!" I smile, knowing she's about to burst through the door. "Mommy!" Eden shouts, sliding to a halt near my bed. She inches to the edge as if she'll startle him, peering up over the mattress. "He's so little."

"He is." I pat the mattress next to me. She climbs aboard, hesitating before giving him a kiss on the head. I nod to Alicia who has brought Eden to the hospital. Dennis moves over to the doorway to talk with her. She peaks in on us, checking out Elisha but I know she can't stay long. "Smell him," I encourage Eden. She wavers before leaning in to sniff him. "What does he smell like?" I ask.

"Like Disneyland."

"Disneyland?"

"Yeah. Right on Main Street where those yummy smells are."

I lean toward Eden's head and exaggerate my own sniffing sound. "You smell like Disneyland, too." She laughs and pushes me away before settling into my side. Elisha looks pinker to me with every minute he's been living outside the womb—about ninety minutes by now.

Eden whispers into my ear, as if telling me a secret. "I thought he would die, too, Mommy."

I give her a squeeze. "I didn't know if he'd live, either. But he did. You lived, too."
~~~

She nods, looking at her brother's head before leaning in to give him a kiss on top of his head. "See, Mommy, I'm kissing his head, not his face just like you asked."

"You are. You're such a great big sister."

She smiles as she sits up a little straighter.

She looks at me with uncertainty in her eyes. "Do we get to take him home?" Her tone suggests that it took all her courage to ask me.

Oh, sweet girl, I think. I look deep into her eyes and whisper back, "We do, Eden. We do." Then I squeeze her to my side as we continue to stare at him together.

"Oh, good." Her relief mingles with my own as we lie there the way I imagine Christopher and Winnie the Pooh might've done while watching the sunset at the end of a gloriously adventurous day.

~~~

I'm carrying my son, all six pounds 10 ounces of him, to the car for his first glimpse of natural lighting. He's in the car seat, the one I've longed to fill for eighteen months but instead sat in its box in the east corner of the garage—the side facing the Sierras. I feel a lightness to my steps as I move towards Dennis who's pulling up to the curb.

I still miss my other son, the older one, the one with feet the size of chocolate minis. I would've loved to meet him. That longing hasn't been replaced. I don't imagine it will ever be.

It feels good to be exerting energy. The emptiness of my arms is no longer. This younger son, the one I wouldn't have met had his older brother lived, is my welcome burden. Stepping up to the car, I pay attention to the installation of the car seat. I wear my mother fussiness like a new uniform, pulling on the belts, the base, the hooks, anything I can see to pull or push—as if his life depended on it. As if mine did.
~~~

Getting into the front seat, my imagination pulls me. I anticipate being woken up in the middle of the night, and I'm giddy. I want to change his dirty diaper. Talk to him. Mark him with my smell, my voice. I want to let him know I'm all his.

Dennis reaches over and squeezes my hand, placing it on his thigh. "Let's go home."

I look into his eyes, the color of Agave, "Let's do this."

Driving south, I think of the son I hold in my heart, the one I didn't carry in a car seat. A rush of fear flows through me as I land on the thought, "I don't know if I'll be able to protect Elisha from an early death. As we pass the graffiti on the freeway on ramp, I say inside myself, "I'm safe; He's safe," until my breathing returns to a steady rhythm. I feel the sun on my face, shining through the front window. The clock reads 10:24.

"I can't wait to begin again," I say to Dennis, looking his way.

"So many firsts," he replies.

I nod. A smile on my face. As I press into my feelings, wondering what's where, and what's going on in my body, I feel energized by what I can only identify as replenishment.

As we pull into the driveway, and Eden flies out the door, I realize it's something more—love. What I'm carrying is love.

Epilogue

He cries in my ear, this youngest son of mine, his toots and gases part of his language. His skin is Italian-leather soft, his hair as coarse as our Sylvester look-alike cat, Oedipus. Eden is drawing with her dad on the couch in the converted garage. I can see them through the open door and hear her expressive voice over her brother's vocalizations, "No, Dad! Oedipus would never eat a mouse! She's way too sweet. She's not that kind of cat."

Mother's Day, today, will never be simple. There will always be one greeting card missing, one launch onto the bed for my wake-up invitation and when they get older, one phone call not received. Yet, Long Beach's death has shaped us into something more than grieving parents. He's left us with a courage to be more human, to need others, and to make space at the dinner table because we don't know what tomorrow will ask us to let go of.

In Southern California, it feels like a storybook day—climbing jasmine leaves swaying in the ocean breeze, a rocking chair available on the front porch, father and daughter engaged in creating marker drawings of our family. And yet, this time around, she leaves out her brother who's been missing for almost two years.

Acknowledgments

Certainly a book that's taken twelve years to birth could not have been done without help. The Montage regulars in my early days who created safety while finding my writer's voice – Maribeth Ekey (who has been in the trenches with me during this writing project), Drew and Nancy Ward, Nikki Grimes, Rick and the late great Gina Mammano Vander Kam, Tricia Elisara, and others who were the faithful voices saying, "Keep going. Keep writing." Also top of this list are my two editors who each grew me as a writer in their own way. Traci Mullins gave this story structure and did a lot of heavy lifting with my first couple of drafts – taking me from a newbie to sharing sensitive content with the reader in mind. Gordon Grice shaped what wasn't working and directed me, like a fine-tooth comb, to tease out the unnecessary and get to the essential.

Also significant were Liz Gonzalez and her class, "Writer as a Witness to Life," which set me on the path of developing the craft of memoir. I'm forever grateful for my classmates who cheered me on as I attempted to share my experiences with pregnancy death for the first time. Suzanne O'Connell was this book's doula. Her careful and consistent guidance to keep writing in the early and middle stages kept me from dropping the project when it felt too difficult to keep bringing words to trauma and grief. I'm also appreciative for the other women of Fierce Writers (with Liz as our leader) who gave valuable feedback during the pre-first draft stages.

It was through her book "Writing Down the Bones" that I first met Natalie Goldberg. In 2011, I traveled to Taos and began my journey of internalizing her wisdom and knowledge as her student. Even as I write this, I'm enrolled in an online class. She cracked open my protective shell that feared taking too long or saying too much. I've been changed by much more than how I write on a page. Natalie's dedication to her calling of teaching writers how to write by persisting in all circumstances to put pen to paper has been everything. I'm grateful for how she continues to show up, being one of the writers "out in front of me."

Jeff Jensen, the world's greatest (and maybe only) text editor, his attention to words and phrasing, made me a better crafter of sentences and his feedback on my first draft, "write what's there without telling the reader how to feel" gave me direction for my first major cuts. Rob Wilder – for cheering me on and speaking into my writing process with his wisdom, encouragement, and care, especially during the year-long intensive when I was finalizing my first working draft. There were many readers over the first several drafts– Cara Castro, Susan Beeney, Grace Brethren Writer's Group with Katherine Lo and Jeremy and Carey Bear who dove in with detailed feedback and conversations about publishing and the craft of writing long after we stopped formally meeting. Susan Davis, you so generously reshaped my *Relationship with God and Disturbed by God* poem. So many writers in groups, retreats, classes, and individual writing sessions, who heard pieces of my story. If you're reading this, thank you for your specific words and listening ears that helped me find my voice and style, as well as sort out what was alive on the page.

The Graces – Shannon Walker for all the typing hours of journal entries for me, Mandy Ream for cheerleading every twist and turn, especially the rewriting process along with your company in the writing (and as a member of Thrive, too), Alicia Porter for acceptance, support, and seeing me in the writing process, and Amy Jensen – I feel you celebrating from behind the veil. This group held my grief and lived the words on these pages. Thrive – Shelly Millsap, Mary Van Geffen and Cheryl Mathieu – celebrating, encouraging and pushing me over the finish line of this project. Christal Daehnert, sitting in the insecurity, the procrastination and the writing with me until I found the timing within to bring it into the world.

I'm grateful also to Chris Sowers for his final feedback, formatting, and detailed work with the interior and pacing of the book, Tracy Hiatt Grice and My Mom for their copyediting contribution, and Robin Massey who attended to many details to get this book to publication. Ali of Mali and Friends – created the tender images inside this book along with the book cover.

Holding gratitude for the following people who bear witness to my life and are living my story with me – my family. Dennis – your full permission to share my perspective while we keep discovering what it means to love one another. Eden and Elisha – you keep me honest and aren't afraid to shine a light on where I need to grow. Mom and Dad – forever grateful for your recognition of the ongoing loss alongside us. Brian and Kennan, you showed up with words, hugs, an open home to regroup and start healing. Sharon, Lisa, Cory, Rachael, Ryan, Tony, Sara, Aunt Michelle, Gina, Michael – for stopping everything to attend to us (especially with out-of-the-oven brownies) and mourn. Kerby and Anna – your words, "We're helpless and had to do something so here's a book" make me hope someone reading this can now share mine as an act of love. Bryce and Shannon – for getting in the grief well with us. And my Court nieces and nephews who bless me with the gift of themselves – Bo, Ky, Demetri, Krue, Amelia, Mackenzie, Whitney, Kiersi, Sidney, and Courtney along with my Malmin/Weber crew – Austin, Kylee, Caleb, Megan, Natalie, Emily, Jacob and Alison.

My community of friends, some of whom have already been named, you bring me joy – especially over campfires and walks. I would be lost without you. UCLA CAPS – you supported me in devastation and celebration. I'm so grateful for the way you held me the year after Baby Long Beach died. To my professional book club, Trang Leete, Mary Manix, Lisa Rowley, Maribeth Ekey (yes, I know

I'm mentioning you twice), and Sharon Lewis-Bultsma who stepped into the well of fear, trauma, and grief during the rewriting process with words of wisdom and reminding me of the "why" to write – you held many tears and kept me going when I wanted to quit. Sheri Douds – you have faithfully rooted for this project. Katie Wood – you came alongside me with enthusiasm and pointers for logistics. Mara Saranpreet Luthane – you drove for writing and lunch faithfully while I finished this project. Laurie Ledbetter – your emphatic, "I think you should title it 'Still," gave me the start of my title.

I'm forever grateful for being pulled by God's Triune love at the age of five when I became enraptured by the magic of spirituality. Thank you to the Grace Brethren Church Community who have walked beside me and my family for 26 years, including during this significant loss.

Reader, thank you for being here. Without you, my writing would be alone.

Journal Prompts

I remember…
I don't remember…
How I got here…
I'm thinking of…
I'm not thinking of…
(those listed above are from my writing practice under Natalie Goldberg)

While I may not remember…
The color red
Today, I'll be able to…
Turned out…
The most life-giving thing I did today…
At one point, I…
I didn't know grief could feel like…
In my grief I'm afraid to ask for…
What went right today…
My favorite Halloween costume
Sparks remind me…
It wasn't the….it was the….
I don't want to go through with…
I want to pass this message along…
The color black
I couldn't do my job…
I did my job even when…
We are all…
I regret…
A gentle response would have been…
I have the power to…
I wish I could…

What is missing…
What I've found…
Given what I know…
The joy I've found…
The way I help myself…
The color green
I fell out of step…
Hopeful news
I can combine my knowledge with
I'm waiting for…
I'm not waiting for…
After I left…
It makes sense to…
I understand now…